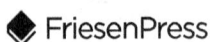

◆ FriesenPress

One Printers Way
Altona, MB R0G 0B0
Canada

www.friesenpress.com

ISBN
978-1-03-915581-7 (Hardcover)
978-1-03-915580-0 (Paperback)
978-1-03-915582-4 (eBook)

1. BIOGRAPHY & AUTOBIOGRAPHY, LGBT

Distributed to the trade by The Ingram Book Company

Raymond and Me

Dan Reynolds

DEDICATION

As I wrote my book, I was in constant thought about the past and the present.

I would like to dedicate this book to my younger self, who couldn't express who he truly was back then, and had to keep everything hidden inside for all these years.

To all the people who have had to keep their true selves hidden, know that you are not alone. This is for you too.

I also want to dedicate it to my loving and supportive wife, Susan. Her never-ending love allowed my life to go forward at a time when I thought love was lost forever and any life choices weren't worth pursuing.

Raymond and Me

INTRODUCTION

I've often wondered how many people in this world have been fortunate enough to experience "true love." Not just the metaphor of what true love is labeled as, but the love for another individual so strong that it binds you together, both of you wanting nothing more than to please, care for, and satisfy the other until you are both content in obtaining that mutual satisfaction.

I frequently think back to when Raymond and I were together. It was a time of suppression and concealment, yet I am extremely fortunate and proud of what the two of us were able to accomplish. Being able to love each other so deeply, and to keep it a secret for so long, wasn't an easy thing to do. It came with many challenges, secrets, and uncertainties, but it was all worth it.

Personally, it caused me to resent some family members for having to hide myself and lie about what my life was truly about. I loved my Raymond more than anyone, or anything, and wanted to tell the world about him and us, but I couldn't. For many years I kept these memories about my past private and strictly to myself, yet the more I kept it hidden, the more

I craved for peace from my inner self, hence my wanting to share them now.

Over the years, I have learned that many people who are not directly associated with, or subjected to, discrimination, hate, or gay-bashing, will simply underestimate its effects on the victim and will disregard the victim's desires of needing comfort as insignificant.

Like so many other gay men of the baby boomer generation, and the younger generation as well, I have had to struggle with an internal conflict of either being true to myself or having the continued acceptance of family and society. For many of us, we simply could not have both.

I, however, have been blessed with an incredibly amazing wife and two beautiful daughters. Since my coming out, they have been supportive and loving beyond belief.

I was also privileged by fate to have loved, and been loved, by the most amazing man I have ever known. We were two lost souls, Raymond and I, alone, stuck in the confines of a homophobic society and that of homophobic Catholic parents.

We were together for well over five, almost six years. Our secret love was known only to a handful of people, which was incredibly sad. We laughed together, we loved together, and sometimes cried together, but our love was deep and true.

This is the story of Raymond and me.

CHAPTER 1
August 1982.

Why tonight? Why did it have to rain?

I stood in the pouring rain, watching my horse as he tried keeping pace with the other racehorses as they passed the three-quarter mile mark. He wasn't comfortable racing in such wet, slippery conditions, and as they raced down the homestretch, it was all he could do to finish sixth in a field of nine. I knew he had tried his best, and for me that was all that mattered, so I wasn't too disappointed.

The rain was still coming down as Doug, the driver, hopped off the sulky and handed me the reins. He was covered from head to toe in limestone mud and all I could see was his friendly smile from beneath all the caked-on muck.

"What a shitty night out. He gave it his all tonight, Dan. He never did like racing when it's slippery and wet, as he hates the mud flying up and hitting him in the face." Doug then helped me climb up onto the sulky and passed me the bucket and blankets, which I'd used previously in the paddock.

"Thanks, Doug," I replied, "hope you have better luck with your other drives."

I then drove my horse from the racetrack back to our barn, which was a couple of minutes' jog away.

"Tough luck tonight, Dan, hopefully better luck, and weather next week," George, my security guard friend, jokingly said, and he opened the gate to allow the horses to exit the racetrack and go into the backstretch area.

My horse had finished "out of the money," as only the top five horses were entitled to part of the purse money.

I believe a horse can tell when he has won a race, as he becomes very proud of himself afterwards. It's also true when a horse loses, especially if he is quite a distance behind the winner. You can sense that he feels somewhat down and defeated.

Once we were inside our barn, I patted him on his neck and gave him an encouraging, "Good boy." He then turned his head and looked at me as if to say, "Thanks, buddy."

By now I was soaked right through. My feet sloshed inside my boots as I walked. I was cold, uncomfortable, and getting grumpier by the minute. I had wanted to get done early, to get back to the apartment and to Raymond.

We had planned on celebrating our second anniversary of our first date together, which was two years ago today. It was Saturday night, and we wanted to go to one of the gay nightclubs in Toronto, but due to an early scratch—or pulling out of another horse from the race—my horse was eligible to take his place. As much as it was such an important date for Raymond and me, I couldn't neglect my job and had to attend the races.

There wasn't a spot on my horse that wasn't caked in sloppy mud. Racing in the mud makes for such a long and tiring night of bathing and cleaning your horse, his tack, and the sulky. The racetrack had a layer of limestone that the horses would race on and leaving the limestone mud to dry was like trying to chip off concrete, so it was much easier to remove while it was still wet.

I grew up with horses from an early age. My father and brother were in the sport, and I followed.

Caring for horses is a tedious job. Feeding them, exercising them, cleaning up after them, and grooming them. In order to take a day or two off, you needed to coordinate with someone to care for them while you were away.

There was good money to be made, but it wasn't always a steady income. I took pride in the way my horses looked, as they were always healthy, fit, and robust.

It was around 10:30 p.m. and I was hoping I could at least be finished by midnight, or shortly after, if I hurried. I stripped my horse of his harness and put a temporary blanket on him while I got his bath water ready as he slowly caught his breath.

While bathing him off, I kept thinking about how Raymond and I had met here at the track, and how fortunate I was to be involved in the horses for that reason.

I wondered if fate would have brought us together if I had worked somewhere else. I didn't want to think of my life without Raymond and if fate had chosen something else for us. Even though I was disappointed with how the evening was turning out, due to the weather and missing the chance of going out to celebrate, thinking about Raymond always cheered me up.

After my horse was bathed, I slowly walked him around for about twenty minutes to help cool him down. Every now and then I allowed him some sips of cool water, and once he had caught his breath and was relaxed, I let him loose in his stall and he began enjoying his hay.

I then began the arduous task of cleaning his leather harness. The wet sloppy mud gets into every seam and stitch and must be washed off with warm water and saddle soap. The limestone draws all the oils and moisture out of the leather, so cleaning it is a necessity.

After an hour or so, I finished cleaning his leather harness and hung it up to let it air dry overnight.

I brought the horse out of his stall and checked to make sure he was thoroughly dry. I then gave him a well-deserved brushing off, combed his mane and tail, and bandaged up his legs for support.

I kept looking at my watch. *Damn, it's 12:30 a.m. already, and I still have to clean the sulky and sweep the shed row.* It was well past one in the morning by the time I left the track and headed back to the apartment, which was a forty-five-minute drive west. As I drove, I kept thinking about Raymond. I had told him I should be home around midnight.

I was hoping he would still be up, but at the same time I didn't want him to be so tired from waiting and convinced myself it was alright if he was asleep. Raymond also worked at the racetrack with the pari-mutuel betting machines and their computer department, but he had the night off, so was at home.

We had two parking spots at the apartment close to the front door entrance, and probably because it was raining another damn car was parked in my reserved spot, which made me have to park in the visitors' area, yet farther away.

Great, the perfect finish to a crappy night! I thought. After saying a few vulgarities about the driver who had taken my spot, I parked the car, and since I was already soaked and somewhat upset for being late, I woefully walked in the pelting rain to the apartment entrance.

Sure enough, Raymond was still awake and watching TV.

He got up off the couch and came to the door where I was taking off my boots.

"Babe, it's almost two a.m. I was starting to get worried. God, you're soaked right through. Get out of those wet clothes and go take a hot shower." He gave me a kiss, and I went to shower and got into my comfy and warm gray sweatpants.

When I got back, I noticed Raymond had set the table for us, a romantic candle in the center, a red rose, lasagna from our dear friend across the hall, and a small cake with "It's Our Second" written on it. We had a quiet meal in the middle of the night to celebrate the two of us. We were both too tired, and just left the dishes in the sink till tomorrow.

We climbed onto the couch and started watching some TV. As I sleepily sat on the couch, now finally warm and dry, I nuzzled up beside my Raymond and contently asked him, "Do you remember that day we met, hun?"

Raymond instantly started to hold me a bit tighter. I could feel his warm embrace while his voice sounded comforting, yet excited, reliving that moment when we first met. "Of course," he said, "it was two years ago today. You were fourth in the fourth, as I like to say."

"I was fourth in the fourth?" I replied.

"Yes, you were looking after horse number four in the fourth race at Greenwood Racetrack, on this day two years ago in August 1980," Raymond answered, and he leaned his head against mine.

While I sat there listening, I couldn't believe how much I was in love with my beautiful boyfriend. His love, sentimental kindness, and handsome good looks were truly one of a kind.

"I had actually seen you a couple of weeks before that," Raymond said, and smiled at the memory. "I was walking into the grandstand on my way to work and had to stop and wait for the horses to pass. You were walking your horse into the paddock, and I thought, 'Damn, what a cute guy.'"

He seemed so happy remembering that moment and he eagerly continued.

"That night while I was working in the grandstand, I kept thinking about you and I tried to get away from work and go back down to the paddock, but I couldn't. I then looked to see who the trainer was of that horse you were looking after in the program, and every night afterwards, I'd look to see if he had a horse racing, and if he did, I'd walk down to the paddock and try to see if you were his groom."

I could feel a lump in my throat as Raymond showed how dedicated and determined he had been in trying to track me down. "You never told me that before, hun. I had no idea you saw me," I said. "All I know is the moment our eyes met, I knew that there was a connection between us, as if there was something in our eye contact that instantly touched my heart, but why would a handsome guy like you even look at me?"

Raymond leaned in close and gave me a kiss. "You're beautiful, babe, as simple as that, and I love you!"

I let my mind wander back to that day two years ago. I recall it being extremely hot and sunny, a perfect night for harness racing.

We had met a few weeks after my twentieth birthday in late August 1980. I was working as a groom caring for race-horses at Greenwood Racetrack in Toronto, while Raymond, who was one year older, worked with the pari-mutuel betting machines in the grandstand there.

We first met at the paddock. In the summer, the large Plexiglas windows of the paddock were removed for ventilation, and to allow the public to come over to the paddock area and view the horses up close before the races.

I was caring for my horse when I turned and saw Raymond

leaning against the window opening. Our eyes immediately locked for a few seconds, but it felt like minutes. Raymond broke the silence and said, "I've always liked this horse. How do you think he'll do tonight?"

I was quite taken by Raymond's stunning looks and wavy golden hair.

"He should do okay tonight," I stammered. "He trained well this week."

Raymond gave me a smile.

I then had to put my horse's bridle on, tighten his equipment, and get him ready to race. Once finished, I eagerly looked back, but Raymond had left.

I never thought any more of it as I knew I was destined to be forever locked away in the gay closet of hell, without any chance of meeting a guy, let alone such an attractive guy as him. My past experiences and the current social stigma of being gay wouldn't allow me to think otherwise.

Yet a couple of nights later Raymond was back at the paddock window while I was with a different horse, and I immediately saw him and smiled. His sincere smile in return reassured me that his intentions were real, genuine, and friendly, while his beautiful blue eyes made me feel so comfortable that I felt he was already hugging me.

"Hey, you're back," I said, as I continued to stare and smile. "Do you like this horse as well?" I jokingly asked.

"I have no idea what horse this is, but I saw you and wanted to say hi. I'm Raymond," he said, and put out his hand through the large window opening.

I can still remember his strong but gentle handshake.

"Hi, Raymond," I said. "I'm Dan."

As we shook hands, we looked deep into each other's eyes, and in that instant, I could sense that something special had just happened. His handshake seemed to transfer a sense of reassurance and kindness into me. My heart immediately started to race. I knew right away from our short introduction that there was something special about our meeting. A feeling that our meeting was supposed to have happened. It felt so natural, as if it was an invitation for it to continue.

People talk about love at first sight, and I can honestly say now that I know what it means, for it is true, as I experienced it at that moment.

"I was wondering if you would be interested in getting something to eat after the races are finished," Raymond asked, somewhat nervously.

I was surprised but, not wanting to break our thought, also nervously replied, "Sure, I'd like that."

"I work in the grandstand, and I'll be done around 11:15 p.m. How's if I meet you by the backstretch guard shack? Would that be alright?" he asked.

"That works for me," I said and smiled back.

After Raymond had left, I was totally bewildered, and I felt like I had no idea what I was doing. The paddock judge suddenly hollered, "Five minutes."

Crap! I hadn't even started getting my horse ready.

I hurriedly got my horse's bridle on, attached his sulky, tightened up his equipment, and was ready.

As I walked my horse by the reins from the paddock down to the racetrack, I continued to reflect on what had just happened.

Did I just agree to go out on a date and on a date with a great-looking guy?

I couldn't believe I had agreed to go out and started getting nervous, yet excited at the same time.

My mind kept racing as I questioned myself over and over. *Why would a guy ask me out if he wasn't gay?*

Maybe he's just overly friendly and needs a friend.
That's probably it. He just wants to be friends.
No, he's gay, I can sense it.
Are you sure?
Yes, he's gay.
God, I hope he's gay.

I tried to convince myself that he was gay, but I was still unsure.

I still had a lot to learn about my gaydar.

Once my horse was on the track, I looked around to see if I could see Raymond anywhere in the horde. I glanced up and down through the grandstand and the crowd, eager to see him. I looked through the multitude of people down near the racetrack railing. I don't even recall watching my horse race as I was still in a bewildered state of mind.

After the race was finished, I took my horse back to the barn, bathed him off, and bedded him down for the night. I glanced down at my watch: eleven p.m. I started getting anxious with each passing minute.

I heard the call of the last race from the grandstand in the barn area, and I knew Raymond would be finished soon.

CHAPTER 2
August 1980.

Once I was done, I quickly made my way from my barn down to the guard shack.

"Where are you going in such a hurry, Dan?" a fellow groom asked.

"Can't stop to talk at the moment, Chris. Will talk tomorrow," I answered.

Sure enough, sitting on the bench was Raymond. His lean, tall silhouette was easy to pick out.

"Hey, I hope you haven't had to wait too long," I said.

"Great timing, as I just got here," he replied. "Feel like going over to McDonald's across the street?"

"Sure, sounds good to me," I said.

"Want to walk or drive over?" he asked.

"It's a nice night. Let's walk," I answered, and we started heading to McDonald's, walking across the parking lot of the racetrack.

The parking lot was practically empty of cars, with only the odd light standard still turned on. Walking in the dim light made me feel more at ease, and I was hoping that no one I knew from the racetrack would see us together and wonder who I was with and ask.

As we walked, we nervously made some small talk. We both seemed a little hesitant and unsure of what we should talk about. Finally, Raymond broke the ice.

"Do you live in Toronto?" he asked.

"Yes, I live at home with my parents. I grew up and still live in Willowdale, a suburb in the northern part of Toronto. How about you?" I answered.

"Yeah, I still live with mine, also. We live west of the city. I would love to move out one day and get a place of my own," Raymond said. "My dad can be difficult to live with at times."

I wondered what he meant regarding his father being "difficult" but was too shy to ask. I just wanted to get to know Raymond and was too excited about being on our date to inquire further.

We reached McDonald's and ordered our meals. We both ordered a plain cheeseburger and fries, while Raymond had a root beer, and I had a Coke.

Even though there were only a couple of other people there at that time of night, we sat down in a corner away from anyone else for some added privacy.

We started talking about work. I mentioned that I was a groom, and practically grew up with horses as my brother and father were in the sport and that I recently got my trainer's license, entitling me to train horses of my own and open a public stable. Raymond mentioned he worked with the computers in the grandstand with the pari-mutuel machines.

"Do you dispense the tickets at the betting window?" I asked.

"No, I work in the computer room. I also remove defective betting machines if they break down and replace them with one that works. I've never placed a bet in my life. I'd be too afraid of losing my money," he said.

As we sat chatting, I noticed the hair on Raymond's arms. His masculinity only increased my desire to want to get to know him more, and I found myself intently staring.

I guess he noticed me looking as he then ran his finger over my hairy arm, casually looked around, and asked, "So when did you realize you were gay?"

My heart stopped. Yet at the same time I was relieved to confirm my hopes of assuming that he was gay also.

It instantly seemed to bring us closer together, and for the first time, I felt comfortable looking Raymond squarely in his beautiful blue eyes, and for an extended period.

I wasn't sure what to say. Then suddenly the truth came out.

"As soon as I knew what my parts were for. I've never been attracted to, nor interested in any woman," I said. "What about you?"

"Much the same," he answered. "I grew up in a very demanding Catholic family and my father has some very opinionated homophobic views, which make my hidden gay lifestyle exceedingly difficult. I would never discuss anything gay at home unless I wanted to hear the wrath of my dad. The negativity at home about being gay has caused me to hide my true feelings to anyone.

"I've never told anyone that I'm gay other than you, right now. I feel comfortable enough being with you to express it. I hope that's alright."

I could see how tense Raymond became discussing his family, especially his father, and I tried to show my concern and sympathize with him.

"Thanks for showing me that trust. I really feel comfortable talking to you about this as well. Your situation sounds like mine, too. No one knows about me, as I've been terrified of someone finding out about my gay thoughts. I was sure I'd never meet a guy. I've never had a girlfriend either," I told him.

"You're not alone." Raymond smiled. "I've never been with a woman either, nor a guy, sadly. It's just been so confusing, trying to understand it all, especially with all the negativity surrounding the gay lifestyle."

We both smiled in such a way as to reaffirm that we understood each other's living situation and that we had developed a very special friendship.

"I'd like to see you again if I could," Raymond said.

"I'd love that," I answered, as I casually looked around and momentarily rested my hand on top of his.

We got up and started walking back to the racetrack parking lot.

As we walked, I could feel the back of Raymond's hand brushing against the back of mine with every step. I was feeling so fantastic that this incredibly handsome guy, actual took an interest in me!

It was difficult for me to believe that this beautiful man had taken an honest interest in me, and he didn't want to hurt me or harm me for liking him in return.

We reached the parking area by the backstretch.

"This is my car here," Raymond said.

I didn't want him to leave and started making any conversation I could think of. "Do you live far from here?" I asked.

"I live in Milton, about forty-five minutes away," he replied.

"Do you work out at Mohawk Raceway as well?" I asked. "That's only about a ten-minute drive away from Milton. That would make it super convenient for you driving to work."

"Yeah, I work out at Mohawk as well. It's certainly an easier drive than coming into the city. Do you stable out there when the horses move from Toronto?" he said.

"Yes, I go with the horses when they move out to Mohawk for the next racing season," I answered.

I desperately wanted to tell him that I'd like to see him again as well and as soon as possible, I hoped.

"If you ever want to meet me," I said with eagerness, "I always watch the races from the grandstand when I'm not racing a horse. I sit at the far east end and up high, where no one else sits." I pointed toward the far end of the grandstand.

"Great, I'll start to look for you up there when I'm on my break," Raymond replied with a big smile.

"I really enjoyed meeting you tonight," I said.

Raymond then got into his blue Chevy Monza. He reached out his hand through the window and we shook hands.

"Thanks for a fun time," Raymond said.

"No, thank you," I replied.

I walked over to where my car was. It was farther back in the parking lot, away from any lights and in the dark. I was so overjoyed that I opened the door and flopped down into the driver's seat. I had never felt so happy in my entire life.

I watched Raymond start to drive away when he suddenly turned around and drove back toward me. He pulled up beside me and got out.

I rolled the window down and cautiously laughed. "What's wrong?"

"A handshake?" he said. "Really?"

He then leaned through the window, looked me in the eyes, and kissed me. "I feel better now. Good night, Dan, and thanks."

I watched as Raymond got back in his car, gave me another smile, waved, and drove away. I sat there for a minute or two, trying to gather my thoughts and emotions. I felt like crying for being so happy and being accepted by another gay man.

What had just happened? My life had changed from me believing I'd forever be living in the dark, cold, lonely closet to suddenly feeling overjoyed. A feeling of warmth and completeness had just entered my body, and for once in my life, I was at ease and proud of being a young gay man.

I drove home and was thrilled at what had happened. I then started to think how I should act once home, should anyone be up.

My parents would often go to the racetrack to watch the horses, so it wasn't uncommon for someone to still be up waiting for me. No one in my family knew about my gay side, and I was definitely too afraid to tell anyone.

I didn't want to look overly excited and make them ask what the reason was for being so happy, especially when my horse didn't do so well. I could never tell them that I'd been on a date with a great guy. I could simply tell them I was on a date with a girl, but that would only create an ongoing, just as complicated situation.

I leisurely walked inside, looking disappointed, but luckily everyone was already in bed.

I made my way to my bedroom downstairs, washed up, and climbed into bed. All night long, I couldn't stop thinking about Raymond, his tall 5'11", 150-pound frame, handsome, chiseled good looks, wavy golden hair, and beautiful blue eyes. His golden hair was offset by the darker hair on his arms.

I'm sure I even got glimpses of dark chest hair close to the top button of his shirt.

While in bed, I started hoping he would remember where I sat in the grandstand at night to watch the races. I was basically a loner and didn't like to be near others, but I knew Raymond was different from everyone else as he fulfilled something that was missing within me.

"Please, please, make him remember," I said to myself, over and over again.

I could barely fall asleep, having this beautiful guy on my mind. Of course, being a typical testosterone-filled young male, I let my mind wander. I tried picturing him naked, being in bed with him. Was he a top or bottom, or had we even figured that out yet, both being gay virgins? I began to smile and chuckle at what I was thinking.

Needless to say, I would never have imagined what fate had in store for us over the next few years and I eventually fell asleep holding my pillow.

"Good night, Raymond."

CHAPTER 3

By the time I was in my late teens and reaching twenty, I had lost any hope that I was ever going to find a boyfriend. How would one look for a boyfriend anyway in a society filled with so much gay discrimination?

As a kid in the sixties, a teen in the seventies, and a young man in the eighties, I saw and experienced the prejudice and hate that many gay men experienced. I soon learned to put up a wall and hide away out of fear.

Gay-bashing was a common occurrence back then. Just six months after Raymond and I met, the infamous Toronto bathhouse raids by police took place. On February 5, 1981, an estimated 200 police officers armed with crowbars and sledgehammers raided four Toronto bathhouses and arrested more than 300 gay men. Referred to as "Operation Soap," it was the largest single arrest in Toronto's history.

It was also a turning point in the history of the LGBTQ community. For years prior to the raid and years after, many, many members of the LGBTQ community were subject to slanderous and derogatory remarks from police, the media, and the public.

It was this negativity and constant taunting that made many members of the LGBTQ community fear for their safety and lives.

This was what I thought would be a normal life for a gay man. One of hurt and bullying, never-ending fear, and of looking over your shoulder.

I started to face the fact that I would be single for the rest of my life and should be content in living within my own gay fantasy world. I was terrified of anyone finding out that I was gay. I had never had a willing gay sexual experience, but knew I was attracted to men at a very young age.

But through it all, I always kept it a secret and never mentioned anything to a family member. If I happened to see an attractive-looking guy, it was never a prolonged stare, but a quick look. If by chance I saw a girl and I was with someone, I'd purposely stare, hoping to show to those around me that I was interested and divert any gay tendencies.

From what I discovered in school and heard on the street, it was alright to make fun of and criticize all gay guys and the gay culture. Should you not join in on the banter and scorn, then you were either thought of as a gay supporter or gay yourself, and subject to the same ridicule, so it was much easier to play along with the game.

This seemed to be the norm for anyone back then. Even my own family never recognized being gay as anything but being abnormal.

I remember being around eleven or twelve years old and watching our next-door neighbor's hot father as he cut his grass.

"Hello, Danny," he would call over the fence.

His shirtless, hairy chest and trail, glistening with his manly sweat due to the summer heat, certainly kept my attention. In my mind, this was a perfectly natural and healthy attraction, and this was "my" normal. I soon discovered that the vast majority of people considered this to be a very abnormal and perverse attraction. A male should be attracted to a female and not another male.

I often thought, *What is "normal"?*

A good friend of mine once said that he views "normal" as "an illusionary construct to give people the sense of security that all is well."

Growing up, there were only about three kids on our street that I considered friends. One day when I was around twelve years old, I went to see if one of them, Jimmy, was free after school to hang out with. I still remember walking down the street. It was fall and just after a new school year had started.

I rang the doorbell and heard the familiar sound of their dog starting to bark. Then his older brother Stephen, who was around twenty, answered the door.

Stephen was always friendly to me, and I especially liked seeing his few chest hairs from the opening at the top of his shirt.

"Is Jimmy home?" I asked.

"Hey, Dan. No, he's not home right now, but he'll be home any minute. Come inside and you can wait downstairs," Stephen said.

Thinking nothing of it, I followed him to the basement.

"No one is home right now, but you can wait in here," he said as he took me into his bedroom. He then shut and locked the door.

A magazine lay open on his bed, showing a man and woman having intercourse.

"Do you like those?" he asked as he nodded at the magazine.

I glanced at them nervously, not knowing what to say or do. I wasn't interested in seeing a girl's naked boobs, but I did catch a glimpse of the naked guy.

Stephen then took off his belt, undid his jeans, and unzipped his fly. "I know you want to," he encouragingly told me.

How does he know I'm interested in guys? Does it remotely show? Do I really portray what a gay person looks like? I was so confused and scared at knowing the answers to those questions.

He grabbed me by the shirt and pulled me closer. "Do it, faggot boy, or I'll tell everyone that you came onto me and that you're a total queer. You like it when I call you faggot, don't you?"

Once again, I was petrified. How did he know my forbidden secret, and would he tell others? What if he told my parents or friends, and what would happen should they find out that I'm gay?

After a short time, he shoved me aside and contently sat on the edge of the bed.

"I could tell you liked it, faggot boy," he said. "I knew you were a little fag, and never forget that I know you enjoyed it, and I'd gladly tell others that you did, too."

"Please don't say anything," I pleaded. "I won't tell anyone. Please, please don't tell."

"If you don't tell, then I won't tell," he said.

He then told me to get out and cautioned me again if I ever told anyone that he'd say I asked for it, and he would tell everyone I knew that I was a queer.

I quickly got myself together and went home.

Walking down the sidewalk, I didn't know whether to cry or accept that I was a queer, like he said. I was so confused and uncertain as to what I should do. I knew I'd never ever be able to tell anyone what happened simply because I thought it would provide evidence that I was queer.

For ages after, I was in constant fear of someone finding out what had happened. I rarely went down to visit Jimmy at home. I did see his brother, Stephen, the odd time on the street, but he didn't acknowledge me whatsoever.

That experience confirmed in me once more that being gay came at a terrible risk, and if found out, the possible shame of family, friends, and others. After that day, I hid further into the closet, deeper into its dark lonely depths, and made sure that the door was closed and locked up tight. I was reluctant to pursue my true inner desires for fear of any kind of retaliation. It's situations like this that can be a lifelong reminder of whether you think it's safe to come out or remain locked away.

A few months went by, and I started feeling safer within my hidden closet.

One day I randomly, and quite accidentally, discovered that my older sister secretly kept a magazine called *Playgirl* hidden away.

I had hit the motherlode of fulfilling a young gay kid's desires when I stumbled upon that. Seeing all that masculine hair, their beautiful muscular physiques, and their appendages all hanging out in full view, undeniably confirmed my gay side. Bless the publishers at *Playgirl*!

All seemed fine until I entered my first year in junior high school the following fall.

I was a small-framed kid, weighed about one hundred pounds soaking wet, was noticeably quiet, and kept to myself back then. I was nervous as to what high school would be like, simply because of its size and any bullying that it might produce.

We were assigned our homeroom and class timetable. I had taken mostly math and science courses. To my disappointment, however, gym was mandatory. I hated gym class, as I was not athletic and had no coordination at all.

That first semester, I guess from being vulnerable and an easy mark, I was soon the target of three jocks. They would intentionally knock into me, and enthusiastically bodycheck me against the lockers in the hallway, all the while calling me "the fag" or "faggot," anything to put me down. Although the word "fag" or "faggot" was used to slander any person they wanted to tease, it made it that much more uncomfortable for me, thinking that they possibly knew I was gay. After a while, if I saw them coming, I'd turn and go the other way.

Halfway through the school year, our classes changed, and I had gym, or Phys Ed. I was terrified when I discovered that those three jocks were in the same gym class.

It was the first day of gym and the last class of the day. The teacher made us play football in the snow and I had no idea of the rules or concept of the game. Somehow, I managed to put on the equipment—pads and protective gear. It was literally flopping all over on me as I ran because I was so small.

Out on the field, the three jocks had a heyday, laughing at me, slamming me into the ground, tackling me, and calling me names—surprisingly, with no disagreement from the teacher.

After gym class, our teacher made us all hit the shower. I had never seen naked guys before in real life, other than that one day when I was forced to go down on that guy, but he hadn't been totally naked.

Once I was in the shower, the three jocks who constantly tormented me entered the shower area. I tried to hide my noticeable excitement and wanted to leave.

The one jock blocked my exit and the three of them waited for the other guys in the shower to leave.

"Go watch the entrance," the one guy said to the other, "and tell me when everyone has left the change room."

Then the other two shoved me over into the corner of the shower.

"You're not going anywhere, faggot boy," the one said.

The guy at the shower entrance waved his hand with a thumbs-up and nodded to the other two who were with me. I didn't see the one guy come up behind me, who kicked me between the legs as hard as he could. I instantly fell to the shower floor, gasping to catch my breath.

"You fucking queer," the one said, "I've waited to do this for a while now," and they proceeded to kick me all over, my stomach, sides, between my legs again; everywhere except above my shoulders and face.

"I knew from the start you were a fucking faggot."

After their multitude of kicks, I could no longer feel the pain of them hitting me. All I can remember is the slapping sound of their wet feet against my wet skin and hoping it would soon end.

They finally stopped, turned off the showers, all took a turn spitting on me, and with one final kick between my legs, left me alone. At that point, I uncontrollably threw up and just lay there, too afraid to move. When I tried to get up, I was in so much pain that I couldn't. I heard the rowdiness talk in the change room stop and figured everyone had left.

After a while, I then heard someone come into the shower.

I looked up and saw another student, an older big muscular Black guy in his tracksuit and runners.

"Fucking bastards," he said, as he helped me up and took me over to the change area. He sat me on the bench, got a towel, and cleaned me up. He then helped dry me off and got me dressed. I remember sitting there in pain, and that's when I finally broke down and started to cry.

The Black guy put his big arms around me and gently hugged me. Then he put his two big hands against each side of my face. He looked at me and said, "It's going to be alright, kid. You'll be okay. I know what you're going through."

I have no idea who that beautiful young Black guy was, but I believe he must have been a senior in our school, being the immense size he was.

All I remember was his huge size, his kindness, and his reaffirming to me that everything would be okay. I then tried to walk back to my locker without getting anyone's attention from being in so much pain. I remember it took me forever to walk home in the snow and cold.

The following day, I was so sore that I could hardly move without it hurting and I was covered in bruises. I was worried if there was any damage done, as I had never seen the parts between my legs as swollen as they were. They were at least twice their normal size.

I was too scared and embarrassed to tell the truth as to what had happened, so I simply told my mother that I wanted to stay home as I didn't feel good, and I stayed in bed while my parents went to work. I was also scared of going back to school for fear of getting another beating from those three jocks again.

Lying in my bed, I thought about what it was like to be a gay man out in the real world. How could God, or the powers to be, instill in you the urge to be attracted to another man, while at the same time, giving society the approval of disallowing it? Weren't there any gay couples in the world who lived happily together, in peace and contentment? I was so confused.

I knew on our own street there were two men who lived together in the same house, yet my Catholic mother condemned them for doing so. Maybe they were just roommates, but my own mother already took it upon herself to think they were gay and criticized them without knowing the full truth or story. Back then, much like today, it's much easier to condemn someone's lifestyle than it is to accept them if it goes against your beliefs.

After a couple of days, I had to go back to school, but was terrified about running into those three guys again. It still hurt to walk and even though some of the swelling between my legs had gone down, I'd never felt them so sore nor seen them so large.

On my first day back, I cautiously walked down the halls, always on the lookout. It didn't take long before I saw the three of them coming. With so many kids in the hallway, there was no room for me to turn around in time and go hide among the crowd.

I watched them walk closer and closer. The one guy glared over at me, but not one of them said a word, nor showed any kind of intimidation. I wondered what was going on and why didn't they say or do something. Later that day, and with a note from home, I eagerly missed gym class.

The following day, again, the three jocks ignored me and never said a word. Their ignoring me started to make me nervous as I thought they were planning some major punishment for me. Yet they ignored me for the rest of the school year and never looked my way. Even when I was back in the gym, they purposely left me alone.

Looking back now, I'm quite convinced that my big Black savior friend must have had a few intimidating words with them, as that's the only explanation I can think of.

I never did find out who he was, and often wondered if he was a fellow gay guy who knew what had happened. Whoever he was, I was, and still am, thankful for the compassion he showed to me.

Once again, I escaped back into the depths of the cold, lonely gay closet. Being so young and vulnerable, I had no reason to think things would ever change, and I made it a point never to allow myself the pain or possible shame of anyone finding out about my true sexuality. Many men of my generation grew up gay, but due to pressure from society, family intimidation, or gay-bashing, like I experienced, hid their gay side by marrying women, just like Raymond and I eventually would do.

Yet looking back these many years later, the beautiful time I had with Raymond was worth any slander or abuse that was thrown my way. It's my belief that the abuse and gay-bashing that I experienced while growing up only strengthened my love for Raymond. Because of his trust and loyalty, it made my love and commitment absolute.

It was as if the Gay Gods had sent Raymond to rescue me from the gay closet of darkness. It also confirmed, and reassured in me, that the love between two compassionate men was not only possible but could be a truly wonderful experience.

CHAPTER 4
August 1980.

Every night when I wasn't racing, I'd walk from the backstretch, around the perimeter of the outer track, and to the grandstand. I'd then purchase a bag of Lays potato chips and a Coke and sit at the far end of the grandstand facing the turn into the homestretch, watching the horses warm up and reading the racing program.

This night, however, was different. It was the day after Raymond's and my first date. I desperately wanted to see him again and was eagerly waiting for him to show up.

Halfway through the evening, I was losing hope that Raymond was coming. I began thinking of the worst. *This is too good to be true. Why would a handsome guy like him be interested in skinny me?*

I once again started dreading the thought of returning to the depths of that lonely closet. *How long will it take—if I ever do—to find another Raymond?*

Suddenly someone unexpectedly grabbed me by the shoulders from behind and said, "What's a handsome guy like you doing in a place like this?"

I instantly recognized Raymond's voice, smiled, and grabbed him by the hand. He jumped over the wooden seats and sat beside me.

"Hope I didn't startle you. This is my first break of the night and it's been super busy in the grandstand tonight. I should have gotten something to drink," he said. "I'm so thirsty."

I passed him my Coke, and he took a drink from the straw.

"Thanks, I needed that," he said.

There's something about sharing someone else's drink and allowing each other's mouth on the same glass or straw that seems to give each of you the comforting thought of saying, *I'm willing to share this because I really like you.*

"How was your day at the track?" Raymond asked.

"It was okay; nothing too exciting. Feed them, exercise them, clean them out, then do it all again tomorrow. Very exciting," I said, teasing him and trying to show my humorous side. "I have to admit I didn't get much sleep as I kept thinking about last night."

"Neither did I!" Raymond said. "And thanks again for last night. I really enjoyed myself. I was starting to believe I'd never find anyone who'd be interested in going out on a date with me."

"Surely you must have dated before?" I said. "You're such a good-looking guy."

"Nope, not really. No one has grabbed my attention till now, but I'm sure glad you did," Raymond said.

We sat there for Raymond's entire twenty-minute break, talking and enjoying each other's company.

"I have to go back inside now. Meet here tomorrow?" Raymond asked.

"I'll be here and waiting for you!" I said.

Raymond smiled and gave me a wink, then quickly went back into the grandstand.

The next couple of weeks were ones of sitting in the grand-stand talking and getting to know each other. Some nights we would venture back over to McDonald's for a bite to eat. As our relationship grew, we eagerly looked forward to our nightly get-togethers, which made our days worthwhile.

Every meeting only deepened our fondness for each other.

"Do you have any brothers or sisters?" Raymond asked one night.

"I'm the youngest of four kids in my family," I said. "The oldest is my brother, who's ten years older than me, and then I have two sisters in the middle. What about you?"

"I have one older sister, Rosalind," Raymond said. "I'd love for you to meet her one day."

Rosalind, or Rozz as she was affectionately known, would play an important part in our relationship going forward, and I'm forever grateful to her.

Talking about our families, we learned that we had a lot in common regarding our family's views on homosexuality. Raymond grew up in a small town west of Toronto. He wasn't into sports and was often pushed by his father to be more aggressive, and forward, in his manly demeanor, as that was what was expected of boys, in his father's mind.

We talked about what it was like when we first discovered our interest in men. When Raymond was around ten or eleven years old, he recalled a certain friend of his father, who worked in his father's construction company and would often visit his parents' home.

His father's friend was a big, muscular, and hairy young man and would always greet Raymond, saying, "Hey, Ray, how's my little buddy?" Then he'd grab Raymond and give him a headlock in his hairy armpit and rub the top of his head with his knuckles. Raymond mentioned the guy always wore a tank top to show off his hairy physique and how he could smell the guy's body odor, which was something of a turn-on.

Raymond was in the same situation as I was regarding hiding his gay side from his family. In fact, he was more confined due to his parents' domineering Catholic upbringing.

As a youngster, his parents forced him to attend church every Sunday and go to Sunday school. Because of his height, being almost six feet tall entering junior high, Raymond had no issues in school and the other kids apparently treated him with respect, even though he was rather gentle and shy.

While in school, he excelled in math and the sciences and was extremely interested in computers when they were first becoming popular. He was a natural with numbers and enjoyed the challenge of taking calculus all through high school.

Raymond said his father was an exceptionally large man, and his views were totally unsupportive of anything gay. He wasn't afraid to let his opinions be known regarding homosexuals and thought they were all cursed by the devil himself. Raymond kept a completely low profile regarding anything gay simply out of fear. Listening to the extent to which his father would go to show his homophobic hatred, Raymond could not eliminate any reprisal from his own father, whether verbal or physical, should he find out about his son being gay.

I believe it was this constant feeling of fear and uncertainty that caused Raymond to want to spend so much time away from home.

I could sense whenever he spoke of his father, he'd tense up and become agitated. Yet when we'd talk about other things, he'd be happy, relaxed, and always smiling.

One night, Raymond didn't have to work, nor did I have a horse racing that evening, and Raymond had driven into the city and to the track, just to spend the night with me in the grandstand. I'd often watch the races, just to keep abreast of the other horses' performances, should one of my horses ever compete against them.

"What should we do tonight, Dan? I don't really feel like watching the races. Have you had dinner yet?" Raymond asked.

"Actually, all I've had tonight is this bag of chips and a pop," I said.

It was Saturday night, and since we didn't have to work on Sunday, we decided to go out for dinner.

"There's that small restaurant down on Queen Street a way that serves awesome steak. We could even walk to it. It's only a couple of blocks," I said.

"Sounds great. Let's go," Raymond answered.

As we walked out of the grandstand, I jokingly said to Raymond, "You know, after the races are over, the Jockey Club should announce over the speaker, 'Thank you to all you losers who lost your money, for it's you that keeps us in business.'"

"That's too funny, but it's the truth!" Raymond chuckled. "I could never bet on the horses. I'd be afraid of losing my money."

It was a beautiful night in mid-September as we walked the few blocks to the restaurant. While we walked, Raymond mentioned he, his sister Rozz, and his parents were going up to their cottage for the next few days but would be back next Thursday.

I was hesitant in what I wanted to say for fear of it sounding too forward, but I said it anyway: "I'm really going to miss you, Raymond, even if it's just for a few days."

Raymond paused in his walking, turned, and looked at me and said, "You have no idea how much I'm going to miss you,

Dan. I'll be thinking of you the whole time I'm up there."

We both smiled and wanted to show our affection for each other more, but we knew better than to do it out in public. After we reached the restaurant, we got seated, and the waitress brought us some menus.

"Good evening, guys. How are you tonight?" she asked.

"We're good thanks and hungry." Raymond smiled.

"Our special today is the prime rib with your choice of baked or mashed potato, along with mixed vegetables," she said.

"That sounds good to me. I'll have the prime rib with a baked potato, please," Raymond replied.

"How do you like your steak?" she asked.

"Medium to well done," Raymond answered.

"And for you?" she asked me.

"I'll have the exact same with baked potato and medium to well done as well," I said.

The waitress asked me what I would like to drink. "I'll have a Carlsberg Light," I answered.

"And for you?" the waitress asked Raymond.

"I'll have the same," he said.

"I'll be right back with your drinks," she said.

We laughed at our similarities with what we liked.

Cautiously, Raymond looked around to see if anyone was close enough to hear us speak, then said very quietly, "Have you ever wanted to tell anyone about being gay, to simply have someone listen to you and understand how difficult it can be at times?"

"Yes, but to be honest, I'm too afraid to, and kind of ashamed of what I went through already, to tell anyone," I said, and casually looked around, making sure no one could hear us.

Just then, the waitress came back with our beers. "Here, guys," she said.

"Thanks," we both answered.

Raymond then went back to our discussion. "If no one knows that you're gay, then you shouldn't be ashamed of yourself, Dan. And even if they did know, that's not your worry. You were born the way you are, and there's nothing wrong with that."

"There's more to it than just being who I am," I replied, and proceeded to tell him about what happened when I was younger. "I was forced to perform oral on a guy when I was twelve, and then was beaten up in the gym showers when I was fourteen for getting aroused at the sight of the other guys," I said. "I was, and still am, afraid that someone might find out that I'm gay and will want to retaliate in a prejudicial, harmful way."

"Oh my God, Dan, why didn't you tell me about this before?" Raymond said, as his loving blue eyes showed me how gentle and caring he was.

"It's something I'm not comfortable telling. In fact, I've never told anyone about either one till now," I confided. "I'm not sure why, but I often wonder if I give off these 'gay' vibes, or if I come across to others in a way that they perceive me as 'gay' in their mind."

"You're an amazing guy, Dan, and I never want, nor will ever allow you to ever get hurt again," Raymond said as he smiled and raised his beer.

I smiled, raised my beer, and we touched bottles.

"Thanks Raymond," I said.

"I was confused also, and afraid of what my internal thoughts were about being attracted to men," Raymond replied. "Like I said, my father is a complete homophobe and enemy of anything gay. I'm terrified of him finding out. I felt I had to try to confess to someone just to know that I'm not alone."

I could tell this was very upsetting for Raymond to talk about, so I let him take a pause and then asked, "What did you ever do? Were you able to tell someone?"

"One afternoon, a couple of summers ago, Rozz and I were up at the cottage, sitting on the dock, dangling our feet in the water. Rozz and I have always had a very special trusting connection, so I asked her if I could tell her something in the strictest of confidence. I asked her that whatever her response was to please, please, not to let Dad know what I said."

"Rozz looked at me and said, 'I think I know what you're going to say, Raymond. Is it anything regarding your hesitation of wanting to date someone?'

"'Yes, something like that,' I said.

"'It's okay if you're gay, Raymond. I've had my thoughts for a while now. You're my brother, and I'll always love and support you,' Rozz answered.

"'But how did you know?' I asked her.

"'I've seen how you look at guys, and it's not the same way you look at girls. You have a natural attraction and smile when you see a good-looking guy. Don't forget, I have that same look of attraction, seeing good-looking men also,' she told me."

Raymond mentioned how they both had laughed. They then gave each other a hug of reassurance.

"When you do find him, be yourself and be happy. Just never let Dad find out, as I don't trust him in what he might do. His views are dangerous in my opinion and evil toward all gay men," Rozz had told him.

"It was a relief to tell her. Just to be able to let someone know how I was feeling inside of me seemed to lift some of the weight off my shoulders," Raymond said.

We finished dinner, paid our waitress, and started walking back to the track. Our conversations and time together seemed so natural and fun, as if we couldn't get enough of each other.

"I didn't realize how late it was. It's almost 11:30 p.m.," Raymond said, "What should we do?"

"Have you ever seen the horses up close?" I asked.

"I've never been to the barn area before," Raymond said.

"Do you want to go back to the barns and see them?" I asked.

"I'd love to," Raymond answered, and we continued walking back to the track.

Even though he worked in the grandstand with the pari-mutuel machines, he had never really seen the horses up close. The closest he ever came was being by the paddock, looking through the window.

We walked back from the restaurant to the backstretch. As we walked, we deliberately brushed hands against each other.

We got to the backstretch guard shack, where my security guard friend George met us.

"Evening, George. How's things tonight? I'm just showing my friend Raymond here the horses. I won't be too long," I said.

"Hey, Dan, all is well, thanks, and that's quite alright. Take your time. Nice win the other night, by the way," he said.

"Thanks, George," I replied.

The backstretch had twelve barns, each with approximately a hundred stalls. Raymond and I walked down to my barn. It was empty of people, as no one was racing that night and it was very quiet.

I often felt sorry for the horses as the barn lights were almost always on. It must have made it terribly difficult for them to totally relax in the constant brightness.

I showed Raymond the horses. He was a bit intimidated by them at first, but soon became accustomed to being around them.

"This is the horse that brought us together," I jokingly said, "you know that day when you shook my hand through the window and introduced yourself."

"I love this horse, then!" he said and gave him a pat on the neck as the horse gently nudged him back.

I then showed Raymond around and the equipment we used, and told him what it was like working there. "This is the tack trunk I use," I said and opened it up and showed him what was inside. Multiple brushes for grooming, hoof picks for cleaning out the soles of the horses' hooves, different liniments for their legs and muscles.

"Wow, I never realized how intense it was, caring for a horse," he said.

He then jokingly asked, "How do you get rid of their poop?"

I then explained what it was like to be a groom and how you used a pitchfork and wheelbarrow to clean out the horse's stall and then put down some fresh straw on top.

"Kind of gross. I'll stick to the pari-mutuels," Raymond said, smiling.

We eventually walked down to my tack room. At the ends of each barn there were small, enclosed rooms called tack rooms. Some trainers kept equipment in them, but most were used as living quarters for grooms.

"These here are tack rooms," I said. "Let me show you inside mine."

Like many other grooms, I had converted mine into a small apartment. It had a bed, a small fridge, and a nightstand.

"Wow, this is amazing. It's like a little sanctuary in here," he said.

"I enjoy coming in here, locking the door, and getting away from it all," I said. "I'll often stay here the night instead of going home."

We stood there, looking at each other. My heart was

pounding so hard I swear Raymond could have heard it beating. He stepped toward me and put his arms around me. We embraced and began to passionately kiss each other. I had never kissed anyone on the lips like that before and was unsure how good it was, but let nature take its course.

I raised my hands and put them on each side of his face.

"Oh my God, Raymond, I've waited for you my whole life," I said.

I ran my hands through his beautiful golden hair as we continued to kiss. I didn't want to let go.

He broke our embrace and lifted off my t-shirt. "Damn, I didn't realize how hairy you were, Dan," Raymond said.

My hands were shaking as I eagerly started to unbutton his shirt. As I undid each button, more and more chest hair was revealed. Once his shirt was off, I was in awe of his sexy and beautiful, hairy physique.

I ran my cheek over his hairy chest and across his hairy pecs, pausing to lick his nipples. I immediately got the scent of his armpit and continued licking my way toward them. I raised his arm to reveal a very hairy jungle.

It was then that I discovered that his beautiful musk was a strong aphrodisiac, and I was instantly addicted to his scent. The more I inhaled his manly smell, the more I wanted to give myself to him.

As I pressed my face in and began licking the hair, I could hear Raymond moan, "Oh my God, Dan."

I broke away as Raymond and I started passionately kissing again. It seemed like we were both in ecstasy, never wanting it to stop. Raymond started unbuckling my belt, as I did his. Soon we were both in our underwear.

Me in my briefs, while Raymond in his boxers.

I grabbed hold of his crotch.

"Holy fuck!" I said, as he pulled his boxers down.

Not only was Raymond handsome and hairy, but he was also incredibly hung.

I slipped out of my briefs.

"You're almost as big," Raymond said. He got on his knees and started to enjoy my manhood. We made our way onto the bed. The two of us rolled on top and underneath each other, my hands and tongue going places I had only fantasized about. We embraced and continued to explore our newfound, beautiful sexual experience.

After we both had finished, we continued to lie there in each other's arms and talked about how wonderful it was.

"I've never had these feelings that I have toward you, Dan. I've never felt the need to tell anyone this, but I'm falling in love with you."

I rolled on top of him and looked into his eyes. "I know what you mean, Raymond, as I'm in love with you as well."

I knew, then and there, that we were destined to be together. We had so much in common, but the most rewarding part was that I felt secure in knowing he was there.

It was as if he was my savior, my knight in shining armor, and I'd do anything to protect him from the evils out in the homophobic world. I believe that it's this connection of wanting to protect each other that makes the bond between LGTBQ+ couples so strong and devoted.

As we lay there, Raymond said, "I've fantasized about this for so long, yet I never realized it would be so much more enjoyable. It's difficult to explain."

"I know what you mean." I laid my head against his hairy chest.

After a few more minutes, we got up, got dressed, and made our way back to the parking lot.

Raymond got in his car, and I leaned through the window. "I don't know how I'm going to get through the next few days without seeing you," I said. "I'm going to miss you so much."

"I now wish I wasn't going, as I'd sooner spend my time with you. I love you, Dan," Raymond answered.

"I love you as well, Raymond," I said.

As we got into our cars and waved our goodbyes, we both knew our lives had changed, and changed for the better.

CHAPTER 5
August 1980.

After our first night of making love, it was as if my whole world wasn't complete unless I was in Raymond's company. When we were together, I was at peace with myself. When Raymond and I were apart, I was lost and alone. Our lovemaking seemed to bond the two of us closer than either of us could ever explain. It was a love beyond compare.

The next couple of days, I was in a world of my own, unconscious of what was going on around me, and I desperately waited for Raymond to return on Thursday.

My usual day would start at around six a.m. I would feed my horses their breakfast, and once they were finished, each needed to be exercised.

These horses were standardbreds that would pull a sulky behind them in a race. I'd start by brushing the horse off, then harness him up, attach him to a jogging cart, and then jog him five or six miles daily.

Once finished his jog, I would then remove his harness, bathe him off, and put a light woolen blanket on him. While he was cooling off, his stall would be cleaned out, and fresh straw added. The horse would then be given some hay and let loose into his clean stall. I would repeat this for each horse under my care.

Once they were cooled down and dry, they would each be taken out of their stall, brushed again, and any physiotherapy that was needed would be done.

Many horses had slight injuries that would need to be addressed, just like any athlete. Often it was a ligament or joint issues that needed to be tended to. They would be bandaged, or support wraps applied around their lower legs, and returned to their stall for the day.

It was often a long day, finishing in the afternoon, only to return later in the day if you had a horse to race in the evening.

Once Thursday arrived, I quickly made my way over to the grandstand. The first race didn't start until 7:45 p.m. but I was sitting up in the grandstand at seven p.m., waiting, waiting to see my Raymond again.

Finally, I saw Raymond walking my way.

He was smiling from ear to ear, and once he was near, we gave each other a big hug, not caring if anyone saw.

"I'm so glad to see you!" he said.

"You have no idea how much I've missed you," I answered back. "Did you have a good time while you were up there?"

"It was okay. Usually, it's just Rozz and me hanging out down at the lake. I'd love for you to see it one day," he said. "While up at the cottage, I was constantly thinking about you. Whatever I was doing, I wondered what it would be like if we were doing it together. Going swimming, having breakfast and dinner, even while I was in bed, I'd think of you. That last one I thought about a lot! I then realized how much I missed seeing you and that I'm wanting to be with you every day."

"I know what you mean. I couldn't stop thinking about

you as well. I'm so glad you're back," I answered. I desperately wanted to kiss him and show my affection, but knew it was simply out of the question to do so in public.

"Even my sister Rozz asked what was on my mind, as I looked like I was always deep in thought. She jokingly said, 'If I didn't know better, little brother, someone would think that you were deep in love by the way you're acting.'

"I excitedly told her that I've met a great guy, and can't wait to get back to see him," Raymond said.

"You mentioned me to your sister?" I froze, not knowing what she'd think, and then nervously asked, "Was she alright with that?"

"She was so excited knowing that I've finally met someone and asked me all about you. I told her how we met, and what you're like. I babbled on and on.

"She wants to meet you," Raymond mentioned. "She invited us over to her place next Saturday night for dinner, if you would like to go. She has an apartment here in Toronto and works at a bank downtown."

"Do you think it's okay? I don't mind going, but I'm nervous about anyone knowing that we're dating," I said.

"Rozz is different, as she totally understands our situation and is totally supportive. I know you'll fall in love with her. There's nothing to worry about," Raymond reassured me.

"In that case, I'd love to go. Shall we meet here at the track and drive to her place?" I asked.

"Sounds perfect," Raymond said. "I have to get to work. Meet you here on my break?"

"I'll be waiting," I eagerly answered back and watched as he walked away with his long, confident strides. I felt so proud to be his boyfriend.

We agreed to meet back at the backstretch at around six p.m. on Saturday to head to Rozz's place.

That Saturday, I sat in my car, waiting for Raymond in the track's parking lot. When he pulled up and I got out and jumped into his car, I quickly glanced around to see if anyone was near before giving him a kiss on the cheek.

I had purchased a large bouquet of flowers to give to Rozz.

"Aw, are those for me?" Raymond coyly asked.

I pulled one daisy from the group and said, "This is yours. The rest are for your sister."

Raymond laughed, put the flower behind his ear, and we drove to Rozz's place. Once there, we parked in the visitors' parking and walked to the entrance.

"I hope she likes me," I said.

"She's going to be so glad to see you. Don't be so nervous," he said as he buzzed her apartment from the lobby.

"Hey, Rozz, it's Raymond and Dan."

"Come on up, guys," she answered.

I could tell she had a very quiet and loving tone in her voice, which helped reassure me that once we met, she would accept me as her brother's boyfriend.

Once in the elevator, Raymond reached over and held my hand. "Your hand is all sweaty," he laughed.

"I'm nervous, okay," I answered, and wiped both of them on my pants.

We got to the door and knocked. Rozz opened it and immediately welcomed us in.

I could smell dinner cooking and it smelled delicious.

"I've heard so much about you, Dan," she said, and gave me a hug.

"These are for you," I replied and handed her the bouquet of flowers.

"Aw, how sweet of you," she said. "These are so pretty. Thank you, Dan. Let me put these in some water. You've chosen a very loving man, Raymond. I can tell."

I immediately started to blush. Raymond then grabbed my hand and led me to the couch.

"What would you like to drink? I have beer, Coke, and, of course, root beer for Raymond. What can I get you, Dan?" Rozz asked.

"I'll have a Coke, please," I answered.

"Root beer for me, Rozz," replied Raymond. "Can I help you with anything?"

"No, you sit with Dan. I can manage."

Rozz came back with our drinks and some small turnover munchies.

"Here, you two. You can start on these." She then went back into the kitchen, came out with the flowers in a vase, and placed them on top of the one end table. "These are so pretty, Dan. Thank you so much."

"You're very welcome, Rozz," I answered, and gave her a shy smile.

We sat and talked about how we met and how Rozz thought we made such a cute couple.

"I want you to know, Dan, that I fully understand the relationship that you and Raymond are in, and I totally support it. There's nothing wrong with two men falling in love with each other. I only wish other people in this heartless society would be more understanding. I'm so pleased to see that Raymond has finally found someone, and I'll always support and do what I can to help you both," Rozz said.

I certainly felt comfortable listening to Rozz and could tell she was sincere about her feelings toward us.

"Thanks," I said, "for years, I've hidden away in that cold closet just like Raymond has. It's difficult to explain how great it is to at least come out to Raymond, and yourself, and feel at ease without any fear of reprisal. It's sad to think that you have to keep your 'gay life' out of everyone's sight and thoughts. The only time you can ever let your guard down is in situations like right here."

"It must be difficult for you both," Rozz said. "I have a friend who is gay, and his life can be a challenge as well. Rest assured, I'm here for you both, so feel free to come for a visit if you two ever need to escape the homophobic world."

"Let me check on dinner," she said. "We're having roast beef. I hope you like it."

"My favorite," I said.

Raymond looked over. "Mine as well."

We both smiled.

Rozz worked as a loans officer at the bank close to her apartment. She mentioned that she wasn't presently dating anyone but was happy with her life.

We had a great evening with Rozz. She was so pleased to see Raymond finally happy.

"Thank you, again, Dan, for making my little brother so happy. You have certainly filled an empty void in his life."

Surprisingly, I felt so at ease with Rozz that I answered back, "Well, he's my man now, and I'm forever grateful to have him in my life."

Raymond lifted my hand and kissed the back of it. "And I'm your man as well, babe," he replied.

"Thanks, hun," I said.

By this time in our relationship, we had developed nicknames for each other. He called me his babe, while I called him my hun.

"Wow, it must be serious if you have nicknames for one another," Rozz teased.

When it was time to leave, Rozz gave each of us a big hug. "I'm so glad for you guys. Drive safe and know that I love you both," she said.

I then fully understood what Raymond had meant about

his sister and how understanding she was. Raymond and I got in the car and headed back to the track.

"Your sister is such a sweetheart, hun. I felt so at ease being with her and being able to show my affections to you without any need to worry," I said.

"I told you that you'd like her. Want to know what she said to me about you when we were in the kitchen?" Raymond asked.

"Should I be worried?" I joked.

"She advised me that she could see a natural connection between us, a bond that has brought us together. Basically, she suggested that I keep you." Raymond smiled and reached out his hand.

"She really said that, hun? You're really going to keep me around for a little while?" I teased.

"At least till we get back to the track. I'd hate to see you walk," Raymond laughed.

It was around 10:30 by the time we got back to the racetrack, and the last race was just about to start.

"Did you want to beat the rush, hun, or wait a while before heading for home?" I asked.

"Do you have anything in mind about how we could wait out the hour?" Raymond replied with that sparkle in his eye.

"We could walk down to the barn and check on the horses, give them some hay and fresh water, and maybe do an inspection of the tack room," I said with a huge grin.

"Yes, I think you're right. I'll do the inspection from top to bottom," Raymond said.

We walked up to the guard shack where my security friend, George, was standing watch.

"Hey, George, how's the night going for you?" I asked.

"Hi, Dan, we had a nasty fall in that one race. Did you see it?" he replied.

"No, I wasn't watching the races tonight. I was out with Raymond here. What horse was it? Is the driver okay?" I asked.

Anytime there was an accident, I was always shaken up, as you get to know so many of the horses and drivers. There was always an ambulance and crew at trackside, as well as an attending veterinarian available should an accident ever occur, as they could be quite dangerous for both horse and driver.

"Everyone is fine. The horse walked away, a bit sore, however, but he seemed alright. It was near the back of the pack. Only one horse went down," he said.

"That's good. I hate seeing those falls, as they're so frightening to watch. Raymond and I are just going to check on the horses," I said.

"Have a good night, Dan and Raymond," George replied and curiously gave me a smile.

We casually walked down to our barn. There were a couple of horses racing out of our barn that night but from another stable at the opposite end of the shed row. Every horse trainer was assigned a certain number of stalls for his stable. These were then arranged together, so there were a few stables within each barn.

I then showed Raymond how much hay each horse was to get and how to simply toss it over the horse's stall door. As Raymond started giving them hay, I started changing their water buckets with cold, fresh water.

Once finished, we cleaned up the shed row and walked down to the end of the barn.

Luckily, no one was around to see us, and we unlocked the tack room and went inside. We once again enjoyed each other's company and soon fell asleep together. Fortunately, I woke up about a couple of hours later. It was one o'clock in the morning.

I shook Raymond and quietly said, "Raymond, wake up. It's one in the morning."

I had to try waking him once more, as he was such a sound sleeper. "Hun, get up. We fell asleep. You have to get home."

Raymond woke up and sleepily pushed me back onto the bed.

"I don't want to go home. This is my home, with you," he said.

"Wouldn't that be amazing if we did live together, hun?" I replied. "Just imagine how wonderful it would be, always being together."

We both snuggled up that much closer after fantasizing about our pretend household.

We walked back down to the parking lot. Raymond got in his car as I casually looked around and then stuck my head in the driver's window.

"Drive safely, hun. I love you, Raymond," I said, and then gave him a kiss.

"I love you, too, babe," he replied, and we both drove home in our continued state of happiness.

CHAPTER 6
Spring 1981.

After dating for a few months, Raymond and I discovered one of the gay nightclubs in the city.

We loved going there and tried to go as often as our work schedules would permit.

Tonight was a warm, spring, Saturday night, and the horses were racing at Mohawk Raceway out in Campbellville. Raymond and I would still meet up in the grandstand when racing out there, and since it was an enclosed grandstand, we would venture to the far end, hopefully away from anyone.

"I don't feel like watching the races tonight. Let's go into Toronto and to the club," Raymond said. "What do you think?"

"I'd love to go, hun. I'd have to get changed first."

I answered, "I have fresh clothes back in the tack room."

"I have to change on the way, also. Do you mind if we stopped at home first?" Raymond asked.

"Are your parents home? With everything you and Rozz mentioned about your dad, I'm somewhat nervous, to be honest," I said.

"Sooner or later, you're going to meet them. They don't need to know about us. I'll just say that I'm driving you home because you had car trouble at the track, and that we're going to go have something to eat first. That's why I need to freshen up. They won't figure it out."

Raymond then drove me from the grandstand back to the barn area, which at Mohawk was quite a distance away.

Once at the guard shack, I leaned over from the passenger seat, looking out the driver's window.

"Hi, Art, I'm just checking on the horses. Only be a minute or two," I said to the security guard.

"Hi, Dan, no problem. Go on through." He lifted the gate.

Raymond and I checked on the horses, and I then quickly got into a fresh shirt.

We then drove into Milton to Raymond's parents' home. With everything Raymond told me about his homophobic father, it was all I could do to remain calm. I kept wondering if he would think I was a gay guy, and not knowing any better whether he'd lose his temper at both of us.

"Relax, babe. It looks like you've seen a ghost." Raymond chuckled.

It was around eight p.m. when we finally arrived and went inside.

I heard a deep bellow come from somewhere. "Raymond, is that you?" his father asked.

"Hey, Dad, I'm just going to get a fresh shirt," Raymond replied.

We walked into the living room where his parents were sitting watching television.

"This is Dan," Raymond said. "His car broke down, and I'm driving him home. We're going to go get something to eat first. I'll be right back."

"Nice to meet you, Mr. and Mrs. Scott," I said and reached out and shook their hands.

I watched as Raymond's father got up out of his chair and stood.

He kept getting taller and taller as he stood until he seemed to dwarf everything around him, including myself. His father was at least six foot four, weighed over 300 pounds, and was a construction worker.

He reached out his hand. My hand completely disappeared within his grasp.

"Nice to meet you, son," his father said in his deep voice.

"Do you work at the racetrack also, Dan?" asked his mother.

"Yes, I'm a groom in the backstretch. Lucky for me, Raymond saw me with the hood of my car open, and he drove over to me," I tried to sound as convincing as possible.

Just then, Raymond returned. He was wearing a fresh top and dress shorts.

"All set," he said. "Let's go."

"Enjoy your evening. It was nice meeting you," I said.

"Drive safely, Raymond," said his mother. "Nice meeting you, Dan."

Once back in the car, I mentioned to Raymond how intimidating his father seemed. "I felt like I was staring at Hercules," I said, "and what's with his voice? I've never heard anyone with a voice that deep. He sounded like Darth Vader. Hell, I think your mother has a deeper voice than I do."

Raymond laughed. "Yeah, Dad's kind of intimidating, alright, and he uses it toward people also, and with him being such a homophobe, you can understand now why I could never let him find out about us.

"It's terrible to say, but I honestly think if he found out that I'm gay, he'd probably beat the crap out of me."

From that moment onward, I was terrified of his father.

Visions of my past, and the possible violence against Raymond or me, unsettled me.

"Forget about my dad and let's go have a good time," Raymond said.

We drove into downtown Toronto and to the club.

I recall we would go there as often as we could, simply because once inside, we could let our guard down, be ourselves, and have a good time.

When there, no one would judge you, nor condemn your lifestyle. We were all one big brotherhood, and everyone was free to relax for a while.

Over time, we became friends with the doorman, who was also one of the bouncers, a huge pussycat of a man named Robert.

"Hey, guys, good to see you again," Robert said and invited us in.

"Going to show us more of those slick-footed dance moves, Raymond?" he joked.

Raymond was an incredible dancer. He'd make up dance moves to the lyrics of the different songs and dance them through. Certain songs became our favorite to dance to. Songs like "Oh Mickey You're So Fine," by Toni Basil, "The Heat of The Moment," by Asia, and John Mellencamp's "It Hurts So Good," all bring back fun memories.

Tonight was no exception.

We sat enjoying our beer at our table when the song "Don't Stand so Close to Me," by The Police came on.

"Let's dance, babe!" and Raymond grabbed my hand as we went onto the dance floor.

When they'd sing, "Don't stand so close to me," Raymond would scowl his brow, then turn and stare, all the while pointing and shaking his finger at me. I can still see Raymond's thin hairy legs jumping off the floor while wearing his black-and-white Keds ankle-high sneakers, or as he called them his AHS.

We soon became regulars there and loved going.

One evening, we were at the club having a fun night out. We had just finished dancing and were sitting down when a big, hairy, muscular guy, or as they are often referred to in the gay community, a "bear," came over to our table and asked Raymond to dance.

"Hey, good-looking. You're quite the dancer. Care to hit the dance floor with me?" he asked.

Raymond thanked him but declined his invite.

The big guy shrugged and walked away.

A couple of minutes later, the guy was back, asking again.

"At least let me buy you a beer, then," he said.

"Thanks, but no thanks. I'm with my boyfriend," Raymond answered.

The big guy reluctantly went back to the bar.

"Damn, he's persistent," Raymond said.

"I don't like him. He's trying to pick you up," I angrily said, trying to hide my jealous streak.

"Don't worry, babe. He's had one too many beers and is all talk," Raymond answered.

We sat enjoying our beer when the guy came over a third time. He grabbed Raymond by the arm, pulled him to his feet, then said, "Come on, cutie, just one dance. I'm sure your little boyfriend won't mind, will you?" He glared and laughed at me.

Even though this guy was easily twice my size, I jumped up from the table and tried shoving him off.

"Fuck off!" I yelled. "He doesn't want to dance with you!"

The humongous guy grabbed me by one arm, picked me up, laughed, and then proceeded to throw me across the dance floor. I lay there and watched as Raymond tried to avoid him and make his way to me as other patrons stared in astonishment.

The two bouncers, Robert and Big Johnny, rushed over after seeing what happened, grabbed the guy and started to escort him out.

"It's time for you to go. We don't allow any roughhousing here," said Robert. Luckily, the guy didn't resist and left without any further confrontation.

"Are you okay, babe?" Raymond asked. "What were you thinking? He could have hurt you."

"No one comes between me and my man."

I had a terrible jealous streak back then, and still do to this day.

Raymond helped me up and gave me a hug.

To our surprise, as Raymond and I stood up holding on to each other, the crowd of guys around us started to cheer and applaud.

"The splendor of youth!" someone yelled.

"More like the splendor of stupidity," Raymond said, as he grabbed hold of my rear end and returned to our seat.

"I'm thirsty. How about another beer?" Raymond asked.

"Sure, I need something to calm my nerves after that," I replied. "Do you need any money, hun?" I asked.

Raymond looked and still had a couple of tens in his wallet. "I'm loaded."

"I know you're loaded, but do you need any money?" I jokingly replied as I grabbed his crotch.

Raymond leaned over and kissed me and went to the bar and got us another beer.

When he returned, he was followed by a cute-looking Asian guy around our age.

"Do you mind if I join you? I'm Eddie," he said.

"Please, have a seat," Raymond said as we shook hands.

"I'm Raymond, and this is my boyfriend, Dan."

"Nice to meet you, Eddie," I said. "Do you come here often? I don't recall seeing you here before."

"This is my first time here. Actually, it's my first time at any gay bar, so I'm still sort of nervous," Eddie said.

"You're more than welcome to join us," Raymond said.

"Thanks," said Eddie, and sat down with us. "That was quite the fight you had. That guy was huge."

"I'm still shaking from it." I laughed and stuck out my hand, showing it quivering still.

"He was an asshole," said Raymond.

We all had a drink and started to get to know each other. Eddie was in a similar situation to ours.

He was a young gay man trapped and hidden inside the closet because of his domineering and homophobic Asian parents, particularly his father.

I believe Eddie's mother knew he was gay, but for fear of reprisal from his father, she never said anything.

After another drink, Raymond and I were back on the dance floor. We motioned for Eddie to join us, but he shook his head.

"I can't dance at all. I have no rhythm," Eddie said.

We all laughed and practically dragged him onto the floor. Both Raymond and Eddie were laughing as they watched me in my attempt to dance and sing.

We all sat back down and were having a great time. "How are you enjoying your first gay bar adventure?" Raymond asked Eddie.

"I'm having an amazing time," Eddie replied. "Thanks so much for allowing me to join you. It's the first time I've ever actually felt relaxed about being my gay self. It was so liberating and fun."

"That's great," I said. "We should meet up again."

Raymond mentioned to Eddie that we often went there on Saturday as we didn't have to work the next day and that he was more than welcome to join us.

"Thanks, guys. I'll certainly make a point of being here. My parents own a restaurant in Chinatown. One night I'll take you there."

It was around one o'clock in the morning when we all decided to head for home.

"Thanks for a fun night," Eddie said. "I really enjoyed myself and hope to see you guys here again. Will you be here next Saturday?"

"Let's plan on it," Raymond said. "Meet you here around ten p.m.?"

"I'll be here," said Eddie.

Afterwards, Raymond and I drove back to the track. As we drove, I gently placed my hand on Raymond's inner thigh and asked, "What's up, big fella?"

"I swear you can read my mind, babe. Are you asking him, or me?" he jokingly said.

"Both," I said, "and I think I got the answer I was looking for from each of you."

As we drove, the more intimately excited we became, anticipating some fun. We secretly stopped by the tack room and enjoyed each other's nakedness again. Once finished, we continued to lie in each other's arms and wished how we could be with each other every day.

"I luv ya, babe," Raymond said.

"I love you more," I responded.

"Do not," Raymond said.

"Do so," I replied.

"Do not, do so, do not," we quietly bantered back and forth, chuckling.

"Our first quarrel," I laughed.

Raymond rolled on top of me. "Let's have make-up sex!" He laughed, and we started at it once again.

"I do love you, babe. More than you'll ever know," he said.

I hugged my Raymond close and tight. "I know, hun, and I hope you know how much you mean to me."

We lay in each other's embrace, content and secure, never wanting to be apart.

We then got dressed and Raymond went home to his parents while I spent the night in the tack room. I lay there, imagining how wonderful it would be if we could live together and whether it would ever be possible. Forgetting about the homophobic state of the world, I wondered what it would be like to come home to each other. Waking up beside my Raymond and kissing him good morning, then going to bed and kissing him good night. I desperately wanted the chance to look after and care for my man. Helping with the household chores, doing laundry, and cooking his meals, celebrating special days together.

In my delirious state of pleasure, I soon fell asleep.

CHAPTER 7
Summer 1981.

Once again, the horses were back racing out of Greenwood Racetrack in downtown Toronto. Moving from one racetrack to another, and transporting your stable, made for a busy day. All your equipment had to be packed up and moved. Usually, a transport truck designed specifically to transport horses was hired. They could carry ten or twelve horses at a time. Along with the horses, the truck would ship the harnesses, tack boxes, racing sulkies, and training sulkies, plus a groom's personal items from his tack room, like bed, clothes, etc.

Some grooms would even get a ride, sitting with the driver in the cab.

Moving day was usually on days when there was no racing at the track to make it less hectic for all involved.

We had moved into our barn and because there was no racing that night, I didn't get to see Raymond, which made me terribly lonely.

The next day, while at work in the backstretch, I was constantly thinking about him, and since there was racing that evening, I knew Raymond would be working in the grandstand and I eagerly couldn't wait for the races to start.

Luckily, I had no horse racing and once six o'clock rolled around, I quickly made my way from the backstretch to the grandstand. As I walked to the grandstand, I started thinking about how long we had been seeing each other. It was difficult to believe that we had been seeing each other for over a year and were entering our second year together. How could time go by so quickly?

I was in such a happy mood, waiting to see him that I visualized about running up to him, jumping into his arms and wrapping my legs around his waist.

Just then, I saw Raymond walking toward me. I could instantly tell something was wrong and my joyous feeling instantly vanished.

He sat beside me and started fidgeting back and forth, running his hands through his hair while not wanting to make eye contact and sighing heavily.

"What's the matter, hun? You seem upset," I asked, worried that he might have bad news and instantly thought something was wrong between us.

"It's my father again. He keeps drilling me about not having a girlfriend. He even asked about you the other day."

"Me? Why me?" I nervously asked as I stared at Raymond. I could feel myself getting all tense at just the thought of seeing Raymond's father interrogating him and asking about us. It was a feeling of both being terrified of his father yet wanting to comfort my boyfriend at the same time.

"Remember a couple of months ago, when we stopped at my parents' place so I could get changed before going out to the club? The night you apparently had 'car trouble'?" he said.

"Yeah, what about it?" I asked.

"My father repeatedly asked who you were, where I'd met you, and why I was always seeing you. I never realized it, but

I'd often tell them that 'I'm meeting Dan and won't be home for dinner tonight,' I just can't take his interfering and constant questioning all the time."

I felt so sorry for him as he sat there, leaning forward, looking at the ground in total despair.

"I'm sorry if I've gotten you into any trouble. What are you going to do, hun?" I asked, nervous of the possibility that his father's actions might jeopardize our new relationship.

"It's not your fault, babe. It's him, and I desperately need to get away. A friend of Rozz's has a one-bedroom apartment that she's moving out of this November," Raymond said. "It's in Milton, and I'd really like to get it, but I'm a bit worried about the monthly rent as it's over four hundred dollars. I added in the extra costs of electricity and parking just to be sure I can afford it. Rozz suggested that I take it. She said she's willing to help me with the first few months' rent if needed."

"That's great," I said. "What if I help as well? I can give you something every month, too. After all, I hope I'll be invited over now and then."

"I was kind of hoping you'd move in," Raymond replied, "like my secret roommate, AKA partner."

When I heard Raymond say "partner," I felt as if I'd just got married, and fell that much more in love with him.

As we spoke, I could see his beautiful smile return and the joy coming back into his face.

"I'm willing to do that, hun," I said. "It would work out, as anytime I'd stay at your apartment, I'd just tell my parents I'm staying at the track for the night. I spend most of my nights at the track anyway. Let's do it!" I excitedly said.

"Oh, babe, I love you so much. This is like a dream come true for both of us. I can't wait to make it happen."

Raymond talked it over with Rozz and the situation

regarding me living with him. She knew we were still dating and was very positive about our relationship. She had no reservations about us living together and encouraged Raymond to get the apartment and get out on his own.

A few days later Raymond signed on the dotted line and we got ourselves the apartment. He had finally distanced himself from his homophobic behemoth of a father, of whom I was terrified after meeting that one day.

I helped move some of Raymond's belongings into the apartment from his parents' place and met his father and mother a couple of more times in the process.

His mother was always friendly and nice whenever I saw her, even showing her support for Raymond getting the apartment. His father, on the other hand, was always stern and direct when I was around, more concerned about the apartment's cost and how Raymond was ever going to afford it on his own. Almost questioning if someone was going to share in the rent.

We set up the apartment and felt as if we had just become a little gay family of our own, in our own small gay sanctuary, away from the harshness of the homophobic world.

We had little to no furniture but were pleased it was our own. Raymond brought his new stereo system, complete with acoustic speakers, to the apartment, along with his collection of LPs and cassettes, in order to practice his dance moves for going to the club.

When Raymond's parents heard he was moving into an apartment, they told him that they would buy him a new couch and coffee table.

"My mom and dad are willing to buy a new couch and coffee table for the apartment, babe. Let's go shopping at

Sears on Wednesday," Raymond said. "My mom told me that she told my dad to give us his Sears card."

"Your mom said that? Wow, that's a surprise. She said 'us,' hun? She really said that?" I asked.

"That's what she told me on the phone, 'us,'" Raymond said. "I'm sure it was my mom's idea to let us go furniture shopping."

"Let's take some measurements for what size we need," I said. "What kind of couch are you thinking of?"

"Anything but leather," Raymond answered. "It's so hot and cold, and sticky."

That Wednesday I arranged for someone to feed the horses and we headed out to one of the Sears stores on the outskirts of Toronto.

As we were looking at the different couches, a nice lady came over to help.

"Are you looking for anything in particular?" she asked.

"I just got my first apartment and was looking at getting a nice comfortable couch. Nothing too modern, but not old fashioned either," Raymond said.

"Congratulations," she said. "Do you have a budget?"

"No, not really, but I know when I see it if I like it," Raymond replied.

As they were talking, I was walking around and spotted a couch and matching love seat off in the corner. I walked over and sat down, got back up, and then flopped down. It felt so comfortable.

It even had a nice coffee table, just the right height to place your feet on. It had soft beige fabric, with big, curled fabric-covered armrests. The bigger couch sat three people, while the love seat had room for two.

I was watching Raymond talking with the salesperson

when he started looking around to see where I went. When he spotted me, I waved and motioned for him to come over.

I could see him say something to the lady and they both started walking over to where I was.

"Try this one out, Raymond," I said, and he sat his tall self down.

"This is so comfortable, ba— ... Dan," he said.

I knew he was going to say "babe" but caught himself short with the lady standing so close.

"I love this one," he said, and placed his long legs on the coffee table.

"This is a lovely couch," the lady said. "It's made with an all-oak frame, and the fabric is also protected with Scotchgard against spills and stains."

Raymond nudged me in the side with his elbow after hearing that remark.

"Would you want the coffee table and the two end tables, also?" she asked.

"Yes, please," Raymond answered.

"Does it come with pillows?" I asked.

"No, but we have an assortment of pillows over here," she said. "Let me get a pillow that I think would match perfectly." She went into the next area and returned with two big and two smaller matching pillows with a bold plaid print.

"What about these?" she asked. "I like the two different sizes to choose from, especially when you're lying down."

"They look great," Raymond said, "and we'll need a couple of lamps also."

The lady walked us over to the lighting section and went directly over to two lamps on display.

"I think these would make a nice combination with the tables. The color of the couch blends with the color of these lampshades," she said.

Raymond looked at me and we both agreed to everything the lady suggested.

"We'll take it all," Raymond mentioned.

"What day would you like delivery? The earliest we can delivery would be this Friday," she said.

"Do you have an opening for Saturday?" Raymond responded.

"Yes, that would work also," she said. "There's an opening for later in the afternoon."

She gathered up all the needed delivery and address information.

"Will this be on your Sears card?" she asked.

"Yes," and Raymond handed her his father's Sears credit card.

She handed Raymond the paperwork and thanked us both for the sale.

"I really like that, hun," I said, making sure no one heard, and went back to try it out once more. Raymond followed and sat right up against me.

"Yup, I like this. It's comfy cozy, babe," he said and grabbed my hand for a moment and then let go. "Imagine the stories this will hold." We both giggled at each other.

We started walking back to the car.

"I'm hungry," Raymond said. "I feel like a burger."

"Let's stop in town at Burger King. I feel like a Whopper," I replied.

"I already gave you a whopper, babe, but let's get a burger," Raymond laughed. "I'll have to speak to the super about using the freight elevator on Saturday. I'll talk to him in the morning."

Once we got in the car, we continued our conversation. "It was really nice of your parents to purchase that for you, hun, but I'm still afraid of your dad, no matter how nice he seems," I said. "I'm sure your mom and dad will want to come over and see the new furniture. I'll make sure I won't be there when they do."

Raymond chuckled, and like always, whenever we would talk about his father, he became fidgety and nervous, especially when talking about his father visiting the apartment.

"I know, babe, I'm afraid of Dad also, but if they want to help me get started, then I'm not going to say no. I'd never rely on it, but my father is very well off financially, so I know he can afford it. That's why I wanted to get the extras for us as well," Raymond mentioned. "He basically inherited most of the construction company once his father passed away. He's doing alright."

We got our burgers and continued driving back to the apartment. We always ordered the same, fries and a cheeseburger, with lettuce, pickles, and mayo. The only difference was Raymond would always get root beer while I got a Coke.

The next morning Raymond arranged to use the freight elevator and got a key from the super.

Once Saturday came, I was up extra early and went and exercised the horses as quickly as possible, finally finishing around one p.m.

I raced home, but the delivery truck hadn't arrived yet. "I hope they get here soon, hun. I can't wait to see it all set up," I said.

"Me too, babe," Raymond replied.

We waited for another couple of hours, then the buzzer finally sounded.

"Sears to make a delivery for Raymond Scott," the guy said.

"I'll be right down," Raymond said. "It's finally here, babe." Then he left.

The apartment was covered in carpet, and we had rented a carpet cleaner and had given it a thorough cleaning after moving in. Everything was ready for our new couch, and I eagerly waited for it to get there.

A few minutes later, the delivery guys carried the main couch into the apartment.

"Right over here, guys," I said and pointed to the open spot against the wall facing our little black-and-white TV on the stand. After another couple of trips, everything was set up.

"Just make sure everything is here that's on your receipt, and then sign," the guy said.

"One couch, love seat, coffee table, two end tables, two lamps, and four pillows. Yup, it's all here. Thanks, guys," Raymond said.

"Do you guys each want a Coke?" I offered. "I have some in the fridge, if you like."

"Sure, that'd be great," the one guy mentioned.

I gave the guy the two bottles of Coke.

"Thanks a lot. Enjoy your new furniture, guys," he said, and they both left.

We finished setting up the couch and moved the loveseat to the other side, making it a bit more open and easier to get onto the main couch.

"Ok, that TV has just got to go," Raymond said. "It's super tiny and a pain to watch."

"One day, hun. One day we'll get a big one. Right now, I want to enjoy what we have." I flopped down on the couch.

Raymond came over and sat beside me. We both cuddled against each other.

"We did it, babe. We have our own place," Raymond said and put his arm around me.

Although I still lived with my parents, I told them that it was such a long drive to the track that I wanted to save money on gas and was going to spend more nights in the tack room at the racetrack, when in reality, I'd be spending them at the apartment.

That night, to celebrate moving into our own new place, we eagerly made love. We felt so liberated from the homophobic world outside, safe and secure within our own small sanctuary where we could enjoy being a loving gay couple, free from the harm and judgment of society.

The night was filled with an incredible recollection of affection. We were a couple, a proud gay couple, full of love and admiration for each other. All the negativity that I had felt and had dealt with in my past was overshadowed by the love we had for each other.

I recall the next morning writing in my journal the following sentiments. It was difficult for me to believe that fate had brought Raymond into my life.

For who was I to say, when true love would come
my way?
I only hoped one day that you would be mine.
Your glance is like heaven, and anytime you're near,
I want to say I love you, in a hope that all will hear.
The moment we met, I knew true love had come
my way,
Your affection captured my heart, and your smile
asked me to stay.
Be beside me forever and as partners we shall share,
the beauty of life together and we won't care if others
should stare.
For you are my life, my rock, a glorious blessing
from above,
You are my soul mate, my best friend, and the true
reason I am loved.
Whether we're in the passion of the night,
or the sunshine of the day,
I'll forever be there with you,

my true love, my one love,
my ever-loving Ray.

Raymond, I love you.

CHAPTER 8

We were very fortunate to have met a lovely older lady, who lived across the hall from us. Mrs. Hutchinson was a widow in her sixties and lived alone. After a while, we affectionately called her Mrs. H for short.

We had first met Mrs. Hutchinson when Raymond and I were moving into the apartment.

We had finally moved our stuff into the apartment and were exhausted, sitting on the only two chairs we had at the time, when there was a knock on the door.

"Who could that be?" I asked.

Raymond looked through the peephole and then opened the door. There, standing and holding a casserole dish, was a friendly looking older lady.

"Welcome to our little neighborhood," she said. "I'm Mrs. Hutchinson. I live across the hall from you, dear. Here is a little something for you."

She gave the casserole to Raymond, who put it in the kitchen.

"Nice to meet you, Mrs. Hutchinson. I'm Raymond," he said.

"I thought you'd be too busy to make dinner, so tell your wife she can relax. I know how hectic moving is," she said.

"I'm not married, Mrs. Hutchinson," Raymond said, and called for me. "Dan, come here."

I went into the kitchen as Raymond reached for and held out my hand as he introduced me.

"This is Mrs. Hutchinson, she lives across the hall. This is my roommate, Dan. Neither of us is married," Raymond said.

"Nice to meet you, my dear," she said.

You could see some bewilderment on her face, but she seemed understanding and nonjudgmental.

"I'll bring the casserole dish over later, Mrs. Hutchinson, and thank you so much. That was very nice of you," I said.

"Don't mention it, my dears, now go enjoy your dinner. Good night."

"What a nice lady," Raymond said.

"Do you think she knows about us, hun?" I asked.

"Well, after me holding your hand the entire time as we spoke, I'm pretty sure she knows now." Raymond chuckled. "I felt totally at ease with her. She seemed so kind and genuine."

Over time, we became good friends with Mrs. Hutchinson. She would often knock on our apartment door and say, "Hello, dears, I've made too much lasagna. You might as well enjoy it." She'd say this with a straight face, with the casserole dish completely full, and without any portion removed. We both truly believed that it made her feel wanted, knowing she was somehow helping to feed us.

One Saturday afternoon I was driving back from the track when on the off ramp of the highway there was a man selling flowers. Being the sentimental fool I was, and still am, I thought I'd stop and buy some flowers for Raymond and the apartment.

As I looked at the many different bouquets, I asked how much they were. The man said, "Seven-fifty for one, or two for twelve dollars."

I then thought I'd buy two, one for Raymond and one for Mrs. Hutchinson. I got home, went upstairs, and went inside.

"I'm home, hun," I said, and Raymond came out of the bedroom and gave me my usual welcome-home kiss.

"These are for you. I thought they'd help brighten up the place as well," I said. "I also got these for Mrs. H. She's always bringing us food and thought it would be nice to return the niceness."

"Babe, you're such a sweetheart," he said.

We both decided to take them over to her and knocked on her door.

"Well, hello, dears. Come in, come in," she said.

We went inside. "These are for you, Mrs. H. We wanted to thank you for all the kindness that you've shown us since we moved in. You've really made us feel welcome. We hardly know anyone else in this building. Everyone seems so private," I said.

I'm not sure when the last time she had gotten flowers was, but they sure put a smile on her face.

"Oh, dears, these are so beautiful. Thank you so much. You're so sweet, the both of you. Now sit down and I'll put these in water, then make us tea."

We enjoyed our visit with Mrs. H and then went back home.

"Thanks again, dears, that was very kind of you," she said, and gave us both another hug.

A few days later, I was down getting Raymond's mail. The only mail was Raymond's *Billboard* music magazine, which he always looked forward to receiving and reading cover to cover, often reading it two or three times.

Just then, Mrs. Hutchinson arrived. "Good afternoon, dear. How are you?" she would always say.

"I'm good thanks, Mrs. Hutchinson. How's your day going?"

She mentioned she was doing well, and then out of nowhere she said, "Dan, dear, I know that you and Raymond are partners, and I want you to know that I understand. I can see the joy on your faces when you're together.

"My nephew is a homosexual also, and I'm fully supportive of you. But tell me, dear, what's so important that you need to run to the basement sometimes? Twice now you've passed me going full throttle down the stairs."

"I'm not going to hide it from you, Mrs. Hutchinson. Raymond and I are partners, and we do love each other. I love him more than anything I know. We both greatly appreciate your kindness and support.

"As far as racing to the basement goes, I run downstairs to hide whenever Raymond's father comes to visit unexpectedly and rings us from the lobby. He's not as understanding as you are. In fact, should he ever find out, he would gladly use violence, instead of words, to show his displeasure at Raymond and I being together," I said.

"Raymond's father grew up in a different generation, dear. Back then, homosexuality was thought of as repulsive and dirty, so I understand your fear about him, Dan. Feel free to knock on my door, dear, should you have to get away," she said as she gently reached for and held my hand.

"It hasn't changed a great deal over the years but thank you for your kind support," I said.

"Be happy, my dear, to love and, more importantly, to be loved, is the greatest gift to share with each other," she said.

Mrs. Hutchinson gave me a hug and then said, "I have to

get dinner ready, dear. I'm making lasagna, you know."

I smiled and chuckled to myself and said, "Thanks, Mrs. H." I thought of what Mrs. H. said and its meaning. "To love, and more importantly to be loved, is the greatest gift to share with each other."

This made me start to wonder what life was truly about. As so many people, and philosophers, have questioned, "What is the meaning of life?"

For me, I realized, and ultimately discovered, that when someone's love is so strong that it takes hold of your heart and soul, and in return your own love takes hold of theirs, then to me, that is the true meaning of life. For what good is your life if you are not loved and free to share your own love in return?

Only once did I try to hide with Mrs. H. I recall the buzzer in the apartment going off and Raymond's father saying, "Raymond, I'm on my way up."

I raced out the door in my bare feet and knocked on Mrs. H's door. I was unsure if she was home or if it was just taking her a longer time than normal to answer the door. I was standing there, bouncing from foot to foot in anxious worry, like a little kid needing to use the washroom. I then heard the ding of the elevator come to our floor, most likely carrying the Beast Dad from Hell up from the lobby. Instead, I continued racing down to the end of the hall and then down the stairs.

Raymond's parents never did find out about us till many years later, but I'm almost sure that they had their suspicions while we were together. I, on the other hand, often wondered about my own family, as I never brought a girl home until I was twenty-six years old.

As a kid, I wasn't interested in sports and would sooner skip rope with the girls on the street while the other boys played road hockey. My father, upon his own initiative, signed me up for baseball one year when I was around eight or nine years old. I hated it.

The overweight coach would constantly yell at me. "What the hell are you doing, kid?" His equally overweight son, who played on the team as well, would enthusiastically punch me in my stomach while sitting on the bench and say, "You asshole."

I had as much of a chance of hitting a baseball with a bat and making it to first base as I did getting to first base with any woman. Hell, I don't think I even knew what first base meant back then.

The team I was put on was sponsored by the local church. I'm not sure whether the coach or his son held any religious views, but from their aggressive nature, they didn't seem to follow the saying "be kind to your fellow man."

Years later, I often thought I was having an internal battle with fate, which was allowing me to be gay, versus man-made religious beliefs that condemned it. Let the battle begin and may the best man, or force, win.

CHAPTER 9

The more I met and learned about Raymond's father, the more I believed he was sent from hell to purge the world of all gays. He and his wife were devout Roman Catholics, attending church every Sunday. He made it perfectly clear regarding his opinions on homosexuality, and it wasn't nice. It was a sign of the devil, and it wouldn't be tolerated.

For some reason, he always seemed to have something offensive to say about gays whenever I was there just to make me feel uncomfortable and scared. I felt like he was waiting to crucify me, almost as if he knew I was gay. I was not only terrified of his size but fearful of what he would ever do to Raymond, should he ever find out about the two of us living together. As Raymond had said, I know that his father would have tried beating the gay out of him and wouldn't care that he was doing it to his own son. I honestly believe that his father thought if he was brutal, forceful, or possibly violent toward a gay person, then it would defeat the gayness in them, and they would then be "cured."

Whenever I was staying at the apartment, which was quite often, Raymond and I had an emergency plan in place should his father or mother ever unexpectedly come visiting. Upon hearing the buzzer from the lobby and hearing the loud growl of "Raymond, it's your father," I'd immediately throw anything of mine behind the couch, race down the three flights of stairs to the basement and hide in the lockers.

I'd stay there till Raymond came down to get me. For a small guy, I got pretty good at running down the stairs, missing every other step.

Usually, Raymond's parents would telephone in advance of coming over for a visit, but his father liked to show up unexpectedly once a month or so, almost as if he was spying on his son.

One night we were in the apartment watching *Wonder Woman*, Raymond's favorite show, when there was a knock on the door.

"Who would that be?" Raymond said, as he got up off the couch.

"Probably Mrs. H," I replied.

Raymond jumped up and looked through the peephole.

"Fuck, it's Dad!" he quietly yelled over to me and motioned me to go safely hide. "He must have walked in while someone was leaving."

I knew immediately what that meant and raced to hide in the bedroom. Once he knew I was safely hidden, Raymond opened the door.

"Dad, I wasn't expecting you. What are you doing here?" Raymond asked.

I could hear his father's deep voice. "Is that cologne I smell?"

"Yes, Dan was here earlier, and he just left."

His dad then interrupted. "From what your mother and I have noticed, you two seem to enjoy being around each other quite a bit. You two are always laughing, shoving, or touching each other. How often does he come over here? I hope there's nothing going on between you two, as we've never seen you with a girl.

"You better not have thoughts of being a homosexual, as you know my God-damned stance on that. Maybe you should come to church with us this Sunday and see Father Glen and talk about it. You haven't been to church in quite a while," he said.

From the tone of his voice, I could hear Raymond's father getting louder and angrier.

After a few minutes, he finally ended his lecture by saying, "Dan seems very feminine in nature, and I don't really care for him, to be honest. I wish you would stop hanging around with him, as I just don't like it."

Hearing him spew his ignorant and insulting words, I felt myself getting angrier and angrier by the second, and felt like busting out of the closet, for other reasons, and to defend my Raymond. Unfortunately, I knew if I went into the living room and his father saw me, it would just make a very bad situation that much worse, and I was also scared of what could happen.

Finally, Raymond angrily asked his dad to stop. "Dan and I are just good friends, and we like our company together. It's nothing more than that."

His father abruptly said, "Your mother wants to know if you want to go to the cottage with us on Saturday."

"I can't. I have to work this Saturday night," Raymond quickly responded.

Nothing more was said, and I heard the apartment door shut and lock, then Raymond came and got me.

"He's finally gone, hun. Did you hear what he said?" Raymond asked.

I stepped forward and hugged my Raymond. I could tell he was upset, as he was trembling.

"Why does he have to be like that, babe? Why can't he accept me for who I am? I'm sorry you had to hear that. I'm truly sorry, babe. That's just him being his rude, homophobic self," Raymond said, his eyes tearing up.

I continued to hold him tight. I knew how scared he was of his own father and his homophobic nature.

"As long as we're together, then we will be happy, and that's all that matters to me," I said, trying to reassure him. "I don't care what he thinks of me. It's you who I love and want to be with."

Raymond stared me in the face while holding me tight. "Next summer, I want to go to the cottage for a few days with you. Just you and me. No one else up there. Just us, together, all alone. We could go swimming in the lake, skinny dipping in the dark, stay up late, watch movies, and then snuggle up in bed together," Raymond said, starting to smile again.

"I'd love that, hun. That would be so much fun," I said.

"I'm going to ask Rosalind's help in trying to arrange for us to go to the cottage, without 'them' knowing. I know she has our backs, and she'll try to make it happen," Raymond said, beginning to relax.

CHAPTER 10
Spring 1982.

Raymond and I were sitting in the apartment watching TV. Raymond didn't have to work on Wednesdays and even though I had finished my barn work earlier, around noon, I still had to go feed the horses their dinner around five p.m. or so.

"I'm heading back to the track to feed the horses their dinner, hun, I'll be back in about an hour," I said.

"Ok, babe, I'll be here," replied Raymond. "Are you getting pizza for dinner?"

"Yup, I'll stop on the way home at Domino's," I answered.

Wednesday night was one of our favorite nights, simply because neither of us had to work, as there was no racing that night. The track was about a fifteen-minute drive away, which made it much easier than heading into Toronto. I drove to the track, fed my horses their dinner of oats and hay, and gave them fresh water, cleaned up the shed row and ventured back home.

I then stopped in town and purchased a large double cheese pizza, along with a couple of Cokes and some Mug root beer, which was Raymond's favorite brand.

After making my way to the lobby, I realized I had forgotten my entrance key and buzzed upstairs.

As soon as I buzzed upstairs, another guy walked into the lobby just when I was asking Raymond, "Hey, hun, I forgot my key. Let me in."

Raymond responded, "Only if you have pizza, babe," and unlocked the door.

The guy looked a bit baffled as he must have found it odd that two guys were calling each other, "babe" and "hun." I turned to him and said, "She has a bad cold."

"Well, I hope 'she' feels better soon" he said with a raised eyebrow and emphasizing *she*.

"Thanks," I said and quickly went upstairs.

This night, however, when I got there Rosalind was there. I walked in and saw Raymond with a huge smile on his face and holding a tiny, dark-haired kitten.

"Look at him, isn't he adorable, babe?" he said.

"Where'd he come from? Whose is it?" I asked.

"I brought him," said Rozz. "A colleague of mine at the bank has a cat that had kittens. You two need some company, and besides, at least the two of you can now say you've experienced some pussy."

We all laughed and took turns holding him.

"What shall we name you?" Raymond asked, as he held him to his face and giving him more kisses.

"Let him name himself," Rozz said. "Get to know him first."

I got some plates from the kitchen, and we all sat down and started to enjoy our pizza. Raymond put the kitten down on the couch and poured his Mug root beer into a glass. It foamed up like root beer typically does.

The kitten was sitting on the couch and then jumped over onto the coffee table. We watched as he walked over to Raymond's glass of root beer and stuck his nose in. He then took a sniff and began licking up the foam floating on top of the glass.

"Oh my God," Rozz said. "Look at that."

"He just named himself!" Raymond shouted. "He's now Mr. Muggs!"

"Mr. Muggs it is," said Rozz, and we all started to laugh.

Raymond was really taking a liking to this little guy, and it made me happy. Rozz put her hand on my thigh, seeing my enjoyment.

"I even brought you a litter box, bowls, and some kitten food, so don't forget to feed him," said Rozz. "Dan, you already know how to feed animals so you're in charge. Eventually, he'll need his shots and to get neutered."

"I'll ask the vet at the track where we can take him to get fixed," I said.

"Do you remember when we went to visit Aunt Liz and her cat had the kittens?" Rozz asked Raymond.

"How could I forget it?" Raymond answered. "Dad had a fit in the car."

Rozz and Raymond then told me about when Raymond was little, around five or six years old. They had gone to visit their Aunt Liz and her aunt's cat had kittens. Raymond wanted to take one home, but his father adamantly refused.

"We don't need no damn animals in the house," his father said. Raymond then got upset and started to cry.

On the car ride home, Rozz mentioned that Raymond was still crying because he wasn't allowed to have a pet kitten. Rozz said she still remembered sitting in the back seat staring at her father. Her father was getting more agitated and angrier, listening to Raymond's crying. She recalled her father telling their mother to, "Shut 'your' little girl up."

His mother tried to calm Raymond down, to no avail. Finally, in a loud deep voice, his father bellowed, "God damn it, boy, are you still crying over a damn cat? Now stop it!"

Rozz confirmed their father's overbearing demeanor, and his constant position that men should be men and women had their place. His views on Catholicism were almost zealous in nature, adhering to going to church every Sunday. His views on homosexuality, in her opinion, were mean, hateful, and possibly violent.

Without the opportunity to grow up with a pet when he was younger, I then understood why Raymond was so attached to our new son, Mr. Muggs.

"I'm finally a daddy!" Raymond said.

"Well, you're older than me, you know, so you really are my daddy," I replied.

We both laughed, and laughed harder yet when Rozz said, "I don't get the joke. Raymond's not old enough to be your father, Dan."

We then started to explain some of the gay culture to Rozz, who then found it somewhat amusing. "An older gay male is often referred to as a daddy, while a younger gay male is a son." Raymond chuckled.

While Rozz was there, Raymond mentioned how he wanted to take me up to their cottage, and what had happened that one night when their father confronted him about us hanging around together so much.

"I want to go up and show Dan the cottage," Raymond said to Rozz. "Just Dan and me, no one else. Do you think you could help and arrange something? I'd hate to think what Dad would do should he ever find out that two gay men spent the night up at his personal Shangri-La."

"Well," Rozz paused, then continued, "you can have your choice of either being whipped, tarred and feathered, or simply beheaded. But really, I shouldn't joke, as he's totally merciless when it comes to gay men."

I sat there in a frozen stare again, thinking about their father.

"I'm sorry, Dan, I didn't mean to distress you," Rozz then continued, "Mom and Dad are going away in a few weeks for a heavy construction equipment convention in Detroit—bull-dozers, graders, and stuff like that. They'll be gone for a couple of weeks as the convention lasts a week itself. I'll nonchalantly confirm with Mom that I want to go up there myself for my vacation. You two should go and have a good time, relax, and have some fun with each other. Go for the entire week."

"I've never taken an entire week off work before," I said.

"If you've worked for the same employer for a year, then you're entitled to it," Rozz said. "Have you worked for the same guy that long, Dan?"

"I've been there for over a year now. I'm going to ask him tomorrow for some vacation. I want to get away for a fun time. Let's do this, hun," I said.

"I'll arrange it with Mom and let you know, Raymond. This is going to be great," Rozz said. "I'm getting excited just thinking about helping to plan it."

I loved Rozz. She was nonjudgmental and accepted us both. She loved her brother dearly and was always willing to support him and listen to the plight of all gay men. She was ahead of her time regarding gay equality.

Maybe it was the hate that she'd witnessed toward gay men while growing up in her own family that gave her a more understanding and sympathetic outlook on the situation. Raymond and I both loved her dearly.

The next day, I asked my boss if it was possible to have a week's vacation, which he thoroughly agreed with. He was quite pleased that I was taking some well-deserved time off. All I had to do was to tell him when.

CHAPTER 11
Summer 1982.

A few days later we were in the apartment when the phone rang and Raymond answered; it was Rozz. As he spoke, Raymond started giving me the thumbs-up sign and nodding his head.

"Ok, thanks again, Rozz. Love you, bye." Raymond then hung up the phone.

"Perfect, Rozz said that Mom and Dad are heading to that convention a week this Saturday. They're leaving for Detroit on Friday, July 30th and won't be back until Saturday, August 14," Raymond said. "We're heading up to the cottage, babe, and for the entire week!"

"That's great, hun. I'll ask for that week off from work," I said.

"I'm sure I can swing getting the time off work as well," Raymond said.

Soon it was all arranged. Raymond and I both had the week off. We started planning what we needed to take. Rozz came over to help us pack and to also take care of Mr. Muggs for the week. It was about a forty-minute drive to her work from our apartment, but she said she didn't mind the extra drive. She said she would just leave early to beat the morning traffic.

"Raymond, don't forget there's that small convenience store in town where you can get all your cold stuff, like milk. Here's my work number at the bank if you ever need to get in touch with me during the day," and she handed Raymond her business card.

"Just call me here at the apartment when you get there to make sure you arrived safely," she said.

Raymond picked up Mr. Muggs and gave him a kiss on his nose, "Be good for Auntie Rozz my Muggins, we'll be back soon."

We finished packing up Raymond's Chevy Monza and headed up north. For whatever reason, Raymond always drove when we were together. Whether it was because he was a bit older, or maybe because I thought of him as the alpha male in the relationship, I never questioned it and simply took my spot in the passenger's seat.

Rozz waved goodbye from the curb as we drove off.

"How far is it?" I asked Raymond.

"It's at least a couple of hours or more of a drive, babe," he said. "Sit back and relax."

Luckily, we had beat most of the Friday cottage travelers rush by leaving early. A few hours later, and after driving in sweltering heat and on many unpaved dusty side roads, we arrived.

Their cottage overlooked the lake and was quite beautiful, half log cabin and half cobblestone. It had three bedrooms, a bathroom, a full kitchen, and even a sauna room down by the lake.

We unpacked the car and carried the food and supplies into the cottage.

"Let's go for a swim, babe," Raymond said.

"I'd love that. I'm soaked with sweat from the drive," I answered.

We undressed and got into our trunks. The cottage was quite remote, a fair distance from any other neighbors. It was almost private. We walked down the path to the dock.

"That's the sauna over there," Raymond said. "We'll have to try it out one night. Sit in the sauna, then jump into the lake. Makes you sleep like a baby."

We got to the edge of the dock, and both jumped in together. We started enjoying the cool water refreshing us from the very hot summer's day and car ride.

I felt like the happiest man in the world looking at Raymond and his wet, hairy self.

"What?" he said.

"I'm just happy that I'm yours," I replied.

"Ahhhhhhhhh!" he yelled and lunged at me, pulling me under the water. We came up laughing. We were both holding on to each other and just in the moment, kissed.

"You have no idea how much I love ya, babe," Raymond said.

Hearing how much Raymond cared for me and loved me always gave me shivers and I embraced him hard and put my head against his wet chest. "I love you more, hun," I whispered, holding back my emotions and not wanting to cry. It was a precious, intimate moment that remains in my memory still.

"Are you getting hungry, babe? I'm starved," Raymond said.

We got out of the lake and went back to the cottage, toweled each other off, and slipped back into our shorts. We then decided to make hamburgers for dinner, along with Cokes and, of course, Mug root beer.

I recall there being a huge stone barbeque on the back patio with a stone chimney well over twelve feet tall.

Raymond did the barbequing while I got the plates and table ready. I then set the table outside and brought out the buns and condiments, while Raymond brought over the burgers.

"These are delicious, hun. They're so juicy it's leaking all over," I said.

"I'm the same way when you're around," Raymond jokingly said, trying hard not to laugh.

"You're a pig, a tall beautiful, and please don't ever change, adorable pig," I laughed back.

After dinner I washed the dishes and cleaned up the kitchen.

"What a beautiful night," Raymond said. "It's so hot. Let's go for a quick dip in the lake."

"Sounds good to me," I said.

From the cottage, Raymond turned on the lamppost on the dock. We once again got into our swimming trunks, headed down to the dock along the cobblestone path, and quietly slipped into the refreshing water.

"That feels so good," I said. "The water is almost warm."

Raymond stared at me for a moment, as if he were doing something, then suddenly threw his trunks onto the dock.

"Your turn, babe," he laughed.

I reached down and tossed mine aside as well.

"Now that's really refreshing," Raymond said.

We swam for a few minutes, touching, groping, and quietly laughing so as not to make much noise in the quietness of the night. The spot nearest the dock was only a few feet deep, with just our shoulders above water. I walked over to Raymond, and as we embraced, we slowly and passionately began to hug and kiss.

"Let's go inside, babe," Raymond said.

We then went to reach for our trunks when we realized we had tossed them a few feet too far onto the dock and out of reach. We both started laughing as we walked quickly up the steps in the buff, and under the light of the lamppost, grabbed our trunks, and quickly ran up to the cottage. Once inside, we continued to laugh at our streaking.

After drying ourselves off, Raymond brought out the Jiffy Pop popcorn and began gyrating it back and forth on the stove. The smell of fresh popcorn soon lingered in the air as he poured the popcorn into a big bowl.

I got us each a cold pop and then curled up on the couch with Raymond.

"What shall we watch, babe?" Raymond asked, as he turned the dial on the TV. "We don't get many stations up here, so we're lucky to get even one station that comes in clear. Here's a classic."

We settled back into the couch and started watching the movie *Psycho*.

"I love this movie," Raymond said.

"It's a bit scary, but I'll watch it," I answered. "I always get creeped out watching this movie, especially when the car sinks into the swamp,"

I curled up tight against Raymond during the entire movie, enjoying the feeling of security, knowing he was there protecting me. Even any imaginary monsters that may be lurking weren't as scary while Raymond was near.

We sat intently watching the movie with our popcorn, Raymond with his Mug root beer, and me with my Coke.

"I have to go to the john," Raymond said, and he got up and left me alone.

I sat there nervously watching the movie, anxiously waiting for him to return. He then snuck up behind me, and while wearing a shawl wrapped around his head and shoulders, jumped over the couch and sat beside me. For no reason other than to scare the crap out of me, Raymond tugged on my arm and said in an old, pitiful-sounding frail voice, "I'm home, Norman dear."

I turned and suddenly jumped out of my skin, "You fucker!" I yelled.

He started howling with laughter and soon I began to laugh as well as I leaned over and pretended to punch him all over.

"I'm sorry, babe, but I couldn't resist," Raymond said, as we continued to laugh.

"Well, you're lucky I love you, fucker," I replied, and leaned over and gave him a kiss.

We continued watching TV for a while and then decided to go out on the back patio for some fresh air. It was about one o'clock in the morning and still a beautiful hot night outside with not even a breeze. All you could hear was the gentle sound of crickets and the nightlife out in the darkness, highlighted by the light of a full moon shining overhead. From over the lake, you could also hear the unforgettable, lonesome sound of loons in the distance. We sat down on the outside bench, enjoying the moment.

"It's so beautiful up here, hun," I said and rested my head against Raymond's shoulder.

"I love it up here, especially now that we can finally be alone like this," Raymond said. "Stay here. I'll be right back."

He went into the cottage and came back with his portable cassette player.

"Dance with me babe, dance with me under the moonlight," Raymond said, and put in a cassette tape and turned it on.

He pulled me up off the bench, and we began to dance. We started slow dancing to the Righteous Brothers singing "Unchained Melody." As we danced, I couldn't help but think how life was so perfect. *Here I am, dancing with my man, my lover, my savior, my best friend, under the passionate glow of moonlight.*

I can still feel him against me. His warm, soft touch and the smell of his beautiful affection are still vivid in my mind to this day. I didn't want this moment to end. It was beyond my description. It was euphoric.

"This is going to be our song, babe," Raymond said. "Wherever we are, whether together or apart, whenever we hear this, we'll think of each other."

"I'm going to remember this moment forever, hun," I said, and continued to hold him close. I remember closing my eyes and letting Raymond slowly guide us gently back and forth.

"Oh my, it feels like something else has a big hunger for someone's touch," I said as Raymond pushed himself against me. We finished dancing and excitedly went to bed.

It was an unbelievable night of sharing each other's passion. By this time, we had figured out who was the top and bottom in our relationship, and although we sometimes flipped, our positions of choice were quickly decided upon. Raymond always enjoyed taking the upper bunk, while I eagerly enjoyed the lower.

To this day, should I hear the Righteous Brothers sing "Unchained Melody," I can't help but get emotional. For me, it's a feeling of both joy and melancholy, especially when you listen to its loving lyrics. It's that one word that hits so close to my heart, that single word, "need."

When I hear them sing "I need your love," it completes the definition of what true love is, in that you both need and are yearning for each other's love but are also at peace in knowing it is readily available for you both to receive it. It was this mutual love that constantly flowed between Raymond and me that helped make our relationship so strong.

The next morning, I was up before Raymond and had made bacon, eggs, sausages, toast, and tea.

"Raymond, breakfast is ready," I yelled from the kitchen. "Come down to the table, hun."

Raymond sleepily came downstairs, gave me a big hug from behind, and kissed my neck.

"That looks delicious, babe. Let's eat," he said.

"What should we do today, hun? We should go into town and get some milk and bread," I said.

"We can do that," Raymond answered. "There's a small general store a couple of miles away."

We cleaned up from breakfast and drove the few miles to the general store.

"I love this old store," Raymond said. "Come and have a look."

We went into the store and started walking on a much-worn wooden slatted floor that would creak with every step. It was like an old-fashioned store that hadn't been brought into modern times. It even smelled old, like old musty wood mixed with the smells of the different foods being sold.

"Let's get some marshmallows and have a fire in the pit tonight," Raymond said.

We walked around and got a carton of milk, a loaf of bread, marshmallows, and a couple of bags of potato chips and placed them in our basket.

"Look at this, babe," Raymond said and lifted the lid of an old Coke cooler. Inside were glass bottles of soft drinks—Coke, root beer, Orange Crush, 7UP—all standing up in ice-cold water.

"I've never seen one of these coolers before," I said.

We both took a couple of Cokes and a couple of root beers and went up to the cashier.

"Will this be all boys?" the older lady asked. "If you'd like,

93

I have some cardboard bottle carriers if you want more soda pops," she said.

"Thanks, I'll go get a couple more then," Raymond answered.

"Six Cokes and six root beers," answered the lady, and put our groceries in a brown paper bag.

We paid the lady for our groceries and went back to the car.

"It's really hot out today, hun," I said. "Let's go for a swim when we get back."

"Great idea, babe," Raymond answered, and we got in the car and started driving back to the cottage.

"How long have your parents owned the cottage?" I asked.

"My dad inherited it from his father or my grandfather. It was nothing like it is now. Dad's basically rebuilt the entire place. It was just a small little place from the pictures I've seen," Raymond said.

"Was your grandfather anything like your dad?" I asked.

"I never met him," Raymond answered. "He died when I was only one or two years old, I believe. Rozz vaguely remembers him, said he was a nice old fart."

We drove back to the cottage, unloaded our groceries, and put the cold pops into the fridge.

"Now let's go for that swim," Raymond said, and he started undressing right there in the kitchen.

"Is there anything in here you have an appetite for?" he joked.

I then watched his pure white bum wiggle and walk away. I followed him up the stairs and every now and then I'd take a firm grasp onto each cute cheek.

"You're bad!" Raymond kept saying with every grasp.

"But I'm good at being bad," I jokingly replied, and gave his firm cheek a hard slap.

"Ouch!" Raymond laughed.

"Sorry, hun. Here, let me kiss it better." I gave his cheek a well-deserved kiss.

"Better?" I asked.

"A little," Raymond whimpered playfully.

We then got into our trunks and headed down to the lake.

CHAPTER 12

We walked to the end of the dock. Raymond grabbed my hand and said, "On three. One, two, and three!" and we both jumped into the water.

"Ahhh, that feels so good, hun," I said as we swam around in the warm but refreshing water.

Raymond then went under the water and came back up headfirst between my legs, knocking me back under the water. We both then surfaced and started laughing.

Meanwhile, we hadn't noticed the people at the cottage next door were also having a swim. They paid no attention, and the one younger guy gave us a wave from his dock. We waved back.

"Do you know him?" I asked Raymond.

"I think he's the son of the people that live there. I think I spoke with him a couple of summers ago," Raymond said.

I noticed that he kept looking our way. "He seems to keep looking over here," I said.

Raymond and I watched as he got back into the water and slowly started swimming over our way.

"Hey, guys, beautiful day out today," he said.

"It's a great day to be up here," Raymond answered.

"I'm David," he said.

"Nice to meet you, David. I'm Dan, and this is Raymond."

"I think we met last summer," David mentioned to Raymond. "You were here with your sister, I believe."

"That's right, now I remember," Raymond said. "Rozz and I were on the dock there when you came by."

"Is your sister here with you?" David asked.

"No, it's just Dan and me up here for the week," Raymond said. "We needed a break from the city."

"I know what you mean. I'm up here with my parents, but I would love some time up here alone as well. I love it up here."

"We're having hamburgers on the barbeque later tonight, then a fire. Feel free to join us if you want, David," Raymond answered. "Say around six or seven o'clock?"

"I'd like that," David replied. "I love my folks, but sometimes they get boring, if you know what I mean."

"We sure do. Come join us for a couple of burgers," I said. "You're more than welcome to."

"Thanks, guys. I'll see you later, then," David answered, and swam back to his cottage.

"He seems like a good guy," I said. "I hope he's okay seeing us together."

"I think it's alright," Raymond said. "I remember now. Rozz said she thought he was a great-looking guy, but said she thinks he was looking more at me instead of her. I don't think we have anything to worry about, babe."

Raymond and I continued our swim, and after a while, headed back to the cottage all refreshed, yet somewhat tired.

"I feel like a nap," Raymond said.

"So do I," I answered back.

We both made our way up to our bedroom, got out of our wet trunks, dried off, and slipped onto the bed. It was so hot.

The gentle breeze from the ceiling fan made us soon quickly fall asleep. I fell asleep leaning my head on Raymond's chest with one of Raymond's arms around me.

We must have been asleep for a couple of hours.

It was around five o'clock when we both woke up.

Raymond rolled on top of me and gave me a kiss.

His beautiful, aroused body felt wonderful.

"Let's get the barbecue started, babe. I'm hungry."

We put on our shorts and headed out to the back yard. Raymond started cleaning off the grill while I went into the kitchen to start getting the hamburgers ready.

"Where did you put the charcoal, babe? Have you seen it?" Raymond asked from the back window, looking in.

"I brought it in from the car and put it away in the closet right inside the back door, hun," I said. "How many hamburgers should I use? Six should be enough if David comes over?"

"Yeah, that should be plenty, two each," Raymond answered back.

I got the hamburgers ready and started cutting up some tomatoes, got out some cheese and pickles, and cried while chopping onions. I put them all on a plate and put it back in the fridge. I knew Raymond liked it when I fried some onions, so I made an extra pile for him. I got out the frozen French fries and put them aside, ready to be put in the oven.

I then went out to check on the barbeque as tears were rolling down my cheeks from the onions.

Raymond suddenly stopped what he was doing and with a worried look, asked, "What the fuck is the matter, babe? What's wrong?"

"I've missed you so much, hun," I jokingly sobbed.

"Ha, onions!" Raymond laughed. "I can smell them, but since you've missed me." He stepped forward and gave me a kiss on the lips just when David arrived.

"Don't mind me, guys," David said. "I'm cool with it."

"Sorry, David," Raymond answered.

"Sorry for what?" David asked, "Because you kissed Dan? Please, I only wish I could bring my boyfriend up here."

We both looked somewhat shocked, but relieved at the same time.

"I brought a few cold beers. Mind if I put them in the fridge?" David said.

"Sure, here I'll show you inside," I answered.

I walked David into the kitchen and placed the beers in the fridge.

"You have a boyfriend also?" I asked.

"Yeah, I've been seeing him on and off for a few months now," David replied. "We live about a hundred or so miles apart, so it's been a challenge. How long have you and Raymond been together?"

"Almost two years now," I proudly answered. "We met in August 1980."

"That's great," David said. "Do you see each other often?"

"Almost every day, we have an apartment together. No one knows except for a few close friends that we're a couple, though," I said. "It's difficult keeping it a secret, but so far, no one has questioned it. I'm sure some have their thoughts, though."

We each grabbed a beer, and I took one for Raymond. "Here, hun." I handed him a bottle.

"Thanks, babe," he replied.

"You have a boyfriend as well, David?" Raymond inquired.

"Yeah, as I was telling Dan in the kitchen, we've been seeing each other for a few months now. It's a long-distance relationship and has its challenges. You two are so fortunate to have what you have in being able to live together."

"We're very lucky, aren't we, babe?" said Raymond, giving

me a squeeze. "The barbeque is ready. Can you bring out the burgers?"

I went and brought out the burgers, and on my return, I stumbled and dropped one on the ground.

"Crap, I'm sorry hun, I dropped yours," I joked, and picked it up, wiped it off, and put it back on the plate.

"The heat will burn off the germs." David laughed.

I went and got the condiments from the kitchen, and fries from the oven. As I brought out the fries and condiments on a tray, I heard Raymond deliberately tell David, "I'll give that burger to Dan," he said.

"It was your burger," I said, "but if you want, I'll gladly eat your big meat to keep you happy."

I heard David sputter on his beer and start to chuckle.

I then set the table, and we all sat down.

"This is great," David said. "Thanks for inviting me over."

"Not a problem. You're more than welcome," Raymond answered.

"Are you up for the weekend?" I asked.

"Yes, I came up with my parents from the city," David answered.

"Do they know about you and your boyfriend?" Raymond asked.

"Actually, they do. They're very understanding about it but asked that I don't flaunt it among relatives and friends, which is fine with me."

"You're lucky. I'd never be able to speak a word of it to my folks," Raymond said, "unless I wanted to be disowned and possibly tormented till my death."

"Is it really that bad?" David asked.

"Oh yeah," I replied. "I'm terrified of his Goliath of a dad."

"That's too bad, as it's made my life so much more comfortable with them knowing and accepting it," David said.

We finished the burgers and started to clean up.

"We were going to have a fire down by the lake in the fire pit," Raymond said. "You're more than welcome to stay."

"Sure, let me go get a couple more beers," David replied. "I'll be right back."

David left for next door as Raymond and I cleaned up the kitchen.

"What a nice guy," I said. "He's so lucky that his parents are so understanding of him. Imagine if ours were, hun."

"We'd have it all if they did understand, babe," Raymond answered.

We finished cleaning and putting everything away when David showed up at the back door with some more beers.

"This should keep the mood going," David chuckled and put them in the fridge.

"What's a fire without marshmallows?" I said and grabbed the bag from the cupboard.

"Raymond, can you get the small Styrofoam cooler from the one closet? We can fill it with cold water and put the beers in it," I said.

"Good idea, babe," he said and went and got the cooler. He put the beer in and topped it up with some cold water.

"I think there's a few ice cubes left in the freezer tray," I said, and Raymond got them out and dumped them in as well.

"All set?" asked Raymond. He then flicked on the outside lamppost, and we all started walking down the path toward the lake.

David carried the beers in the cooler, Raymond the fire starter, bag of firewood, and matches, while I had the difficult task of carrying the marshmallows, the bag of potato chips, and extra-long forks.

"Able to handle that, babe?" Raymond joked.

"Fuck off, hun," I answered, and we all laughed.

The fire pit was a few feet off the path and near the lake. It was surrounded by three log benches, which had once been big tree trunks that had been cut lengthwise and firmly anchored down, about ten feet away from the fire. Between each log bench was a short log standing upright and used for a table.

We sat our cooler and snacks down.

Raymond then got out the fire starter, kindling, and firewood. It wasn't long before he had a good fire going.

We contently sat around the fire, having our cold beer and enjoying each other's company.

"Another beautiful night," Raymond said.

"What do you guys do for a living?" David asked.

"We both work at the horse racing track," said Raymond. "I work with the pari-mutuel betting machines in the grandstand, while Dan works with the actual horses."

"That's interesting," David said. "I've never been to a horse race before. How did the two of you meet?"

"We met at the track," Raymond said. "I was walking into the grandstand one day and saw Dan walking a horse from the track up to the paddock area. I was smitten by his cute looks. I then waited for him to return on another day, and luckily by chance, I saw him in the paddock again and introduced myself."

"I still remember seeing Raymond for the first time," I answered. "I was unsure if he was talking to me when he said 'Hi' as he's such a looker. I didn't think he was looking at me."

"Stop it, babe. Our eyes locked the moment we saw each other," Raymond said. "We finally went on a date a couple of days after we met at the paddock."

"That's sound so great," David said, "as if fate kept trying to push you together."

"How did you meet your guy?" I asked David.

"We met in university and had some fun while there. We kept in touch afterwards and finally started to be more serious a few months ago. We're considering moving closer to one another, but we want to make sure we're really meant for each other. I have a good feeling about us. We get along great when we are together," David said, "and I'm always thinking about him."

"Where do you two live?" Raymond asked.

"I still live in Toronto with my parents, while Philip lives in Kingston. That's where we met. I'm thinking of moving out there," said David.

"What do you do for a living, David?" I asked.

"I work in a bank, so I'm hoping to get a transfer down there, if possible," replied David.

"Another banker," Raymond joked, "my sister works in a bank. She's the only one in my family who knows about Dan and me."

We roasted a few marshmallows but soon all agreed the flavor of beer and marshmallows was not that great of a combination and instead started passing around the potato chips. We all opened another beer and continued talking about life and fun stuff.

"I'm getting a buzz on." I giggled.

"Let's go for a swim," Raymond said.

"I'm game." I started to giggle even more.

"I didn't bring my trunks," David said.

With that Raymond stood up and said, "Neither did I," and dropped his shorts, showing off his hairy birthday suit.

I knew immediately what David's reaction would be when he saw Raymond naked, and I quickly glanced over at him.

David's eyes almost popped out of his head upon seeing Raymond's exceptionally large appendage hanging loose in the light of the fire.

"Holy crap! How do you manage to fit that thing into your pants every morning?" David joked.

"With some help from me, of course," I proudly said, and we all continued laughing.

"Guess it's my turn," and David stood up and dropped his shorts, then his underwear, as I did the same.

Raymond then turned around as his white but incredibly cute rear end took off toward the dock.

We all slowly got into the water, not wanting to make any noise, and started to relax and take in the cool, refreshing water.

"The water is a bit chilly tonight," I said.

"Damn, that means shrinkage," David joked. "The last thing I need coming out of the water beside Mr. Full Size Extra Large over here is shrinkage," as he nodded toward Raymond and jokingly said, "lucky bastard!"

"Actually, I'm the lucky one when you think of it," I said.

We all had a good laugh and Raymond grabbed me and pulled me under the water. I surfaced and then said, "I've also learned how to hold my breath underwater for quite a while since I've been up here, haven't I, hun?" and we continued to laugh.

"Oh, lucky Dan, lucky Dan," David said.

We finished our swim and climbed back onto the dock to go inside. Raymond poured some water on the fire, and we grabbed our clothes, covered our crotches, and quickly walked back up the lighted path to the cottage. I went inside, brought out a couple of towels, and passed one to David.

"I should be getting back home," David said. "I'll let you two enjoy the rest of the evening together. Thanks for a fun night, guys. I really enjoyed myself."

"Feel free to stop by tomorrow. Have a good night David," Raymond replied.

As he was walking away, David stopped, turned, and said, "Hey, lucky Dan, make sure you do everything that I'd do with that thing! Have a fun night, guys." He gave us a thumbs-up.

Raymond and I went back into the cottage. It felt like a hundred degrees in there. We turned on the fan and put on the TV. The swim must have made us super relaxed as we soon fell asleep on the couch with the TV on. Raymond's head was on the pillow against the arm rest, while I fell asleep with my head lying on a pillow against Raymond's bum.

We must have slept that way for a couple of hours until Raymond woke up and nudged me to go to bed. We sleepily walked up the stairs, stripped off our shorts, flopped into bed, snuggled up to each other, and continued our sleep.

CHAPTER 13

The next morning, we both woke up full of energy. I lay against Raymond, twirling my finger in his chest hair.

"What shall we do today, hun?" I asked.

"Well, right now I know what I want to do," Raymond said, and eagerly proceeded to roll over on top of me. His aroused self was even larger than normal, if that was at all possible, and we passionately began to kiss and caress.

"God, I love you, babe," Raymond said.

"I love you so much too, hun," I answered.

Raymond then rolled onto his back, and I eagerly climbed on top of my man, feeling his hairy chest against mine, while smelling his magnificent body. We kissed and caressed, and eventually got into our favorite position, where we could both kiss and watch each other's enjoyment, while I straddled him. After what seemed like ages of pleasure, we both erupted in a breathtaking moment of lovemaking.

Once finished, we both lay in each other's arms enjoying the moment, both completely content and satisfied in knowing that nothing could, nor ever would, break the deep love that we shared for each other.

After our morning playtime, we went downstairs for some well-deserved breakfast.

"Feel like some bacon, sausages, and eggs, hun?" I asked.

"Love some," Raymond answered. "I'll get the kettle on."

As we started making breakfast, there was a knock on the back door. Raymond went to the door, and I heard him say, "Hey, David, come on in."

"I thought you guys would like some freshly baked rolls. My mom made them this morning. She's always up early baking," he said.

"Want some breakfast, David?" I yelled from the kitchen as I was cracking the eggs into the fry pan.

"I don't want to be a bother," David said.

"How do you like your eggs?" I yelled back.

"Over easy is fine, and thanks," he said.

"Come and sit down. I was just getting our tea, or would you prefer coffee? We have both," Raymond asked.

"Tea is fine for me as well," and David sat down at the kitchen table.

"Get David a plate, hun. I'm getting the eggs and toast," I asked Raymond.

"You two remind me of an old married couple anticipating each other's moves while going about your daily chores," David joked.

"You know, David," Raymond said, "if I could, I'd marry Dan tomorrow." Raymond came up behind me and gave me a loving hug while I gently and deliberately backed up into him.

"And what do you say to that, Dan?" David asked.

"Why wait for tomorrow?" I said. "Let's do it now. If it wasn't for all the bigotry and homophobic hate gays encounter, there would be lots of same-sex married couples."

"One day, it will be possible," David encouragingly said.

"Do you really think so?" I asked. "After everything the gay community has gone through, you think that will ever happen, David?"

"I honestly do," said David. "We've made great strides within the gay community already, even a first Gay Pride Parade, but it's a generational thing now. This older generation, with its set-in-stone ways, has to make way for the freer thinking and nonjudgmental attitudes of our generation. Once our generation is in power in parliament, in the press, and we can make the changes, then it will happen, but not until then."

"Wouldn't that be amazing," I said. "Oh, hun, it gives me goosebumps just thinking of it."

I brought over a plateful of eggs and toast as Raymond brought the bacon and sausages.

"You could feed an army with this amount of food," David said.

"We somewhat worked up a very large appetite this morning, didn't we, babe?" Raymond said with a sly grin.

I smiled and started to blush.

"Oh, lucky Dan, lucky Dan," David joked.

We all started enjoying our breakfast.

"Any plans for your Sunday, guys?" David asked.

"Just lying around the backyard and going in the lake," Raymond answered.

"What are you up to?" Raymond asked David.

"Probably drive to the general store. My mom asked me to go as she needs some things. Other than that, just lie around also."

"Do we need anything from there, babe?" Raymond asked.

"Feel free to come with me if you want, even just for the ride," David suggested.

"What do you feel like for lunch? If you wanted burgers, we'd need hamburger and buns," I said.

"Let's all go," Raymond said. "I saw they had a meat

cooler. Maybe we could get some steaks for dinner. Feel like steaks for dinner, babe?" Raymond then looked at David. "Feel free to stay for dinner as well, David. Unless you have plans at home."

"Have you ever had marinated teriyaki steak?" David asked. "I make an incredible steak. Let me cook tonight."

"That sounds so good," Raymond said, "doesn't it, babe?"

"I'll make some salad and do some vegetables," I said. "Let's look for a dessert while we're there—maybe an apple pie and ice cream?"

"I'll see if my mom will bake us a pie," David said. "She loves cooking and is somewhat bored being up here. She was up early at five o'clock this morning to make the rolls."

As we were finishing breakfast, David said, "Let me go get my things, and I'll meet you back here, say, in about twenty minutes. Is that okay?"

"We'll be ready," Raymond answered.

"Thanks for breakfast, lucky Dan!" David hollered as he was leaving.

"Welcome," I yelled back.

"Pass me the notepad, hun. I'll make a list of things we need for the week," I said. "Do you want hamburgers for lunch, or what do you feel like?"

"Sure, that'll be fine. Get some more onions," Raymond said, "I like how you diced them up and fried them, babe."

A few minutes later, David walked back in the back door. "I'm all ready. Mom's making us an apple pie."

"Ice cream, babe, put down ice cream for the pie," Raymond said.

"Get me the Styrofoam cooler to keep it from thawing, Raymond," I said. "We'll buy a bag of ice as well."

We gathered up the cooler, grabbed our wallets, and went to the front.

"We can go in my dad's car," David said. "I drove it over."

"Now that's a nice car," I said as we got into his father's Lincoln Town Car.

David and Raymond got in the front while I got in the back.

"There's enough room back here that we could make out, hun," I joked.

"Hey, what about me?" David kidded.

"Actually, I honestly think there's room for a threesome back here," I laughed.

"Now you're talking," David said, smiling. "Have you ever done that before, a threesome?"

"Shared each other with another guy?" Raymond asked.

"Yes," David answered. "I don't mean to pry. It's just something that Phillip and I have often talked about, but it's never materialized."

"We've only done it once before, with our friend Eddie, but we would never do it separately as we're a package deal, aren't we, babe?" Raymond said.

"Of course, hun. I would never share my piece of perfection," I answered.

David laughed and said, "From what I recall, there's definitely more than enough perfection to go around."

We all laughed as we drove to the store.

"I've never tried it before," David said. "Just never been in the situation."

I joked from the back seat. "Are we going to have to pay you somehow for you making dinner tonight?" I asked.

"Damn right!" David laughed in return. "I'm just teasing you both."

Raymond looked back at me while David was driving and gave me a wink, confirming everything was okay.

We arrived at the store and went in to do our shopping.

We brought the pop cartons back and filled them both again with six Cokes and six root beers.

"Did you want any pop, David?" I asked.

"Sure, I'll have a couple of Cokes, please," David said before he went and got some steaks at the meat cooler.

"Look at those beautiful, thick T-bone steaks," David said. "Could I get three of those large T-bones, please?"

The butcher behind the counter wrapped up the steaks in brown wax paper and tied it with string.

Raymond got some hamburger meat, and I got the buns.

"Grab that small bag of charcoal briquettes, babe," Raymond said. "We'll need more for the barbeque."

We made our way to the checkout.

"Let me purchase our dinner tonight, guys. I want to contribute somehow," David said, and paid for the meat and vegetables, everything that he needed for dinner.

"I'll start getting the steaks marinated once we get back to your place," David said. "I take the teriyaki sauce and mix it with a bit of lime juice and then add the other secret ingredients that I've tried."

David seemed to get so excited about how to prepare dinner, as Raymond and I let him enjoy his explanation.

"The barbeque has to be extra hot to sear it at the start," he said.

"You're like a chef giving a lesson," I said as we walked to the car.

"I love to cook and try different things," David said. "I get it from my mom. She's always in the kitchen. She's probably making our apple pie right now, knowing her."

"Ice cream!" I yelled, "I forgot the ice cream."

"I'll go back," said Raymond. "You guys wait for me in the car. I'll only be a second."

David loaded up the car and put the steaks in the Styrofoam with another bag of ice.

As we waited for Raymond, David said, "I hope I didn't embarrass you by talking about getting together, Dan. you looked a bit upset in the rear-view mirror, and I'd never want to harm you and Raymond's relationship."

"I'm fine," I said. "I just start to get jealous sometimes when someone comes on to Raymond."

"Raymond's a very handsome man, but I'm really attracted to you," David said.

Dumbfounded, I didn't know what to say, then said, "Please don't tell Raymond that."

"Sorry, but I already did," David replied.

Just then, Raymond returned and put the ice cream into the cooler.

"What's up guys?" he said. "You look like a deer in the headlights, babe."

"David and I were just talking," I said.

"Oh yeah, about what?" Raymond asked.

David then mentioned how he was attracted to me.

"I know that," Raymond said.

"Why didn't you tell me?" I asked.

"Because I knew you would get upset just like this," Raymond said. "Babe, you have no idea how many guys I see look at you, and yes, I get jealous too, just like you do with me, but we are a team—nothing, and no one, is going to break us apart."

Due to how much negativity and teasing I'd gotten when I was younger, I never thought myself physically attractive and couldn't help showing my devotion to Raymond at that moment. I practically threw myself into the front seat and kissed him.

"You know I love ya with every inch of my love," Raymond

teased and then kissed me while bracing me so I wouldn't fall into the front seat.

"Whoa, now that's a devoted love," David said. "You two really are a team, aren't you?"

Desperately wanting to change the topic, I asked David what year his father's Lincoln was.

"It's an '82. He got it last fall. I love driving it even though it's a bit of a boat being so big," David said.

We drove back through the countryside to the cottage.

Once inside, David asked for a bowl and measuring cup. "I can do this out of memory now," he said. "Dan, can you pass me that shopping bag over there, please? It's got all the ingredients in it that I need."

I got the bag and looked inside. "There's a lot of stuff in here."

"It's my secret recipe, some herbs and spices, a bottle of teriyaki sauce, and a couple of limes," David replied.

He seemed to love mixing and whisking the ingredients, and once finished, gave it a small taste.

"Here, taste this, Dan," and David dipped in a spoon and put it up to my mouth.

"That tastes delicious, David," I said.

David then got the steaks out, gently rinsed them off, and patted them dry. He then placed them in a deep bowl and slowly poured the marinade into the bowl, covering up the steaks.

"What smells so good?" Raymond said as he came into the kitchen.

"You should taste this marinade David made. It's really good, hun."

Raymond ran his finger through the marinade bowl and had a taste.

"That is really good, David," Raymond said. "You should bottle it and sell it, call it 'David's Delight!'"

"Maybe one day I will," said David, with a proud and content smile. "These steaks have to marinate for a few hours." He placed the steaks back in the fridge.

"Time for a beer and some relaxing time down by the lake," David said. "Who wants to join me?"

"Count us in," Raymond said, and we all went and got into our swimming trunks.

I grabbed the cooler, filled it with some cold water and ice cubes, put in a half dozen beer, and we headed down to the dock.

"We should check out the sauna, babe. We haven't had it on since we've been up here," Raymond said.

"You have a sauna here?" David asked.

"Yeah, it's that building over there," Raymond said.

"I'd love to try it out," David said.

"Let me go start it up," Raymond answered, and went over into the sauna. A couple of minutes later, he stuck his head out the door, "It's all ready whenever you guys are. Babe, bring me a cold beer for in here," Raymond asked.

I grabbed a couple of beers, and David and I went into the sauna. The steam was quite intense but was somewhat soothing at the same time.

As I expected, there sitting on the tiered cedar bench was Raymond in his glory and his beautiful birthday suit.

"Hey, it's a sauna. It's mandatory to dress this way, isn't it?" Raymond laughed.

"Good Lord," said David, looking at Raymond, "he's even bigger when he's awake!" and then dropped his trunks and sat down with his beer.

"Come on, lucky Dan, take it off," David encouraged.

I stripped off my trunks, climbed up to where Raymond was, and sat beside him.

It wasn't long before we could all see the definite pleasure that the sauna was causing our nakedness.

We sat enjoying our beer and allowing our sweat to build up.

"This is so relaxing," David said, "in its own relaxing sort of way, of course."

We sat there for a few minutes, enjoying the heat while sweating and drinking our cold, but slowly getting warm, beer.

"Now, let's go jump in the lake," Raymond said as he got up and quickly tried putting on and pulling up his trunks.

"Damn," Raymond chuckled, as he fumbled, trying to get everything tucked back inside.

"What'd I say?" David said. "Oh, lucky Dan, lucky Dan," and we all started to laugh.

We followed Raymond, dashed to the dock, and jumped into the water.

"Oh, fuck, that's cold!" I yelled.

Raymond started laughing. "But it's supposed to be really healthy for you, babe."

"I agree with lucky Dan," David said. "I'd sooner be back in the sauna."

We all got out of the water, went back to the cottage, and started getting dinner ready.

Raymond oversaw the barbeque while David got his steaks out of the fridge, and I started the vegetables.

I set the table out on the patio, and it wasn't long before we were having a great-tasting teriyaki barbequed steak.

"This tastes absolutely delicious, David," I said, and Raymond agreed. "It practically melts on your tongue."

Once the main course was finished, we cleared the table and David brought out his mom's apple pie. I got out the ice cream and we spoiled ourselves once more.

We then all watched some TV, and after a while, David

decided to head for home.

"Thanks for another fun evening, guys. See you tomorrow," David said.

"See you tomorrow, David, and thanks again for making dinner," we both answered.

Before long, Raymond and I were once more cuddled up on the couch and again fell fast asleep.

CHAPTER 14

Soon it was Saturday, and time to head back home.

We cleaned up the cottage and made sure there wasn't the slightest indication that we had ever been there.

David came over to say goodbye, and we exchanged telephone numbers to keep in touch.

"I really enjoyed our company together, guys," he said. "I only hope Philip and I can achieve what you guys have."

"It takes two to make it work," Raymond said and reached out for my hand. "I'm sure you and Philip will have no problem at all."

We exchanged hugs, and David left.

Raymond and I packed up the car and headed back to the city. While driving the long journey back home, I relaxed in the passenger seat, put my feet up on the dashboard, and started writing some thoughts down in my journal.

Up at the cottage that week, I realized how wonderful life can be when everything seems to fall wonderfully into place.

I soon thought of these words, which still apply today, as they did back then.

"When you have contentment in your life, then you have inner peace, which makes you see the beauty that surrounds you, and life is good."

Raymond, I love you.

Raymond brought contentment into my life. He gave me meaning and purpose, which allowed me my inner peace. Once at peace with myself, I could see how beautiful the world can be. The world would be a much better place if others could see the beauty in their fellow man, instead of looking for their faults first.

We arrived back at the apartment to an incredibly happy Mr. Muggs and Rozz.

"How was it, guys?" Rozz asked. "Did you have yourselves a good time?"

"It was amazing," Raymond said. "We had such a fun time. Thanks again, Rozz, for helping to make it all happen."

We both gave Rozz an enormous hug.

Raymond then lifted Mr. Muggs up and gave him some much-needed welcome-home kisses.

"Did my Mugginses miss his one daddy?" Raymond asked.

"That reminds me," Rozz said. "The vet left a message to remind you about your appointment to get Mr. Muggs fixed," she said.

"That's right, hun," I said, "I totally forgot about that. He's already had his first shots, but now it's the deepest cut of all."

"My poor boy is going to be ball-less," Raymond said, and held him tight.

"It's best before he starts spraying all over the place," Rozz said.

Rozz gathered up her stuff, and we walked her down to her car.

"Thanks again, Rozz, for everything," Raymond said, and we both gave her another hug.

"Don't mention it, guys," she said. "You needed a break."

She then got in her car and drove home as we waved goodbye from the curb at the apartment entrance. A couple of days later, Raymond and I dropped Mr. Muggs off at the veterinary clinic recommended by my horse vet for his operation.

"Good morning, guys," the receptionist said. "Is this Mr. Muggs?" she asked.

"The one and only Mr. Muggs," Raymond said, and handed her Mr. Muggs, sitting quietly in his cat carrier.

"He'll be fine," she said. "He'll be ready to go home at around three o'clock today. You can pick him up then."

Raymond said goodbye to his Mugginses and then dropped me off at the track.

"I'll phone from the pay phone once I'm done, hun." I wanted to give him a kiss, but with so many people walking around the area, I didn't want to take the chance and instead gave him a quiet "I love you" and got out of the car. Raymond then continued on his way home.

Later that day, Raymond came and picked me up. I was a bit late in calling, and we went directly to get Mr. Muggs from the vet clinic.

"Hi, guys, let me go get Mr. Muggs," she said, and came back with a very loud and noisy Mr. Muggs inside his cat carrier.

"Sounds like someone is a little annoyed," I said.

Raymond then looked inside the carrier and greeted Mr. Muggs, where he instantly went quiet.

"He just missed his daddy, that's all," Raymond said.

"These are his antibiotic pills," the receptionist said. "Follow the directions on the label. Here is some spray to put on his stitches. It helps heal, plus he's wearing his little cone collar to stop him from licking as well.

"You can probably take the collar off after a couple of days, but it's important that he not lick the stitches out."

We paid our bill and started for the car.

Now and then, Mr. Muggs would let out a lonesome howl, and once Raymond responded, he was quiet for a while.

Back home in the apartment, Mr. Muggs seemed to be more relaxed, and for the next few hours, spent the entire time on Raymond's lap.

Raymond would take the collar off while Mr. Muggs was resting on his lap and give his neck a scratch, to which Mr. Muggs would erupt in a loud purr.

After a few days, our ball-less Mr. Muggs accepted his loss, never bothered licking, and went back to being his normal, adorable self.

CHAPTER 15

While living in the apartment, I enjoyed writing in my journal about things that happened. I would write bits of poetry about Raymond and myself, usually regarding an experience that we had encountered. Often, I'd write them down again on a small note, and leave them on Raymond's pillow.

Once there was a problem with the betting machines at the track one Saturday evening, and he didn't get home till about two o'clock in the morning. As I always did when I was at the apartment, I stayed up for him. He came home and was exhausted. I felt so bad for him. I made us a cup of tea, then we went to bed.

It wasn't long before he fell asleep on my chest. The next morning, I wrote in my journal the following words while they were still in my thoughts.

> Lying with my man, I feel his touch and gentle shove,
> The feeling of our security, as we're both wrapped
>   in love.
> Our bodies lean upon each other in joyful peace,
> We're cuddled up, warm and naked under the fleece.

I hear him sigh, knowing he is at rest.
My man is exhausted and falls asleep on my chest.
I look at my angel, asleep and content.
He'll sleep in my arms until tomorrow is sent.

Raymond, I love you.

I wrote so many of these poems for him, and although they might seem foolish and sentimental, he always smiled and thanked me for them.

I'm a true believer that good people deserve to be with good people, and that fate tries its best to bring a loving couple together. It might take a while, but it is definitely worth the wait.

CHAPTER 16
October 1982.

It was mid-October, a few weeks before Raymond's birthday and a couple of weeks before the Halloween party at the club. Raymond and I were snuggled up together on the couch one night.

"Did you still want to go to the Halloween party at the club in a couple of weeks?" I asked.

"I sure do, but what should we dress up as, babe?" Raymond asked.

"It would have to be something simple," I said, "as we can't walk down the street wearing our costumes."

"What if we go dressed just in our regular clothes?" Raymond replied, "we'll go as a 'straight' couple."

"That's actually funny," I said. "What if we go as two baseball players?"

"What does baseball have to do with Halloween, babe?" Raymond asked. "Besides, we're not into sports."

"Well, my dad has an umpire's mask at home, and a couple of baseball gloves. We could go purchase two Blue Jays jerseys.

"I still don't get it. That sounds boring. Why go as baseball players?" Raymond asked.

"You can wear one with 'Pitcher' printed on the back, and I'll wear one with 'Catcher.'

"Now I get it. I love it!" Raymond laughed. "Do you think the guys at the club will figure it out?"

"Sure, they will," I said. "Plus, who doesn't know of The Blue Jays here in Toronto, and everyone at the club definitely knows the difference between a pitcher and a catcher, as they're either one or the other," I joked.

"In that case, I'd better go to the bullpen and start warming up my bull. Pass me some balls!" Raymond excitedly said, and he proceeded to tickle me all over.

He knew how ticklish I was and that I would agree to anything he asked, if only he'd stop with the tickling.

"Let's play ball!" Raymond laughed, and we carried our game play from the couch to the bedroom, where we played a few innings.

A few days later, we drove into Toronto and got ourselves the two Blue Jays baseball jerseys of "Pitcher" and "Catcher," along with two Blue Jays caps.

On the way home, we stopped by Rozz's place to say hi and have a quick cup of tea. We showed her the two jerseys. She thought they were great costumes and had a good laugh with our sly pitcher and catcher humor.

I later secretly borrowed my father's baseball mask, two gloves, and a baseball, and took them to the apartment to take to the Halloween dance.

A couple of weeks later, we drove into Toronto and to the club, wearing our jerseys and matching royal blue sweatpants. I had a small Blue Jays duffle bag carrying the mask and gloves.

Once inside, it didn't take our friend Robert long to figure it out.

"Hey guys, happy Halloween!" Robert said as he spun each of us around and read the names.

"Raymond, or should I say Mr. Pitcher? I always knew you were a pitcher to Dan's catching glove." He laughed and motioned for his other friends to come over and see.

"Hey, guys, come and have a look at Ray and Dan!"

I quickly took out the mask and slipped it on.

"I love it. The mask almost adds a bit of kink to it, don't you think?" Robert said.

They all had a fun laugh at our costumes.

The club was decked out in a Halloween theme with fake cobwebs all over, jack-o'-lanterns, and skulls.

Eddie showed up dressed as Dracula. He had tucked his cape up under his jacket and into his black dress pants. He then pulled out a set of plastic fangs from his pocket and put them in his mouth. With a definite slur, he proceeded to try to say, with his Chinese accent, "I'sh wantchs to schuck yoursh blood." We all soon started to laugh, listening to how Eddie sounded with his fake fangs in.

"Who wants a beer?" Raymond asked, and after Eddie and I nodded, he went and got our drinks.

We were all having a good time when Laura Branigan started to sing "Gloria."

"This is my new favorite song," I yelled out, and we all went to the dance floor.

Raymond and I had danced to this song a few times, and he had already mastered the lyrics and put in his own dance routine.

"I love how this song starts with the electronic synthesizers," Raymond said, as we started dancing.

I started singing, directing it at Raymond, and reaching out my hands as if asking him the lyrics. He would then move his body to the rhythm of the music and to the meaning of the lyrics.

He would then clench his fist, raise his baby finger and thumb, and hold his hand up to his mouth and ear, pretending to be talking on the telephone. Finally, near the end of the song, when the trumpet hit a crescendo, he would look skyward, and then air play a trumpet pretending to finger the valves.

We all sat back down, laughing and enjoying our beer, trying to cool off.

"That was awesome," Eddie said. "I've heard that song before, but never paid attention to the lyrics."

"We have her album in the apartment," Raymond said. "How do you think I practice my dance moves?"

Finally, around 1 a.m., we decided to leave.

"Dan and I are heading for home, Eddie. Are you leaving or going to stay for a while?" Raymond asked.

"I think I'll go join Bill and his friends for a while," Eddie said. "See you next Saturday?"

"Call us at the apartment and leave a message, and we'll let you know," Raymond answered.

We gave Eddie his usual hug and headed back to the car.

CHAPTER 17
Late fall 1982.

As the seasons changed, so did the location of the horse racing. In the fall and early winter, the horse racing calendar moved from Greenwood Racetrack in downtown Toronto, to Mohawk Raceway in the small town of Campbellville, Ontario, about fifty miles west of Toronto. I much preferred racing out of Mohawk, as it was a quick fifteen-minute drive from the track to the apartment.

Raymond's birthday was in November, and I always tried to get him something special.

"I'm trying to think whose birthday it is, hun, but I just can't remember," I joked one night while sitting on the couch.

"Maybe you have to think a bit harder," Raymond replied, "as it's someone very important, and they deserve lots of attention!"

"Probably some relation that I've totally forgotten about," I said. "It's no big deal anyway."

With that, Raymond lunged and body-slammed on top of me while we sat on the couch.

"Just don't forget, it's better to give than receive," he joked.

"Then, by all means, give it to me, give it to me!" I laughed.

The next day, I thought about planning something for Raymond's birthday. As much as I preferred having a quiet birthday for myself, Raymond enjoyed having more of a party atmosphere and having friends around to celebrate his special day.

Raymond had already left for work at the track, and since I wasn't racing, I decided to stay home that night.

Seeing that I was alone, I decided to knock on Mrs. H's door and asked a favor of her.

"Dan, dear, come on in. What can I do for you?" she asked. "No racing tonight?"

"Raymond already left for work at the track, but I'm not racing. I'm staying home tonight," I said. "I was wondering if I could ask a favor of you? Could I get you to make Raymond a birthday cake for his birthday? I know how much he loves your chocolate cake."

"I didn't know it was his birthday. I'd love to do that for him," she said. "When is his birthday, Dan?"

"It's next Wednesday," I replied. "I was going to invite a couple of friends over. Feel free to drop by as well, Mrs. H."

"I better make a triple layer, then," she said. "How old will Raymond be?"

"Thanks, Mrs. H. He's turning twenty-three," I replied, and gave her a peck on the cheek.

"Just a baby," she smiled. "Leave it with me, dear, and I'll take care of it for you. I'll let you know if I need anything."

Once back in the apartment, I called Rozz at work.

"Hello, Miss Scott speaking," she answered

"Hi, Miss Scott, it's Mr. Dan," I joked. "How's your day going?"

"Hey, Dan," she answered, "all is good, thanks. What's up?

Is everything okay there?" she asked.

"Yes, all is good, thanks, and I apologize for calling you at work, but I was wondering if you would like to come over to the apartment next Wednesday for Raymond's birthday?" I asked.

"That's right," she said. "I'm glad you called, Dan, as I almost forgot Raymond's birthday was coming up. Certainly, I'll drop by. Do you have any idea what he wants for his birthday?"

"I know he's been hinting at the latest album from Duran Duran, called *Rio*. He already has their first album called *Duran Duran*, plus, he also likes the Ramones, *Pleasant Dreams* album," I said.

"He likes the punk rock group the Ramones? Good God," and she let out a funny sigh. "Let me look at the local record store. I'm sure they'll have either one," she answered. "I've got to run, Dan. Thanks for calling, and I'll see you next Wednesday. Love you." She hung up.

I then called Eddie at his parents' place.

"Hello?" said a very soft-spoken lady.

"Is Eddie home, please?" I inquired.

"Who is speaking, please?" she asked.

"It's his friend, Dan," I answered.

"One moment please," and I heard the phone receiver be placed down on the table.

A few seconds later, Eddie was on the phone. "Dan! What's going on, buddy?" he asked.

"Hey, Eddie, I was wondering if you would like to come over to the apartment for Raymond's birthday next Wednesday. It's nothing big, just a couple of friends," I said.

"Wouldn't miss it, my man," he answered. "Is everything okay with you guys?"

"All is great," I answered and then asked, "How's things at home with you?"

"Don't ask, I'll tell you all about it next Wednesday," was his reply.

"Come over whenever you're free," I said. "You know you're always welcome here, any day and at any time of day."

"Thanks, man. See you guys next Wednesday," he said and hung up the phone.

I knew Eddie and his parents often didn't see eye to eye on things, but he sounded okay, and I never thought anything of it.

Just then, there was a knock at the door.

I peeked through the peep hole, and it was Mrs. H.

"Hey, Mrs. H," I said.

"Dan, dear, how many people are you having over for Raymond's birthday?" she asked.

"So far, it's you, myself, Raymond's sister Rozz, and our good friend, Eddie, so a total of five, including Raymond," I said.

"Let me make a big lasagna for dinner as well. Everyone loves lasagna," she said. "It'll be my little birthday gift."

"Aw, thanks, Mrs. H. That's so kind of you. I know every-one will enjoy your lasagna as Raymond and I love it," I said.

"Perfect," she said. "Back to the soaps on TV. Chat later, dear." And she went back across the hall.

Later that afternoon, the phone rang. I would never pick it up out of fear of it being Raymond's parents and would always wait for the answering machine to kick in first. If it were Raymond, Rozz, or Eddie, they'd say, "It's okay, Dan. You can pick up."

"Hey, Dan, it's Rozz. You can pick up if you're there," she said.

I quickly answered the phone. "Hey Rozz," I said. "What's up?"

"I just phoned the big record store on Yonge Street, and they have both albums in stock. I told them to hold them both for me, and I'm going over to get them after work," she said.

"Perfect, Rozz. I know he's wanted either one of them. He'll be thrilled I know," I said.

"Ok, thanks for telling me, Dan," she said. "Back to work. Talk later."

"Thanks, Rozz, bye," I replied, and we hung up.

Now it was my turn to figure out what else to get Raymond for his birthday, and what to plan for our small get together.

Mrs. H was looking after the main course and cake. Rozz had her presents, and Eddie confirmed he was coming over.

Earlier that summer, I had ordered some impressive hardcover books about photography from the National Geographic Society. I secretly hid them away to give to Raymond, one for his birthday, and one for Christmas.

I wrapped the one up, along with a camera tripod that I had bought after seeing how excited Raymond got after looking at it when we were at the camera store one day.

I also got the mushiest birthday card I could find. I remember purchasing a birthday card from the local drug store, "To my Loving Husband" and hoped the cashier wouldn't look at the front of it when I handed it to her upside down, with the price on the back showing.

He already had a subscription to *Billboard*, and I thought about extending it. I also thought about getting him another music magazine and decided to go into town to the local smoke shop to see if I could find a copy of the *Rolling Stone* magazine.

I started looking through magazines in the store and found it. While there, I found a small, stuffed cat with excessively large eyes that looked just like Mr. Muggs and bought that as well.

DAN REYNOLDS

I paid for my birthday presents, went back to the apartment, and hid my secret stash in the back of our bedroom closet.

The following Wednesday, I was up early to head to the track. The alarm went off at the usual five a.m., and I rolled over to Raymond and wished him a happy birthday.

"Happy birthday, hun!" I said and gave him a big kiss and a naked hug.

"Thanks, babe," he answered. "Try not to be too long. I want today to be for us."

I quickly made my way to the track and got done as soon as I could. I got back to the apartment around two p.m., and luckily saw Eddie drive in as I was walking from the car.

"Eddie!" I said. "So good to see you." We gave each other a hug.

"Hey, Dan, I'd never miss an important thing like Raymond's birthday!" He was carrying a present as well.

"I may need you to help me blow up some balloons, if I can get Raymond out of the apartment for a few minutes," I said. "Rozz is coming over and I'm going to ask her to take Raymond downstairs to look at her car or something. That'll give us a few minutes."

"Great idea," Eddie said, and we made our way up to the apartment.

"Let me knock on Mrs. H's door. You can hide your gift in there if you want, and we can surprise him with it later," I said.

"Sounds good to me," Eddie answered.

I knocked on her door and Mrs. H. answered. We were greeted with an always friendly, "Hello, my dears. What can I do for you?"

"Hi, Mrs. H., this is our friend Eddie," I said and introduced him.

"Would it be alright if we hid Eddie's birthday gift in your apartment until our surprise party for Raymond later?" I asked.

"Of course, my dear, come on in," she said.

"Does that ever smell good, Mrs. Hutchinson?" Eddie said.

"That's dinner," Mrs. H said. "Leave your gift here, Eddie, and come get it when you're ready."

"Thanks, Mrs. H.," I said, and we left for across the hall.

"She spoils you two rotten," Eddie said.

"Yes, and I'm very glad she does," I happily replied.

We walked into the apartment as Raymond was lounged out on the couch watching TV.

"Eddie!" Raymond yelled and jumped up off the couch. "It's so good to see you. What are you doing here?"

"I heard it's someone's birthday, and I wanted to come over," he said. "I hope I'm not interfering with anything you two have planned."

"Of course not," Raymond said. "You know you're always welcome here anytime, and thanks for coming. It makes me happy seeing my friends on my birthday," Raymond said.

We all sat down and got caught up in the recent gossip of our lives.

"So, how are things going at home?" I asked Eddie.

"My dad keeps trying to arrange a date with me and one of his friend's daughters. I keep telling him I'm already seeing someone, just so he doesn't go through with it," he said. "The other day, he asked me to bring the girl home for them to meet her. I told him that she's very shy, but I will bring her home soon. I don't know how much longer I can hide it from them," Eddie said, somewhat frightened. "If they ever found out I'm gay, I don't know what they would do."

"I'm not sure what you should do, Eddie," Raymond said.

"But no matter what happens, we're here to support you."

"Thanks guys," Eddie answered.

Just then, the buzzer from the lobby rang, and Raymond answered the intercom.

"Hello?" he asked,

"Hey, guys, it's Rozz," she answered.

"Rozz, now Rozz is here. What's going on?" asked Raymond with a huge smile on his face, finally figuring it all out.

"Just be quiet, hun, and let your sister in," I said, smiling.

He unlocked the lobby door, and Rozz came upstairs.

Raymond waited for her at the apartment door and greeted her with a hug.

"Happy birthday, little brother!" Rozz said and gave Raymond a hug, then handed me the bag with his gifts inside.

Rozz followed me into the kitchen, where I quietly asked her if she could ask Raymond to go downstairs and check out her car or something, as I wanted to dress up the apartment with some balloons.

"Oh, Raymond, would you mind quickly coming down-stairs with me?" Rozz said. "My check engine light came on in the car driving over. I don't know anything about that stuff."

Raymond put on his shoes, and they left for the parking lot.

Eddie and I got out the balloons, and we started quickly blowing up balloon after balloon.

"Wow, you blow really well," I teasingly said to Eddie.

"You're not the first to tell me that," Eddie jokingly replied.

We managed to get about twenty balloons blown up and taped to the walls, with some streamers and a big Happy Birthday sign.

I quickly went and got Mrs. H, and we all waited with our cone-shaped birthday hats on for Raymond to return. Even Mr. Muggs sat there with his little pointed hat on.

The lobby buzzer rang, and I said, "Hello, may I help you?"

"Ha ha, let us in, babe," Raymond said.

I unlocked the lobby door, and we waited for them to return.

Raymond opened the apartment door to a very loud, "Happy birthday!"

"How'd you decorate the place so fast?" Raymond said, "Mrs. H! and look at Mr. Muggs!"

I went over and gave Raymond a big kiss and hug.

"Thanks, babe," he said.

"You're welcome hun. You deserve it."

I helped Mrs. H. go over and get the lasagna and birthday cake, while Rozz got the plates out from the kitchen. Eddie got out the cold pop that I had stocked up with earlier.

We all had a fun time celebrating Raymond's birthday while eating all of Mrs. H's lasagna, and then singing him happy birthday.

He was thrilled with his gifts. "I can't wait to play these," Raymond said. "Thanks, Rozz." And he gave her a hug.

Eddie also gave him a couple of albums, for which Eddie received a hug as well.

I gave Raymond his camera tripod, photography book, and the *Rolling Stone* magazine with the subscription card filled out for a year.

"Thanks, babe!" Raymond said. "I love all of these."

After a fun time, everyone decided to head for home.

"Thanks for coming," I said, and Raymond and I hugged everyone as they left.

The last to leave was Eddie.

"Thanks for coming, Eddie," Raymond said, and we reassured him once again that we would always be there to support him in any way we could.

"Thanks, guys," Eddie said, "I'll let you two continue to

celebrate," and gave Raymond another hug.

Raymond and I cleaned up the place, and then went to bed.

Raymond and I celebrated his birthday in our own joyous private way, and afterwards fell asleep together.

CHAPTER 18
December 1982.

Raymond and I both enjoyed the Christmas season, even though we had to spend most of Christmas Day with our own families.

Leading up to Christmas, I tried to think of something to get Raymond. He loved photography and was always taking pictures. Years later, it was the pictures that he took of him and me that would be the basis for his divorce from his homophobic wife.

"We should take a day off and go Christmas shopping, babe," Raymond said, "get something for Rozz, and maybe Mrs. H and Eddie."

"That's a good idea, hun. Let's plan on Wednesday next week. There's no racing that night, and I should be able to finish early," I said.

The following Wednesday was an easy day at the track, and I was finished extra early, at around eleven a.m. I got back to the apartment, and we drove into Toronto.

"Traffic is a bitch," Raymond said. "Where do all these

people go and come from?"

We finally got to the mall, and after driving around and around searching, we eventually found a parking spot.

We couldn't get over how busy the mall was for a weekday.

"This Christmas shopping is nuts," I said. "There's so many people here. Don't people work during the day?" I joked.

While we strolled through the mall, I happened to see a white shirt with a pink tie and baby-blue sweater pullover in the window of one of the men's clothing stores.

"I could see myself wearing that tie at the club one night," I said. "That looks so sharp. Let's go in and see how much it is."

We went into the store and were greeted by a very cute young guy.

"Can I help you guys find anything?" he politely asked.

"I was looking at that pink tie and sweater combination in the window," I said.

"Isn't that totally eye-catching!" he said, and with a little swagger, went over to the tie rack and searched through them all but couldn't find a pink one.

"The one in the window is the last pink one we have. Sorry, guys. I'm not sure when we'll be getting any more in. It's silk and made in Italy, the best ties we have in the store. It's on sale for twenty-five dollars. Good price for this brand," he said. "The sweater is also on sale. It's twenty dollars. Did you want the one in the window?"

I was a little hesitant about spending that kind of money on myself.

"Thanks," I said, "I think I'll look around first," and we started walking to the exit.

I looked back and Raymond was thanking the cute sales associate, then started walking to catch up.

"Let's go to the camera store over there," Raymond said,

and we went in. Raymond was in his glory with all the cameras, accessories, and photography books there.

"Look at this, babe," he said, all excited, and he pointed into the display case.

"It's the new Polaroid Instant SLR 680. Have you ever seen one before?"

"Only on TV," I said. "Aren't those the cameras that you take the picture, and they develop it right there and spit it out?

"Yeah, wouldn't that be fun at the club, hun?" Then Raymond nudged me and quietly said, "Or in bed?"

Just then, the clerk came over. "Can I help you?" she asked. "How much is the SLR 680?" Raymond asked.

"It takes beautiful pictures," she said, and took one from the display case and handed it to Raymond.

"It's on sale for $315," she said. "Plus, it includes a bonus of two boxes of extra film."

I could see the joy that had been on Raymond's face while holding it slowly melt away with disappointment when he heard how much it was.

"Thanks," he said and handed the camera back to the lady.

"I guess that tie doesn't seem as expensive after all, does it, babe?" Raymond joked.

After walking around, we stopped and had some lunch.

As I sat there, I knew I had room on my credit card, and contemplated going back to get Raymond the camera. But how would I go back to the store without Raymond knowing?

Just then, Raymond said, "I saw something that I want to get for Rozz. You stay here, babe, and finish your lunch. I'll be right back."

"That's fine. I'll wait here." Perfect timing. I quickly finished eating and raced back to the camera store around the corner to purchase the Polaroid SLR 680.

I went in and saw the same lady. "Could I get that SLR 680 camera that we were looking at a few minutes ago?"

"Certainly," she said, and got one from the case, along with the couple of boxes of bonus film.

"It already has a box of film that comes with the camera, so in total there are three boxes of film," she said. "That's a great deal."

She placed my gift in a small bag, and I hurriedly raced back to where we had been sitting. I stuck the camera bag into another bag so Raymond couldn't see it and waited for him to return.

"Get what you wanted for Rozz?" I asked.

"Yup, I'm all done. Let's get out of here. I've had enough of the hustle and bustle of Christmas shopping for one day," Raymond said.

As we were leaving the mall, we walked by the "Get your picture taken with Santa at the North Pole" display.

Suddenly, the little guy elf quickly ran over to greet us. "Merry Christmas, guys. Come and have your picture taken with Santa, together. Santa insists!"

Raymond and I both looked over at Santa, who gave us a wave and a nod, motioning us to come closer as the last couple of kids climbed down from his lap and left. Santa sat in the North Pole in his big, decorated chair. Not knowing why or how friendly he'd be toward having two guys sit on his lap, we cautiously approached.

Santa did his usual, "Ho ho ho," as we sat down, one on each leg. He then asked in a quieter voice, "And what does Raymond and little Danny want for Christmas this year? Ho ho ho!"

Shocked, we both stared deeply at Santa, trying to get past the white hair and beard.

"Robert!" Raymond said, recognizing the doorman and bouncer from the gay nightclub we went to.

Santa Robert squeezed us both into him for a hug. "I saw you two love birds walking through the mall earlier," he said. "When I saw you walking closer, I told my totally gay happy little elf friend to go get you."

Santa then let out another loud "Ho ho ho" as we got up off his knee.

"Have a great Christmas, guys," Santa Robert hollered, and gave us each a squeeze on the ass as we were getting up, followed by an extra-long and loud "Ho ho ho!"

We started to exit the North Pole display when Santa's little helper greeted us. "Merry Christmas!" Then he quietly said, "Hope you have a merry and gay one!" and gave us a big smile and waved us goodbye.

"I didn't even recognize Robert," I said.

"Can you imagine he even asked me out a couple of times?" Raymond said.

Somewhat heartbroken, I said, "Are you serious? And what did you say?"

"What do you think, babe? I said no, of course, and told him, 'Dan and I are a couple.'"

I've always had a terrible jealous streak and was nervous about another man hitting on Raymond, simply because of his *GQ*-handsome good looks.

As we drove home, I was somewhat quiet. He reached out to hold my hand, and I grabbed hold.

"You're mine, babe. I have no interest in any other guy, Dan. It's you and me together, and no one else," Raymond reassured me.

That night I wanted to thank him, and before we went to bed, I wrote him another little poem and gave it to him.

> *I'm lucky to have you and thank you again,*
> *For being my lover and my best friend.*

You're an amazing man that I can't compare,
From your handsome good looks to your beauti-
  ful stare.
There will always be guys that may turn our head,
But at the end of the day, it's you that I want to
  cuddle up to in bed.

Raymond, I love you.

Raymond snuggled up close on the couch as we watched TV.

"For as long as we're together, I'll always be yours, babe," Raymond said.

After a long day, we went to bed, made love, and fell asleep in each other's arms.

CHAPTER 19

As with every Christmas, we over-decorated the apartment, and Mrs. Hutchinson supplied us with an endless supply of Christmas cookies. We had small multicolor lights around each window, out of the way of the curious teeth of Mr. Muggs.

In the one corner of the apartment stood our artificial Christmas tree. It was small, but once decorated, looked incredibly homey.

We received three Christmas Cards that year wishing Raymond "and" Dan, a very merry Christmas. One card was from Rozz, another from Mrs. Hutchinson, and the third from our dear friend Eddie.

All three were signed with "Love."

Raymond and I both loved the holiday season, for it seemed to heighten the magic in our loving relationship. Each of us wanted to show the other how much we cared for and supported each other. It was as if the holidays gave us the opportunity to show the world the joy we had in our lives. For us, it wasn't a religious celebration, but a celebration of being together and showing how much we loved each other.

We had wrapped our gifts to each other, and they were placed under the tree.

I was still trying to find Raymond one more special gift, a new pair of sneakers. One night, while getting ready to go to the club, he mentioned how faded and worn the black fabric canvas was getting on his and that he should get a new pair.

The only brand he'd ever wear were PRO-Keds black-and-white basketball ankle-high sneakers, or as Raymond called them, his "AHS."

Raymond liked the punk group the Ramones, and they all wore PRO-Keds, as did elite basketball players in the NBA.

I looked everywhere but couldn't find them in a size twelve and a half.

He could get away squeezing into a size twelve, but he always said the twelve and a half were just that much more comfortable, or even a size thirteen.

Finally, out of desperation, I called Rozz one day from the apartment, asking if she knew where I could find them. She mentioned there was a sporting goods store near her bank in Toronto, and she would go look.

A couple of days later, she called the apartment and let me know she found a pair of black PRO-Keds, in a size twelve and a half.

"These sure are difficult to find," Rozz said. "I happened to be in the store when they were putting them on the shelf. The young guy said I came at the right time, as these would all be sold out by tomorrow. I'll drop by for a visit on the weekend and figure out a way to bring them upstairs."

"Thanks so much, Rozz. I know he loves those, and I just couldn't find them anywhere."

"Dan, could I ask a favor of you?" she said.

"Sure, Rozz, what is it?" I asked.

"Have you gotten Raymond anything else for Christmas?

The reason I ask is I haven't gotten him anything, and if I could, I'd give him the sneakers, but understand if you want to," she said.

"I already got him a new Polaroid instant camera and some film, so if you want to, feel free to give him the sneakers. Besides, I'm getting close to maxing out my credit card," I jokingly said.

"Those damn bank credit cards." She laughed. "Thanks for letting me purchase the sneakers. It makes it a lot easier," Rozz said. "Thanks, Dan. Love you!"

"Love you as well, Rozz. Bye," I answered.

As Christmas approached, Raymond and I were getting more and more into wanting to spend more time together, if that was at all possible.

It was Christmas, that time of year when you believe in magic and the excitement of watching people unwrap gifts and enjoy the company of loved ones.

I knew I would have to spend some time at home during the holidays simply to continue the illusion that nothing was out of the ordinary, at least in regard to me living with someone, let alone living with a man.

I purchased gifts for those at home and they continued to have no idea of my life with Raymond. Finally, it was the morning of December 24th—Christmas Eve. I had slept over and awoke to the smell of bacon!

Raymond was up early and had made breakfast. It was around five a.m. He knew that I had to go attend the horses, clean out their stalls, and make sure they had fresh water.

The sooner I was able to get my barn work done, the sooner I could get back to the apartment and be with Raymond.

From the kitchen, I heard Raymond holler, "Get up, babe. Breakfast is ready."

I sleepily went into the kitchen and gave Raymond a full body hug from behind.

"Go do the horses as quick as you can, babe, then we can have the day together. Rozz said she may stop by this afternoon."

Raymond had made bacon, toast, and tea.

"I shouldn't be more than a couple of hours," I said, then I ate breakfast, kissed and hugged Raymond, and drove to the track.

It didn't take me long to finish my work with the horses. It was a day off for them regarding exercise, which made the day much easier.

Their stalls were cleaned out, they were brushed, any leg bandages, used for support and therapy, were changed, and they were resting comfortably.

I then drove back to the apartment and went upstairs. I got off the elevator just in time to see Raymond's parents enter the apartment. Thank the powers that be that I saw them in time. I immediately stepped back into the elevator and stood there, peeking around the elevator door as I held it open in a frozen stare. I began second-guessing what I should do next.

They entered the apartment just as the elevator began to ding to indicate the door remained open, and I practically jumped out of my skin. I nervously thought, *What would have happened if I had unlocked the apartment door with a key and walked in with them there? I'm sure there would have been hell to pay from Father Beast, wondering why I have a key.*

Once I thought the coast was clear, I quickly went and very quietly knocked on Mrs. Hutchinson's door. She answered the door in a few seconds, which seemed to last for ages. I kept quickly glancing over at our apartment and figuring out an escape plan just in case they came out.

"Dan, my dear, come in," she said. "You look flustered. What's wrong? Is Raymond's father visiting?"

"Thanks, Mrs. H. Yes, I saw his parents just as they were entering the apartment when I came out of the elevator. I hope you don't mind me dropping over," I said.

"I've told you numerous times, Dan, that you're always welcome. Much more comfortable than sitting in the lockers downstairs, isn't it?"

She smiled, then grabbed me by the arm and led me inside.

"Let me make us some tea."

As the kettle was on, Mrs. H picked up the phone and called someone.

"Raymond?" she asked. "It's Mrs. Hutchinson, dear. I have that special delivery for you. I thought it best that I keep it here for you instead of sending it down to the lockers. Yes, dear, come over when you are finished, and you can pick it up."

She quietly hung up the phone, looked at me, smiled and went back to making our tea.

We had a pleasant visit together. She was a widow and had two sons. Both her children had moved away and had families of their own. She said they would "sometimes" call on special days, but she hadn't seen them in a couple of years.

I felt bad for her. She had one grandchild to whom she would send birthday and special occasion cards, but she also mentioned she had never received a thank you.

I now understood why she'd become so attached to Raymond and me. We acknowledged her birthday, Christmas, and often brought her flowers for no reason other than being a friendly neighbor.

She had a pet cat as company. I can't remember its name, but he would constantly rub against me. I think he could smell the odors of the barn and the horses and would roll and purr at my feet.

As a Christmas gift that year, we bought Mrs. H. a multi-level cat tree and some cat toys. She was so happy and thankful that she couldn't stop hugging us.

She, in turn, had knitted each of us a toque, a pair of mitts, and a heavy sweater.

After an hour or so, Raymond knocked on the door.

"Come in dear, let me make more tea," said Mrs. H.

I asked Raymond, "What's wrong?" as he looked like something was distressing him.

"It's Dad again," he said. "He wanted me to go to Midnight Mass with him and Mom tonight. I said I already have plans, as Dan is coming over."

Apparently, his father once again questioned my association with Raymond, who said he lost his temper and raised his voice to his father, saying, "Am I not allowed to have a close fucking friend? I'm getting tired of this constant, ruthless inquiry into my private life. I'm twenty-four years old and I can make my own fucking decisions. Even when and if I want to go to church."

"You spoke that way to your father?" I asked.

"I'm fucking tired of him trying to rule over me and manipulating my life. I'm sorry, Mrs. H, for swearing," Raymond said.

"What did he do?" I asked, quite astonished that Raymond had finally stood his ground.

"After speaking my mind, I could see Dad's temper flaring. He started glaring at me as he stepped forward and got a bit closer. Mom then grabbed him by the arm and said, 'Let's go, John. I don't think this is either the time or the place. Raymond, we'll be expecting you for Christmas dinner tomorrow,' she said."

"Then what happened?" I asked.

"Dad didn't say a word. He glared at Mom, and they both

started walking to the door. He opened the door and suddenly turned and was about to say something toward me when Mom just pushed him out," said Raymond. "I'm not sure what would have happened if Mom wasn't there. I hope she's ok."

"Are you going to Christmas dinner tomorrow?" I asked.

Before Raymond could answer, Mrs. Hutchinson said, "No, he'll be having Christmas dinner with me. I'd feel more comfortable knowing he is here, and you're welcome also, Dan."

Raymond thanked Mrs. H and said he would love to join her for dinner.

"I don't think I could put up with him at this moment, even if it is Christmas," Raymond said.

You could tell Mrs. Hutchinson was thrilled at not spending Christmas alone.

CHAPTER 20
Christmas Eve 1982.

We thanked Mrs. H again and walked across the hall to home.

"I can't believe him. He just won't stop. No matter. I'm not going to let him ruin our Christmas, babe," Raymond said.

He walked over to the tree, looked through the pile, and brought one of the many presents from under the tree.

"Here, babe, I feel like being happy again. Merry Christmas." Raymond passed me the present, kissed me, and said, "Well, go ahead, open it!"

I gently unwrapped the present, removing the tape and lifting the folds.

"You're the only person I know who won't tear open a gift!" Raymond said. "Drives me crazy!"

Inside was a long box, and I opened it up. It contained the pink necktie we had seen in the men's store when we went Christmas shopping.

Raymond was kneeling in front of me as I opened it.

"That's the one from the store that day!" I cried in excitement. "I thought there weren't any left."

"Do you like it, babe?" Raymond asked with a big smile.

I threw my arms around him. "I love it! This means so much to me, hun. I'm only going to wear it when we go to the club." I started giving him multiple kisses.

"But when did you go back and get it?" I asked.

"When we were sitting having lunch, and I said that I wanted to go get something for Rozz. It's the one from the window display. After you told the salesclerk you would 'look around' and started walking away, I quietly told him that I'd come back and asked if he would put aside the one in the window for me," Raymond said.

"You're so sneaky!" I replied, while thinking, *I did the exact same thing.*

I got up and said, "Okay, hun, my turn," and went and got him a gift.

He sat on the couch and tore open the paper. "This is the proper way to open presents!" Raymond laughed.

Inside was a heavy hardcover book about photography. It had lots of ideas and suggestions on taking pictures and using light effects.

"Babe! I love this. I was going to buy this exact same book!"

Raymond put it on the coffee table and lunged at me. We fell back on the couch, embracing each other. We kissed and enjoyed the moment.

I had told my parents that I was going to spend Christmas Eve night at the track so I could get done early on Christmas Day. They never questioned it, as they understood the care that was needed for the horses. For some, Christmas Day was a lonely time at the racetrack. Many grooms had neither a place to call home nor any family they could visit.

Some would offer to feed your horses on Christmas, so you didn't have to, but I still told my parents I was going to stay the night, at least on Christmas Eve, just to secretly be with Raymond.

Our little Christmas tree was lit and all aglow, as were the string of Christmas lights on our outside railing. It was snowing outside and bitterly cold. We both went out onto the balcony with Raymond tightly holding onto Mr. Muggs.

A small amount of snow had started to accumulate on the balcony, and it made that familiar crunching sound as we stepped on it from it being so cold outside. We glanced out over the neighborhood as I stepped closer beside Raymond and put my one arm around his waist.

"It truly is magical, isn't it, babe?" Raymond said.

As we looked out over the balcony, a feeling of serenity came over me. Even in the bitter cold of the softly falling snow, I was at peace. Peace in knowing I was with my Raymond and our Mr. Muggs, the three of us together and happy. The lights inside the scores of houses were lit, shedding a tranquil haze on the neighborhood and making the falling snow almost glisten as it came down. The multitude of colorful Christmas lights that people decorated their homes with added to the Yuletide glow.

What excitement did those houses hold inside?

I imagined all the little kids anxiously waiting for Santa to arrive. Their parents eagerly looking forward to bringing excitement to their kids with the multitude of toys that they had secretly hidden away, while at the same time, waiting for the kids to eventually fall asleep. Families and loved ones together, celebrating the warmth and magic of what would soon be Christmas Day. As special as it was to be with family on such a special occasion, Raymond and I both felt we would sooner be together than to be with our own families.

I wondered how many gay people and gay couples were out there as well. How many of them were alone, or secretly together, and celebrating the exact same festive joy just like everyone else, but in their own hidden way? In my heart, I wished them all a merry Christmas.

I thought no matter what the outside forces were, whether it was nature's weather, society's outlook, or our own families' attitude, I had my own little family right here beside me to cherish and protect.

"It's you, Mr. Muggs, and me, hun. Us three together in a cold, uncertain world," I said.

I leaned my head on Raymond's shoulder and held him tighter.

Mr. Muggs let out a small meow, giving his approval as well.

We all went back inside to the warmth, and Raymond put Mr. Muggs down on the couch. Mr. Muggs then gave a quick shake, as if he were shaking the cold off his fur, and immediately raced into the bedroom.

We watched some TV and decided to go to bed as it was getting late. We lay in bed, snuggled up together.

Mr. Muggs, now warm again, was curled up in his cat bed, content as could be.

Raymond looked over at our bedside alarm clock. It showed midnight. He then lovingly rolled on top of me.

"Merry Christmas, babe. If you only knew how much I loved you, I'd be the happiest elf in the whole wide world," Raymond said, as he stared into my eyes.

"I do know, hun, because I love you equally as much, plus more," I answered.

It was a special night. So cold outside, and yet we were snuggled up nice and warm together inside. Both of us content in the security of living our life as a couple and not worrying about who in society, or family, frowned upon it or criticized it.

We made love for what seemed like hours. We didn't want it to stop. We were like one entity embraced in love.

Intertwined in passion the way only two gay lovers could understand.

We soon fell asleep and slept contently through the night.

CHAPTER 21
Christmas Day 1982.

The next morning, we woke up with Mr. Muggs standing on Raymond's chest doing his morning meowing wake-up call.

"Merry Christmas, my Muggins." Raymond lifted him up in the air and then kissed him on the nose.

"Merry Christmas, babe," he said.

"Merry Christmas, hun," I answered.

We went out to the living room and sat on the couch.

"Let's see what Santa brought!" Raymond said.

"Let me go first," I answered. I got up and eagerly went and got the gift with the camera inside.

"Here, hun, open this one first," and I gave him his present. It had its own card, which said, "Wishing My Wonderful Husband a Merry Christmas."

Raymond opened the card and gave me a kiss.

"We are a couple, and we are husbands, babe. I love you," Raymond said, and then excitedly tore open the present.

"Oh My God, Dan, it's the camera and film. I love this, but it was so expensive. You shouldn't have got something so expensive, babe."

"If I can afford it, hun, I'd give you anything you wanted," I said and kissed him on the lips.

"What should I take a picture of?" he asked.

"Take a picture of this," and I jokingly dropped my sweats, turned around, and exposed my rear end. He immediately leaned forward and gave me a love bite, a little harder than expected, and I let out a bit of a scream.

"I'm sorry, babe." He laughed.

"I owe you one in return," I said, and kissed him to let him know I was okay. Raymond then went back to the tree and brought out a couple of presents. "Merry Christmas, babe," and handed me the bigger box first.

"Aw, thanks, hun," I said and started to undo the wrapping while Raymond laughed and rolled his eyes.

Once the wrapping was off, I excitedly opened the box. Inside was a baby-blue pullover sweater, just like the one we saw at the store that day.

"The sweater that goes with my tie! I love it, hun. They look so great together. I can't wait to see them on me!" I said. I was so excited and hugged and squeezed Raymond for the longest time.

He then gave me the smaller gift, and I deliberately tore open the wrapping as Raymond started to laugh.

Inside were a pair of navy-colored leather gloves. Inside one glove was a small bottle of my preferred cologne, Polo, while inside the other glove was a cassette tape of one of my favorite singers, Nana Mouskouri.

"I love all of these, hun!" I said as Raymond sat down beside me on the couch, where I leaned in close and kissed his cheek.

"You're welcome, babe. It makes me happy to see you happy."

We sat there together, enjoying the moment. After a while, I had to head for my parents' place.

I so much wanted to stay with my Raymond instead. I wished I had the courage to just come out to my family and say, "Fuck it, I'm gay, and I want to live with my Raymond for the rest of my life."

I then got dressed and hugged Raymond as I was about to leave. "I love you so much, hun," I said and we passionately kissed.

"Have a good time with the fam, babe," Raymond said.

"I'll try my best. Enjoy your dinner with Mrs. H," I answered.

Raymond then walked me to the elevator, where we quickly looked around and kissed each other again.

I drove to my parents' while listening to my new cassette tape in the car. I was already missing my man and almost started to cry, wanting to be with him.

I had Christmas Day at my parents' and wondered the whole day what Raymond was doing, desperately wanting to call the apartment.

I knew he was with Mrs. H, but I couldn't stop thinking of him.

Once Christmas dinner was over at my parents' house, I said I was going to go feed the horses out at the track and probably stay there as it would be getting late.

I drove to the racetrack and fed the horses their dinner, then immediately went to the apartment.

To my surprise, Raymond wasn't home.

I went across the hall and knocked on Mrs. H's door.

"Dan, Merry Christmas, dear. Come in, come in. Raymond's still here," she said, and gave me a hug.

"Is that you, babe?" I heard Raymond call. "Come here, babe. Come look at this."

I went over to where Raymond was sitting on the couch and sat beside him. He was looking at some old photos in an album.

"Mrs. H's father was fascinated with train engines and traveled all over taking pictures of famous trains," he said.

It certainly was a different type of hobby, but at the same time I thought it was very intriguing.

"See this, babe, this is a picture of the train that was used when Queen Elizabeth first visited Canada," Raymond said, "and this is the train that carried Robert Kennedy's coffin after he was assassinated."

"What does it say on the back of that one, Raymond, dear?" Mrs. H asked.

Raymond turned over the photo. "June 1968. New Jersey."

"He would travel a lot on business and always had his camera with him," she said. "I thought you would enjoy them, as I know how much you're into photography as well."

"These are amazing," I said. "What an interesting hobby. I remember my aunt taking me to go see a train that came off the rails once. What a mess. I think I was around six or seven years old at the time."

"I made a chocolate cake for Christmas dinner," Mrs. H. said. "I was tired of those silly old fruitcakes, which no one eats anyway. Let me get you a piece, Dan. Want another slice, Raymond, dear?" Mrs. H asked.

"Yes, please. What's one more?" Raymond replied.

Mrs. H. came back with two slices of chocolate cake and another pot of tea.

We all sat down and discussed our Christmas Day.

"I had a wonderful day," Mrs. H. said. "Thank you, Raymond, dear, for making it so special."

"You're very welcome, and thank you for inviting me, Mrs. H," Raymond said.

"Did you speak with your parents, hun?" I asked Raymond.

"Yes, I called them this morning and said I was staying at the apartment and that I'm fine. Surprisingly, my mom never questioned it," Raymond said.

We finished our cake and cups of tea, and then said good night to Mrs. H.

"Thanks again for a wonderful day, Raymond, dear, and I'm so glad you came over as well, Dan. Good night, dears," she said.

We gave her hugs and walked across the hall to home. A few days later, we celebrated New Year's together with Mrs. H. She was such a sweetheart.

She told us once again that she didn't mind we were a gay couple, and the important thing was that we respected and loved each other.

She then told us something that she said she had never told anyone before. She told us about her late husband, and how terribly abusive a man he often was, both verbally and physically. Getting mad at the simplest of things, like having to wait for dinner if it was not ready when he got home.

She worked as a nurse at a local clinic, and depending on how busy they were, she would often be late getting home, which made it that much more difficult.

She said he died of a massive heart attack one afternoon while he was at work, about fifteen years ago. She said it took her a long time to get over the guilt of him passing, as it was also a bit of a relief for her when he did.

CHAPTER 22
January 1983.

After the excitement of the holidays, Raymond and I settled back into our daily routine of going to work and staying in the apartment. One Saturday night in mid-January, we decided to go to the club.

Of course, I wore my spiffy white shirt, pink tie, and baby-blue pullover for the first time. All our friends complimented me on it. We also met up with our good friend Eddie.

His parents owned a Chinese restaurant in the heart of Chinatown, and Eddie invited us to dinner at his parents' restaurant a couple of times.

I recall one fun evening Eddie, Raymond, and I were having dinner at his parents' restaurant when the server brought a live fish, plucked straight out of the aquarium, over to the people at the next table.

Upon looking at the fish flopping on the wooden board, the Asian gentleman nodded his approval to his server. The server then immediately raised his arm and with one fell *swoosh* of the blade, cut off the head of the fish. The fish's head, now separated from its body, continued to open and shut its mouth and move its gills.

I let out a loud shriek as its head got detached, and Raymond stared in awe with his own mouth wide open, while Eddie laughed at the both of us.

We became good friends with Eddie, and on a few occasions, usually after arguing with his father, he would sleep over at the apartment on the couch, too afraid of going home to his father's abusive chant.

Tonight, however, we could tell something was wrong, and he was very upset. He looked like he was in a coma, staring out at anything with no look of expression, with his eyes all red and swollen.

"What's the matter, Eddie?" we both asked.

"I told them. I told my folks that I'm gay," Eddie said, as he broke down and started crying. "My dad kicked me out of the house."

"Oh my God, Eddie, what happened?" I asked. "How did it happen?"

"My father said that he had arranged for the daughter of a business associate of his to meet me and go out on a date with her, then my mother says, 'Isn't this exciting, Eddie?' and she showed me a photograph of her. 'I've always wanted grandchildren.'"

"They have arranged marriages here in Canada?" I asked, surprised.

"Yeah, it's quite common in many cultures, even here in Canada," he explained and lowered his head almost in defeat. Eddie continued in tears, "I then told them that I'm not going out with her. I'll decide who I go out with."

"'It's time you were married and started a life on your own,' my father told me.

"'I'm not going out with her!' I said."

Eddie told us that he then shoved the kitchen table away and stood up and started walking away.

"'Get back here!' my father demanded and said, 'Yes, you will be taking her out as I've already committed and said that you're looking forward to seeing her.'

"'Go tell her, and her father, that I won't be seeing her. You know why? Do you want to know why I won't be seeing her? Because I'm gay. Yes, I'm gay, and I enjoy the company of men.'"

Eddie said his parents then started talking in Mandarin. He understood what they were saying, and as soon as his mother mentioned that he was a homosexual, his father went into a rage, standing up, pointing and yelling at Eddie.

Eddie said his father told him he was a disgrace to their family's good name, and to get out and never return. "'You're no son of mine,' my father said."

Eddie said his mother wasn't much better, and supported her husband, whether out of fear or disgust.

Raymond looked at me and nodded toward Eddie. "Come stay with us tonight, or until you get straightened out," Raymond said. "As long as it takes."

"Bill just offered to let me stay with him, but I'd sooner be with you two till I get my mind clear, if that's okay," Eddie said. "I need someone to talk with, and you're the closest friends I have."

Bill was in his forties and a very close friend of Eddie's. We knew Eddie and Bill had slept together before, as Eddie had told us, and from what I remember, he'd told us with a huge smile on his face.

I got up and gave Eddie a hug. He was a mess. The three of us sat there talking about the situation and what had happened. Eddie mentioned that he was great friends with Bill but was more comfortable discussing his current life situation with us, as we knew what he was going through and could relate.

I know what Raymond was thinking, as I was thinking the same. What would happen if we ever told our families?

I know my mother, being somewhat of a homophobe herself, would have been non-supportive, criticizing the gay reason for being, and thinking it was totally disgusting.

I'm unsure as to what my father's opinion of me would have been. He was a very level-headed man, and I personally think his view would have been for wanting me to be happy. I don't believe I would ever have been kicked out, even if I had told them, but I didn't want to take that chance.

Raymond and I knew it would cause a cascade of problems for us both. We would be outcast from our families or forgotten about. Raymond's parents' stance was quite clear. We knew if he ever came out of the closet, he'd be disowned, shunned, and probably severely beaten by his father.

Raymond's family was very well off financially, especially his father. Raymond often wanted to break away from his family, not caring about the money, but he was also afraid of what his father would do physically if he ever found out that Raymond was a gay man. His father's fanatical attitude toward homosexuality was downright evil and violent. It was thoughts like this that always had a hold on both of us and one that seemed to keep our relationship closeted.

If his father ever did hit him, would Raymond have the courage to file charges against his own father? It was a Pandora's Box of uncertainty, and one that we both agreed should be left alone.

Raymond, Eddie, and I left the club and drove back to the apartment. Raymond and I drove in our car, while Eddie was in his own. He'd grabbed all his clothes and thrown them in the back seat of his car. Most were still on their hangers.

We helped Eddie with his clothes and belongings and went upstairs and were greeted by Mr. Muggs.

Eddie picked him up and said, "I envy you guys. Thanks for being there for me."

Raymond got some blankets and a pillow and put them on the couch for Eddie. We chatted for a few minutes, and then all decided to go to bed.

As Raymond and I lay side by side, I could hear Eddie quietly sobbing.

"Poor Eddie. He's really fucked up, hun," I whispered to Raymond.

"I know," Raymond said. "Come with me."

We went out to Eddie. He was sitting on the couch, quietly crying. "I have no one," Eddie sobbed.

We sat on each side of him with an arm around him.

"You have us, Eddie," Raymond said. "Come sleep with us. Nothing sexually intended, but I don't want you to be alone."

"Thanks, guys. I think I'm closer to you two than I am with my own family, and after tonight I know so," Eddie said.

We all got into bed. Raymond, being the tallest, was in the middle, while I was on one side, and Eddie on the other. We soon were snuggled up in a relaxing human embrace of security.

Raymond jokingly said, "This would make for a hot movie. We'll call it from top to bottom and back again."

"Stop it." I laughed.

That seemed to have broken the seriousness, and Eddie started laughing as well. After a while, we all soon fell asleep.

It was situations like Eddie's that made me once again thank fate for bringing Raymond into my life.

The next morning, I was up early to go to work at the track.

Raymond and Eddie spent the day in the apartment. Eddie was trying to get his life in order: where he'd stay and what he should do going forward. He had saved up some money and was financially stable for a little while.

Raymond and I both agreed that Eddie could stay with us for as long as it took him to be able to find a place and feel comfortable with his future. I believe he stayed with us for about two weeks.

He offered to pay us for his stay, but we told him we were all friends, and that's what friends did—helped each other in times of need. It was quite enjoyable having Eddie around, as he kept the apartment neat and tidy, and would often cook dinner and do the laundry downstairs in the laundromat.

One day I came home in the afternoon, and Eddie was alone. Raymond had already left for the track to work with the betting machines.

"How was your day, Dan?" he asked. "I think I found a place to stay."

"That's great to hear, Eddie," I answered. "Where did you find a place?"

"I spoke with Bill again on the phone today. He said he wants me to stay with him. As you know, I've spent a couple of nights at his place before, and he seems like a nice enough guy. Do you think I could stay here for another couple of nights?" he asked. "Bill said he needed a couple of days to clean out the one bedroom to make room for my belongings."

"Of course, Eddie," I answered. "Raymond and I are in complete agreement about you staying a couple more days or weeks—it doesn't matter."

I stepped forward and gave him a much-needed hug.

"Thanks, Dan. I don't know what I would have done without you two. You guys are very special to me. I'll always remember this."

"Have you spoken to your parents at all?" I asked.

"Yeah, I called my mom, and we had a long talk," Eddie

said. "She's willing to accept me being gay but asked me to let her discuss it with my dad and give it time for him to understand. She told me to call back in a week or so and in the evening when his father was at the restaurant. I told her I was staying with you guys, and she asked me to thank you both for being such good friends."

I didn't have a horse racing that night and stayed in the apartment with Eddie while Raymond was at work.

Raymond arrived home at his usual time shortly before midnight. Eddie and I were both still up, waiting for him. Eddie then told Raymond about him staying with Bill and what had progressed with his parents.

"That's great, Eddie. Stay as long as needed. You know you're always welcome here," Raymond said.

"Where does Bill live anyway, Eddie?" Raymond asked.

"He lives out in the west end of Toronto, near High Park," Eddie said. "It's a nice house and within walking distance of the subway line. You know I've stayed with him a couple of nights, and even though he's twice my age, I truly feel that he cares about me and is honest in what he says. He asked me a couple of times before if I wanted to move in with him, but that was when I was still living at home."

Over the years, I have met quite a few gay men just like Eddie, who have experienced the same cruelty and rejection from their parents.

After fearfully telling their parents that they were gay, and after courageously "coming out," these proud young men only heard their parents say, "Get out!"

In my opinion, it's totally heartless to view someone you brought into this world, hopefully through an act of love and passion, as so reprehensible and dishonorable that you would actually kick them out of your own family dwelling for nothing more than your own narrow mindedness, prejudice, or homophobic upbringing and/or beliefs.

I often say that when a baby is born that the newborn child wants nothing more than to be held and loved. All the prejudice and hate the child learns are taught by others, and usually by their own family.

We are all born with the ability to love and the need to be loved. Love does not see skin color; love does not care about your age, race, or religion, nor your gender or sexual orientation. But love is often held back when it is overshadowed by someone's discrimination, their homophobia, or their self-righteousness. It's surprising how many people will deny or lack the compassion and adamantly and stubbornly refuse to return someone's love.

The only thing colder than living in the dark and lonely closet by yourself is the cold, heartless act of turning your back on someone whom you once loved simply because you've discovered that they no longer live up to "your own" expectations.

They will soon discover that love is love, and eventually, it will be themselves who will be living in that cold, lonely closet alone, empty of love and compassion, and living a life of solitude and self-pity.

CHAPTER 23
February 1983.

Valentine's Day was approaching! We always liked doing something special on that day, so Raymond and I decided to go to the club to celebrate it.

I thought about surprising Raymond, while at the club, with a song request, and spent one afternoon in the apartment, looking through Raymond's huge album collection. He had his own personal binders that he'd made, sorting his collection. Each binder was titled, like the hits from *Billboard* magazine listings: Pop, R&B/Hip Hop, Country, Dance/Electronic, and Rock. He had two binders for each genre, one for "Groups," and one for "Solo Artist."

He had typed a single page for every album he had, and under the album heading, listed all the songs on it in track order. Each album entry was sorted into its genre, whether it was a group or artist's name, and then each one sorted alphabetically.

He had countless albums to listen to. He often thought he would make a good DJ, and I agreed with him. His knowledge of music, as well as how he arranged the songs in a certain dance sequence, was very professional.

I wanted to find something that would make us think of one another upon hearing it, instead of something more one-sided. Finally, I found the song I thought would work. I had heard it a few times in the car before and thought it was the perfect song for Valentine's Day and for us. Even though neither Raymond nor I had ever had a previous relationship, its lyrics described how we felt upon finding each other.

We had arranged to meet Eddie and his man Bill there.

The club was decked out in its traditional Valentine's Day theme. Lots of gay couples were there, having a fun and loving night out. As we sat at our table, I was trying to sneak away and get to the DJ to request my song without Raymond knowing. I had told Eddie about my wanting to request a song, and he secretly helped with my plan.

"Who's ready for another beer?" Eddie asked.

"Hun, can you get me a cold beer?" I asked Raymond, "I'm dying for a cold drink."

"Sure thing, babe. I'll come with you, Eddie," and Raymond and Eddie headed to the bar.

"I'll be right back, Bill," and I quickly snuck over to the DJ.

"Hey, Tony," I said.

"Dan the Man, what's up, brother?" Tony asked.

"Can you do me a favor and dedicate a song to my Raymond for me?" I slipped him a couple of dollars.

"What's the song, Dan?" he asked, and I whispered in his ear. "Aw, that's a perfect song for you two and for tonight. You got it, sweetie," Tony answered, and gave me a wink.

"Where'd you go?" Raymond asked when I got back to the table.

"I needed a bathroom break," I said.

We sat there enjoying our beer and after a few minutes, and once the last song finished, there was a slight pause in the music.

Tony the DJ started to play a song quietly in the background as he spoke. "I have a special dedication from a special friend to his loving man, Raymond," he said, and Tony started pointing out into the crowd.

"Where's Raymond? Raymond, are you out there?" He continued looking over the crowd until he spotted Raymond waving back.

"This is dedicated to you, my friend, from your loving man, Dan. Enjoy it, you two lovebirds. Now everyone, go grab your love, or the person next to you, get on the dance floor and enjoy this slow dance."

Tony started to play the song, "Even the Nights Are Better" by Air Supply.

"Babe, you are the most romantic person I know. I love this song." Raymond grabbed me by the hand, and we went onto the dance floor.

As we danced around the floor listening to its loving lyrics, different guys gave us a nudge and a friendly smile, acknowledging their approval.

We all went and sat back down to cool off with our cold beer.

"That was so sweet of you, Dan," said Eddie.

"Thanks, Eddie," I replied.

"Yeah, I think I'll keep him," Raymond said. "Will you be my Valentine, babe?"

"Every day of the year, hun," and we gave each other a kiss.

We continued to dance the night away. Suddenly we heard it. That song! That wonderful, heart-tugging glorious song!

We both looked at each other.

"Our song!" we both yelled and immediately hit the dance floor again.

"Did you ask Tony to play this, hun?" I asked.

"I swear I didn't, babe. Fate must be looking down on us."

We grabbed each other close, and I rested my head on Raymond's chest.

The Righteous Brothers started to sing "Unchained Melody."

As we danced, I felt secure in my man's embrace and safe from the world.

"I never want to be out of your embrace. hun. I'll love you forever," I whispered as we danced.

"You mean the world to me, babe. I'll forever be here for you. I love you, Dan," Raymond answered as we began to kiss.

While in each other's arms, I realized that those two lost souls had become a union of one. We had found peace, love, and trust within each other in this ever-challenging homophobic world. We held each other close, and as we danced around the floor, our embrace only magnified the loving need that we both had for each other and the security it provided.

Raymond had brought his camera and took pictures of us together, along with our friends: Eddie and his companion Bill, as well as Robert the bouncer, and a great many others.

CHAPTER 24

At about one a.m., we decided to head for home and got our jackets. We went out the front door into the chilly air as I tried to do up the zipper on my leather jacket.

We had parked a couple of blocks away, and as we got onto the sidewalk, Raymond noticed two guys looking at us from across the street. They had seen us come out of the gay club.

I looked over as the one was pointing at us. He then nudged his friend, and the two stepped closer to the curb, all the while continuing to stare at us. Under the streetlight, I could see they were both wearing long leather coats that went below their knees and heavy-looking leather boots with shiny buckles. Both were easily over six feet tall, and I was terrified that they were concentrating on us.

The one then said in a teasing, high-pitched voice, "Look at the queer pretty boy with his faggot-pink fucking tie. Are you two fags out for a walk?"

Then another guy yelled, "You two queer motherfuckers should die. Rot in hell where you belong, perverts!"

Just then, a group of people came walking down the sidewalk toward them, and the thugs paused their verbal abuse until they walked past. The two gay bashers almost looked annoyed that the people walking by had interrupted them. Even though it was a few years after the bathhouse raids, the incident was still vivid in many people's homophobic minds.

We decided to go back inside the club and wait, hoping they would leave.

"What's wrong?" Robert the bouncer, AKA Santa, asked, "Forget something?"

"There are a couple of gay bashers outside, yelling at us from across the street," Raymond said.

"Damn bastards, let me go have a look and see how far they want to take this," Robert replied, and he angrily went outside with his bodybuilder muscles bulging under his t-shirt.

"I wonder if they're brave enough to say that to Robert?" I asked Raymond.

Robert was a big guy who also worked out at the gym. He was quite the specimen of a man.

Robert came back inside. "I think they're gone, guys, but you can leave out the back door and get onto the side street if you like."

We took Robert's advice and left out the rear entrance. We then cautiously walked down the alley to hook back with the side street, and then up to Sherbourne Street.

"I can't get my zipper up. It's stuck," I said as we continued to walk, with me looking down, fiddling with my leather jacket's zipper.

Suddenly, Raymond stopped and quietly said, "Take your tie off, babe. Take it off. Do it now."

"I like wearing my tie," I said, like a little kid pouting, and looked over at him.

I then felt Raymond's hand clench mine.

"Take it off!" Raymond quietly ordered.

I started loosening my tie from around my neck. "What are you talking about?" I said, but before he could answer, I saw what was causing him his worrisome stare. It was those two gay bashers again. They were standing on the corner, across the street.

Suddenly, the one guy looked over, pointed, and yelled, "Hey, there's the fucking fag with the pink tie!" They quickly started running across the street and started toward us.

Raymond pulled my arm and yelled, "Run!"

Holding hands, we quickly turned and ran as fast as we could back down the side street and into a back alley. The back door to the club would be locked, and no one would ever hear us knocking, so we kept running. Even though I had been a fast kid growing up, I was finding it difficult to keep up with Raymond's longer strides, and I pushed myself, lengthening my strides, trying to match his.

Behind us, I could hear the gay bashers yelling as they chased us.

"We're going to beat the fuck out of you both, you queer fucks!"

We ran down a back street as they got closer.

One of them yelled, "You're dead meat! That tie is mine, faggot."

"This way," Raymond hollered, and we continued running down the dark back alleyways.

I was totally lost. It was so dark that I could hardly see where I was running. Suddenly, I slipped on a patch of ice, tripping with a loud crash and falling into a couple of metal garbage cans. I slammed into the frozen pavement, and something razor sharp cut deep into the inside of my left knee.

"Raymond!" I yelled. I had flashbacks of that day in the high school shower and getting beaten up again. Hardly able to move, I waited for the gay bashers to pounce.

I don't want Raymond to get hurt! I thought and desperately wanted to try to help fight them off. I tried getting to my feet, but a dreadful pain in my knee stopped me from moving, and all I could do was just lie there.

Just as Raymond started helping me up off the pavement, the outside lights on a couple of houses that backed onto the alley turned on.

A very large guy came outside from one of the houses. "Who's there?" said a deep voice in the dark.

Then another guy in the house next door came out, asking, "What's going on out here, Frank? What's all the noise about?"

"I'm not sure, Mark. I heard a lot of yelling. Then it sounded like the trash cans were getting tossed around. I thought someone was throwing them."

Frank and Mark then came down from their small porches, opened the gates, and came into the alley.

Raymond acknowledged them both somewhat cautiously.

"I'm sorry for the noise, sirs. My friend Dan and I were being chased by a couple of unfriendly guys when he accidentally slipped and tripped over the garbage cans. I think he's hurt himself."

"Who's chasing you? I don't see anyone," the one said.

I fearfully looked around and couldn't see or hear anything.

The one big guy walked up and down the alley a few yards and looked around. "I think they're gone, Mark," he replied to his neighbor, and walked back toward us.

"I'm Frank, and this is my neighbor, Mark," he said to us.

Raymond was kneeling by my side with his hand on my shoulder as he looked up at them. "Thanks for your help. I'm Raymond, and this is Dan."

I had torn the knees in my pants, and my one knee was bleeding heavily from the fall.

"Are you okay, son?" Frank asked. "There's a lot of blood there, and that gash looks quite deep."

"I'll be fine once I get home," I said, very frightened, as I looked at Raymond for reassurance.

"Where are we?" asked Raymond.

"You're behind Linden Street," Mark replied. "You two seem nicely dressed. Where are you coming from, and why was someone chasing you?"

Raymond and I once again put our guard up, as we weren't sure whether they were gay-friendly or foe. They each looked around forty and both were a good size physically. We certainly didn't want to give any indication that we were at the club, just in case.

"We were enjoying a fun night out together when these two guys decided to try to pick a fight with us, so we ran," Raymond answered.

"This can be a rough area on a Saturday night," Mark said.

"Yes, it can be, especially with having the gay club around the corner," Frank said with a smile and gave us both a wink.

"I'll pick up the mess, sir," Raymond said.

"That's alright, son. I can clean it up, no problem. Let's get you up on your feet," Frank said.

"You help the boys, Frank, and I'll pick up the garbage," Mark answered.

"Thank you, sir," Raymond said again.

Frank then came over to help Raymond lift me up.

"Where are you two heading?" he asked.

"We parked our car on Bleecker Street," Raymond said. "But now we've lost our way."

"Follow me to the front of the house, and I'll show you a safer way to get back to your car," he replied.

With one arm around each of their necks, they easily lifted me off the ground and walked me through his back gate, between the houses, and out onto Linden Street.

Frank then gave us directions to get back to Bleecker Street and pointed down the street.

"Bleecker is the next street east of here, running north and south," he said. "If someone were chasing you, I'd stick to the main streets where there are more people and traffic, where you can be seen. Go to the end of this street here, turn left, go up Sherbourne and across Howard, then back down Bleecker, and you should be safe."

"Maybe I should walk back with you," Frank said.

"The streets are still fairly busy with traffic, so I think we'll be fine now," Raymond answered.

"Thanks again for your help," we both said and shook his hand.

"No problem at all. Just stick to the main streets, and you should get home safely. Even in the wee hours of the morning, there's always some traffic in Toronto," Frank reassuringly said with a smile.

It took a while to get back to the car due to my limping. We felt like easy prey should the gay bashers come back.

Once safely back in the car, Raymond helped me get inside. I slowly tried bending my knee and winced at the pain getting in.

"That's a lot of blood, babe. Maybe we should go to the hospital, as you may need stitches," Raymond said.

I looked at my knee and could see that where it was cut had somewhat congealed. Even though there was a lot of blood, it had stopped bleeding. I was always interested in equine anatomy and had read many books on veterinarian medicine and procedures, so I felt comfortable my wound wasn't in need of emergency care.

After sitting in the car, I started to relax somewhat. That's when it suddenly dawned on me.

"My tie!" I cried. "Where's my tie, hun?" I frantically started searching all my pockets. "I've lost my pink tie. I must have dropped it after I loosened it. I don't remember taking it off. Where is it?" I stammered. "That was one of my favorite things in the whole world, hun. It means so much to me. I need to go find it."

I started crying at its loss and for being so scared. "This seems like a fucking nightmare we're in." I sat there in the car with my head down, covering my face with my hands, trying to conceal my crying.

Raymond gently moved my hands away and wiped away my tears with his fingers. He then looked straight at me. His beautiful blue eyes gave me comfort, and they helped calm me down. I was then able to stop crying and gather my thoughts.

"I'll get you another one, babe. Don't worry about it," he said, and then leaned in and gave me a kiss on my cheek. "Let's just get home."

As we drove, we started to recall what had happened.

"I couldn't understand what you meant when you kept telling me to take my tie off," I said.

"I knew if they recognized you wearing the tie, they'd be onto us," Raymond said. "Plus, if they did catch us, I didn't want them to strangle you with your tie."

CHAPTER 25

Once back at the apartment, Raymond helped me out of my clothes and helped wash my knee off. It was then that we realized that we had no first aid supplies of any kind at home, not even a Band-Aid.

He helped me get into bed and tried to make me somewhat comfortable.

"Can you get me some ice from the fridge, hun? It'll help with the swelling," I said. "And some Tylenol, if we have any."

Raymond went and got some ice and wrapped it up in a damp washcloth. He also got me a couple of Tylenol and a glass of Coke, plus the two big pillows from the couch.

"Lift your leg up, babe." He placed the pillows underneath my raised leg. "That looks so sore. Are you sure you don't need stitches?" Raymond asked again. "I wonder what it was that cut you open?"

"I don't know what it was, but it hurt like hell. I don't think it needs stitches. The ice is helping, as it's taking some of the hurt away. Thanks, hun," I replied and rested my hand on his. "I love you, ya know."

"I love you also, babe," Raymond said and kissed me on

my forehead. Then he undressed and joined me in bed.

He gently snuggled up close, so we were touching, and placed his hand onto of mine.

"Good night, babe. Love you," he said.

"Good night, hun. Love you, too," I replied.

Neither one of us slept very well that night, but now and then I'd hear the very familiar sound of Raymond's gentle little snores, which would make me smile and quietly giggle.

The next morning, my knee was super swollen and still sore.

"How is it, babe?" Raymond asked.

"It almost feels worse than it did last night," I said. "It still hurts to move, or if anything even touches it."

"I'm going to see if Mrs. H has any Band-Aids, babe. I'll be right back."

Raymond then went across the hall and knocked on Mrs. Hutchinson's door.

"Good morning, Raymond," she said. "What can I help you with, my dear?"

"Would you happen to have any Band-Aids, Mrs. H?"

"Did one of you hurt yourselves?" she asked.

"Dan fell last night and cut his knee open," Raymond answered.

"Oh goodness, bring him over here, dear," she said. "I used to be a nurse. I can help."

Raymond helped me limp over to Mrs. H's place.

"Sit over here, Dan," and I rolled up my sweatpants to reveal a very swollen and very red area around the inside of my left knee.

"Good heavens, that does look sore, my dear. Let me get my first aid supplies."

Mrs. H returned with her small first aid kit. "This might sting a little, dear, but we have to make sure we get it cleaned up and get any infection out," she said.

She gently cleaned it out with some hydrogen peroxide, applied some antibiotic ointment, and then some gauze, and covered it with some bandaging tape.

"When was the last time you had a tetanus shot, my dear?" she asked.

"I'm not sure. Probably not since public school," I said.

"You should go get one, just to make sure. It won't hurt. It looks like you're going to live, dear." Mrs. H smiled. "I don't think it would need stitches, but it is a rather ghastly cut. Just keep icing it and keep it elevated. Whatever happened?" she asked.

Raymond was standing behind Mrs. H as she tended to my knee. I saw him open his eyes a bit wider and begin to slightly shake his head back and forth in an attempt not to let her know the truth. I immediately knew what he was implying.

It was as if Mrs. H had taken us under her wing and felt so happy being a mother hen figure to us. I'm sure she was aware of what gay-bashing was, but I knew her concern for our safety would be paramount.

"I was in a hurry last night at the track and was running to my car when I stumbled and fell in the parking lot," I replied as Raymond nodded and smiled at me. I'm not sure whether she believed my story, but she seemed content in knowing she had helped tend to my injury.

"Accidents do happen," she said. "Now here, take a few of these Band-Aids, the gauze and tape, plus this tube of antibiotic cream. Later tonight, wash it gently with soap and water and reapply the cream. Maybe Raymond can play doctor for you," she said and began to giggle to herself.

"I'm his favorite patient, aren't I, hun?" I said, and she continued to smile.

The two of us gave her each a hug and thanked her again.

"You'll be alright, dear," she said. "I'll check on you later and bring you some dinner."

We walked back across the hallway to our apartment.

"I didn't want her to know what really happened, babe, as she would only start to worry if she ever knew we were being chased and in danger," Raymond said.

Luckily, I had arranged for someone to feed the horses that Sunday, so I didn't have to return to the track at all and was able to rest. We sat on the couch and watched TV most of the day.

Now and then, I'd say, "Oh, Doctor Raymond, could you make me a cup of tea? Oh, Doctor Raymond, could you get me a Coke?"

Finally, on my last request, Raymond subtly replied, "Keep it up, and you'll need a real doctor, babe."

I looked at him with a big, sad smile and a forlorn frown. "But I love you so, so, so, much," I replied.

Raymond put on a deliberately large smile, then stuck his tongue out at me.

"Tease. If you're going to produce it, then use it to seduce it," I answered back with a smile.

That afternoon, there was a knock on the door. Raymond looked through the peephole and saw it was Mrs. H.

"Hello, Raymond dear. Here's some spaghetti for you and Dan, plus I made you a small chocolate cake. I know how much you love my chocolate cake, Raymond."

"Thanks a lot, Mrs. H," Raymond answered, and took the tray into the kitchen.

"How is our patient?" Mrs. H asked.

Raymond led Mrs. H into our bedroom, where I was lying with my leg up.

"How are you feeling, dear?" she asked.

"Much better, thanks, Mrs. H," I replied. "The swelling seems to be going down, plus it doesn't hurt as much. Thanks again for your help."

"Let's have a look," and Mrs. H looked at my wound. "That's much better. A lot of the inflammation is gone, and the swelling is slowly coming down. Keep it clean and covered with the antibiotic cream, dear."

As Mrs. H was leaving, I saw Raymond give her a hug, so I yelled from the bedroom, "Give Mrs. H a hug for me too, hun!"

I felt somewhat at ease knowing Mrs. H accepted our living situation and didn't mind me calling Raymond "hun."

I believe she felt closer to us, knowing that we didn't hide it from her.

"Thanks, dear," Mrs. H replied.

The next day, I was able to walk gingerly and went back to the track and to work. Over the next few days, I mended, and with the help of Raymond and Mrs. H's daily inspection, I was soon back to my normal self again.

CHAPTER 26
Late spring 1983.

"I'm bored. Let's go to the pub for some wings and a beer," Raymond said as we sat in the apartment.

"That's a great idea," I said, and we both threw on our light jackets and went out.

It was a nice night, so we decided to walk the few blocks from the apartment to the pub.

There was a British-style pub in town that we often visited, as we loved the atmosphere. The one server knew us and was always friendly upon seeing us. We became good friends over time.

"Hey, Raymond and Danny, how have you been? I haven't seen you in here for a while. Everything okay?" she asked.

"We've been good, thanks, just busy with life and stuff," I said. "How have you been, Kimberly?"

"Great," she said, and looked casually around, then quietly replied with a huge glowing smile, "I've met this amazing girl. We've been out three times together, and I was hoping to ask you a couple of questions later, if that's alright?"

"Congratulations," Raymond said, "that's great to hear.

Sure, feel free to ask whatever is on your mind."

"Thanks, guys. Want the regular?" she asked.

"Yes, please," we both answered, and she went to place our order.

We always ordered the same thing. Some chicken wings, pierogies, and a pint of Carlsberg beer each.

"Why does she always call me Danny?" I asked.

"Um, because it's your name, duh," Raymond jokingly said.

"But Danny? Other than my sister, no one ever calls me Danny," I replied.

"I think it's cute," Raymond teased. "Oh Danny, Danny, I love your fanny!"

"What's cute? My name or my fanny?" I joked back.

"Both!" Raymond answered. "But your fanny is totally adorable, and it's mine, all mine." We both started to laugh.

"I wonder what Kimberly wants to ask us?" he said.

"I have no idea, but I'm sure curious to find out," I answered.

It wasn't long before she came back with our food, and we were enjoying our meal.

After we finished, our friendly server dropped by our table. "Can I get you anything else, guys?"

"We're all good, thanks," I replied. "Was there something you wanted to ask us, Kimberly?"

"Can I ask you a personal question, and I apologize if I'm wrong, but you two are boyfriends, aren't you? Like a couple, right?" she asked.

It took me by surprise that someone would ask us that in public, and I immediately looked over at Raymond.

"Yes, Dan is my boyfriend," Raymond quietly replied. "Why do you ask?"

She cautiously looked around to make sure no one was close by and leaned in close. "How difficult is it to be a gay couple in the real world?" she asked. "I haven't told anyone that I'm gay, and I'm kind of afraid to tell my parents. I just get so confused. I have no one to talk to about all of this, and then I get so discouraged and start to question myself if I'm really doing the right thing in, you know, in coming out," she said.

"If you and your new girlfriend ever want to talk, feel free to come over to our apartment. Dan and I are good listeners, plus we've been through quite a bit together, haven't we, babe? We'd be more than happy to talk," Raymond said. "We live here in Milton, in the apartment complex."

"That's so sweet of you," she said. "I'd really like to do that."

"Do you live around here, Kimberly?" I asked.

"Yes, I live with my parents here in Milton as well," she said.

"Let me give you our telephone number." Raymond said. "Dan and I are usually free on Wednesday evenings, as neither of us has to work that night." He then wrote down our telephone number on the back of our bill and handed it back to Kimberly.

"Thanks, guys," she said, all excited. "Is it alright if my girlfriend Jill came along also?"

"Of course," Raymond replied, "give us a call and we'll plan for this Wednesday."

We paid Kimberly our tab and left a nice tip.

"You're the nicest guys I know. Have a great night," she said, "and thanks again!"

We left the pub and started walking home. I mentioned to Raymond how we could both relate to her dilemma.

"Even though we're limited in how we can show our relationship and feelings openly to others, hun, we truly are lucky to be able to have each other and show our feelings in the privacy of having our own place," I said.

"I totally agree, babe. I used to think the same as Kimberly when we met. You're falling in love with someone and want to tell the entire world, but you can't show or tell anyone for fear of backlash or something worse," Raymond said. "I can really tell she's confused. Hopefully, she will be able to see it all through."

"We should ask Eddie over on Wednesday and have another input. Plus, we haven't seen him in a couple of weeks," I said.

"Great idea, babe. I'll call him once back at the apartment, if it's not too late," Raymond replied, and we leisurely walked back home.

CHAPTER 27

As we walked back to the apartment, we would stop now and then on the main street, looking at the different shops' windows.

"I never did find a place around here that sells pink ties," I pouted.

"Are you still going on about that tie?" Raymond said.

"Yes, I am. I cherished that tie. It meant so much to me," I said.

"I wonder where you dropped it?" Raymond replied.

"Probably when I was viciously attacked by those garbage cans," I said. "It was a ferocious fight, you know. I was totally outnumbered!"

"Drama, drama, drama," Raymond laughed.

Not wanting to relive that night, we always tried to put it behind us as we both knew it could have been terribly worse. Gay men would go to a gay club for a fun night out, while gay haters would often venture there simply to find their victims. We both considered ourselves extremely lucky.

Suddenly, we both stopped and were standing in front of an electronics store. A large, color, console television sat on display in the shop window. We were both awestruck by the color and picture quality, especially being so used to our little black-and-white set.

"Look at how bright the colors are and look at the size of the screen. That'd be a great addition to our apartment, don't you think, babe?" Raymond said.

"More like, better for watching the bright blues and reds of *Wonder Woman* up close," I replied.

"That too. Just imagine watching Princess Diana of Themyscira in color," Raymond chuckled back.

I jokingly shook my head and then said, "Look at the price, hun. Over 900 bucks. That's a lot of horse feed."

"Do you think we could get it?" Raymond excitedly asked.

"I doubt we could afford it, but something for us to aim for. Put it in the budget," I jokingly said.

We both laughed and continued our walk home, brushing knuckles as we walked, too fearful of ever holding hands in public. Even though Milton was a small town, we didn't want to take any chance of being singled out and targeted. The only time we ever held hands was when we got off the elevator on our floor and walked hand in hand to our apartment door.

Once up in the apartment, Raymond continued talking about the TV.

"If we slide the couch down just a bit, then our new color TV can go right over here in direct view," Raymond eagerly said.

"Yeah, right," I answered. "Let's slide it farther down, and we can also get that new stereo set you want," as I slowly waved my hand in front of the little television just like one of the models on the TV game show *Let's Make a Deal*, when they would show one of the prizes.

"Hey, don't rain on my big color TV parade," Raymond

joked. "Besides, we need a new stereo system anyway."

"We do not," I said. "Your stereo sounds perfect for when you're practicing your dance moves."

"But there's one with an equalizer I saw. It'd be awesome to use," Raymond said. "Then I can adjust the sound frequencies to make it sound perfect here in the apartment."

"I have no idea what an equalizer does," I replied. "All I know is that it already sounds good to me, but let's go to bed."

"But it's so early," Raymond answered. "I'm not tired."

"Who said anything about being tired?" I answered and gave him my sweetest and most innocent smiling stare.

"Race you to the Catherine!" Raymond said.

We had a queen-size bed that we nicknamed "Catherine," after Queen Catherine of Russia and her supposed sexual exploits.

Once there, we eagerly got undressed, and while keeping it in a royal bedroom atmosphere, I jokingly rested Raymond's very large and very excited member in the palm of my hand, where it easily extended a couple of inches beyond my wrist.

"Out of total admiration, I shall start to call him the king, King of the Love Pythons, my liege." And I faithfully bowed down.

Raymond chuckled and then said, "Kneel." Then, using his beautiful python as a sword, gently tapped me on each shoulder and said, "I hereby knight thee Sir Daniel. Rise, Sir Daniel, of the racetrack, and kiss thy king!"

I still remember, in the beginning of our relationship, due to his size, that it took quite a few sessions before I could easily enjoy receiving Raymond. But being the loving and patient man that he always was, he took his time, which made it much easier and totally pleasurable for us both.

For whatever reason, Mr. Muggs would always want to sit on the edge of the bed when we played, making us both feel awkward until one of us would apologize to him and then gently push him off.

After what seemed like a never-ending period of pleasure, we eventually finished, both of us being totally fulfilled from each other's passion. We eventually drifted off to sleep in each other's embrace, joined by a snuggling and very loudly purring Mr. Muggs.

CHAPTER 28

The following Tuesday, there was a message on the answering machine when I got home from the track that afternoon.

"Hi, guys, it's Kimberly. I was wondering if tomorrow is still okay to drop by."

"Jill and I are really looking forward to talking privately with you. Give me a call at my parents' house when you can. They'll be glad to hear a man's voice asking for me." And she let out a giggle and left her phone number.

I then called the number she left back.

"Hello?" a woman's voice answered.

"Is Kimberly there, please?" I asked.

"That's me," she said.

"Hey, Kimberly, it's Dan from the pub. How are you?

"Hey, Danny, I'm great, thanks, and thanks for calling back so quick. How are you? Is tomorrow still okay with you and Raymond?" she asked.

"I'm good, thanks, and sure, tomorrow is fine. Wednesday is our pizza night, so I'll get us an extra-large, and we'll have a fun, relaxing evening," I said. "How about if you come over around seven p.m.?" I asked.

"That's so sweet of you, and yes, seven works great," Kimberly answered.

I then gave her our address, apartment number, and intercom code to use in the lobby so they could call, and we could then unlock the main door to come upstairs.

"See you tomorrow, Danny, and thanks again," she said.

"Looking forward to seeing you both," I replied, and we said our goodbyes and hung up.

We also got a message from Eddie, who mentioned he'd love to come over and said he'd meet us at the apartment Wednesday afternoon.

Eddie knew our schedules and was always welcome to come by at any time.

A few minutes later, Raymond came home. He had spent the morning and early afternoon over at his parents' place, helping his mom with some gardening before he went to work that evening.

"Hey, babe, how was your day?"

"My day was okay. Nothing out of the ordinary. What did you do today?" I replied.

"I had to help Mom clean out some dead bushes in the backyard at home. You want to know something strange?" Raymond said.

"What's that, hun?" I asked.

"My mom asked how you were," Raymond said. "I wasn't sure what to take of it. She asked it sort of nicely too."

"That is strange," I said. "So, what exactly did your mother say? How did it happen?"

"We were in the backyard and clearing out some dead bushes. Mom asked me how things were going in the apartment, and I said it's good. She then asked, 'How's Dan, dear?'" Raymond said.

"I wasn't sure what to say and replied, 'Dan's doing good, thanks.'"

"I'm nervous, hun. Do you think she knows about us?" I said. "What about your dad? She wouldn't say anything to your dad, would she?"

"I'm not sure, to be honest. All I know is she didn't seem annoyed when I looked over at her after she asked how you were doing. In fact, she smiled back at me," he said.

As he spoke, I could see that he didn't seem worried, but almost looked relieved, hoping that maybe his mom did understand and was accepting of our relationship.

"I didn't know what to think. I smiled back at her, and we continued with the yard work. Don't worry, babe.

"I think it was her way of letting me know she's okay with us, but I'd never ask her. I think it's best I just leave it like it is. This way, she doesn't have to feel guilty about her possibly knowing and allowing it, and at the same time not telling my dad. Does that make any sense at all?"

"In a strange way, yes, it does, hun," I answered. "She's your mom, and like Rozz, she cares for you in a different way compared to your dad. When you think of it, she has never once criticized you or questioned you about not being with a girl. It's always been your father. Plus, was it not your mom that suggested we go shopping for the couch, and told your dad to give 'us' his Sears card?" I asked.

"That's right, babe. I never thought of it that closely," Raymond said. "It actually makes me feel better knowing that she might know. The next time I'm talking with Rozz, I'm going to ask her if she thinks Mom has any idea."

For no reason at all, I gave him a hug. "I know, hun, it means a lot coming from your own mom, especially if she is open minded about the two of us being a couple."

"That's a situation that we could talk about tomorrow, with Kimberly and Eddie. They both left messages saying they're coming over."

"That's good. I'm looking forward to seeing Eddie again," Raymond said. "We can have pizza and pop."

"Already planned," I said.

The next day, Raymond and I were in the apartment, getting ready for the girls, when Eddie buzzed from the lobby.

"Hey, guys, it's Eddie. Let me in," he said.

"Hey, Eddie, come on up." I pressed the door unlock button.

Eddie knocked on the door, and Raymond let him in. He'd brought with him a case of Coke and a case of root beer.

"Eddie!" Raymond said and took the top case of pop.

"Here, bring that into the kitchen," Raymond said. "And it's Mug root beer!"

"Is there any other brand of root beer when Raymond is involved?" Eddie laughed.

"I took them from the restaurant," Eddie said. "My father may have kicked me out of his house, but he still works my ass off at the restaurant. Even though he refuses to accept the gay lifestyle, we've been getting along quite well lately. I think my mom had a talk with him. Either way, I feel better being able to at least talk with him."

"That's so good to hear," I said. "I hope you two can patch things up."

We both gave Eddie a hug, and we all sat on the couch.

"It's great seeing you again," Eddie said. "So, what's new with you guys?"

"Much the same—too much work and never enough fun," I said.

"I know the feeling," Eddie said. "We need to go to the club again soon."

"How are things going with you and Bill?" I asked.

"Great," Eddie answered. "He's such a great guy. I'm lucky to be able to live there with him. So far, it's working out well."

"I invited a couple of girls over tonight. Is that okay?" Raymond asked.

"Girls? Females? Are you two converting and switching teams?" Eddie laughed.

"God no," Raymond answered, "it's our server friend Kimberly from the pub. She's a lesbian and wanted to know what life is like being gay in the real world. I thought the three of us could give her a clearer picture of what it's really like and answer some of her questions."

"With what we've all been through, I hope it doesn't scare her and her girlfriend away. All we can do is tell her our own experiences and although it can be difficult, it's always best to be true to yourself," Eddie said.

"They're lucky to have friends like you. I don't know what I would have done without you two," he continued, and gave the two of us a heartfelt smile.

A short time later, the buzzer in the lobby sounded.

"Hello?" Raymond answered.

"Hi, it's Kimberly," was the reply.

"Come on up," he said and unlocked the main entrance door. Shortly after, there was a knock on the apartment door and Raymond answered.

"Come on in, girls," Raymond said.

"Hi, guys." Kimberly waved to us over on the couch.

"Come in and let me introduce everyone," Raymond said. Eddie and I got up off the couch.

"This is my girlfriend, Jill," Kimberly said. "This is Raymond and his partner Danny."

We all shook hands. Raymond stood behind the girls, and I could see him smile and stare at me when she called me Danny.

"This is our good friend Eddie," I said. "He's also gay and

has some insight to offer as well."

Just then, Mr. Muggs came out of the bedroom, stopped, stretched, and jumped up onto the couch.

"And this is our son, Mr. Muggs," Raymond said, and went over and picked him up and nuzzled him up close with some kisses.

"He's adorable!" Jill said.

"He's our boy," Raymond answered.

"Let me order the pizza. How's a cheese and a pepperoni with some garlic bread on the side sound?" I asked.

"Good with us," Kimberly replied, and I phoned the order in for home delivery.

"I love your apartment, guys," Jill said. "It's so homey and comfortable looking."

"Thanks," Raymond said, "Dan's the real housekeeper, aren't you, babe?"

"I try to keep up with him," I joked. "It's really a full-time job picking up all the clothes off the floor."

"I rarely wear clothes around here!" Raymond chuckled, to which Eddie answered, "Always keep the blinds drawn, dude," and we all laughed.

"So, what's on your minds, girls?" Raymond asked.

"Jill and I have been wondering what it must have been like when you told your parents that you were gay, and what their reaction was. We have no one to talk to, and we are both uncertain as to what anyone's reaction might be if we told them we are lesbians," Kimberly said.

"That's an easy question for Raymond, and I to answer, isn't it, hun? Our parents don't know, as we've never told them. Raymond's father is very homophobic, and I doubt we ever will tell him." I said. "We were just talking about this earlier. Raymond thinks his mother may know, but she's too intimidated by her husband to say anything."

"Is that true? Do you think your mom knows now, Raymond?" Eddie asked, as he knew all about our past.

"I think she does," Raymond replied. "I saw her today, and she was asking how Dan was doing. When I looked over, I was surprised to see that she was smiling at me. I was a bit shocked, but I didn't carry the conversation any further."

"Do your parents know, Danny?" Jill asked.

"No, I've never told them," I replied.

"And what about your parents, Eddie? Do they know?" Kimberly asked.

"Oh yeah, they sure know," Eddie responded with a chuckle.

"How did they take it?" Jill asked.

"They kicked me out of the house," Eddie responded. "I had nowhere to go, and Raymond and Dan let me live here for a couple of weeks."

"Oh my God, that's terrible Eddie," Kimberly said. "I would never have thought that would ever happen. Your own parents kicked you out of the house for being gay?"

"You would be surprised how often it does happen," I said. "We've met a few guys at the club whose families have turned their backs on them. It's terribly sad when you think of it."

"What are your parents like?" Raymond asked the girls.

"I'm worried that my mom and dad would be like Eddie's parents. My dad is very homophobic also and is always calling gay guys disgusting slang. I'm just so unsure of what they would say," Kimberly said. "I doubt they would kick me out, but I'm too afraid to say anything."

"What about you, Jill?" Eddie asked. "How do you think your parents would react?"

"I did tell my mom, and she was confused as to what the word lesbian meant. After I explained it to her, she still couldn't understand how a woman could be attracted to another woman," Jill said. "Then my mother says, 'Maybe you'll grow out of it.' Like really? Are they that naive?"

We all had a bit of a laugh.

"But you're right, Jill," Raymond said, "a great many people of our parents' generation are naive and unwilling to acknowledge or accept the gay lifestyle."

"Have you ever thought about moving in together and getting an apartment of your own?" I asked.

"We've thought about it, but we're not sure if we could afford it right now," Kimberly said. "We're both still going to school at Humber College for another year. That's where we met."

"That might be the best thing for you two right now," Eddie said. "It'll give you some time to plan and save up some funds. Give yourself a goal of, say, next summer, or after you graduate. That way, you'll have a good head start financially, and you'll get to know each other that much more. How long have you been going together, anyway?"

"Just short of a month," Kimberly said, "but I know she's the one for me." She smiled, looking over at Jill.

"We can relate to that, can't we, babe?" Raymond said. "With us, it was love at first sight."

"Damn right," I proudly said. "Going on three years now."

"Wow, has it been that long?" Eddie asked. "Didn't mean to make it sound like that, but you know what I mean."

We all had a chuckle.

"And you never had any second thoughts about being with each other?" Kimberly asked.

"Nope, not at all, not a single one. There's something in here," and I touched my chest, "that tells me Raymond is all I need."

"Same with me, babe," Raymond said, smiling in my direction.

"That's how we feel," Jill mentioned, "even if it's only been a few weeks, I know."

"I agree with Eddie," Raymond said. "Give it a year to blossom. Dan and I went a year before we moved in together, although it was out of necessity that I got away from my parents, especially my father's homophobic attitude."

We all jumped when the buzzer sounded.

"Pizza is here," I said, and answered the buzzer.

"Pizza delivery for Dan," the pizza guy said.

"I'll be right down," I replied

I went downstairs, got the pizza, and paid the driver for one cheese, one pepperoni, and some garlic bread, and quickly went back upstairs.

I set the pizza on the kitchen table and got out the plates. Kimberly came into the kitchen to help as well.

"Need some help?" she asked.

"I'm good, thanks. My turn to serve you for a change," I said, and she gave a bit of a chuckle.

"You'll be fine, Kimberly," I said. "Just give it time and save up some money for a place."

"I think that's good advice," she said.

"Come and get some pizza, everyone," I hollered from the kitchen. "There's cold pop in the fridge—Coke, 7Up, or root beer."

We all went back into the living room. Raymond, Eddie, and I sat on the big couch while the girls sat together on the loveseat.

Mr. Muggs, of course, came over, jumped up onto the couch, walked over to Raymond, and then jumped onto the coffee table.

"Watch this, girls," Eddie laughed. "He's going to show you how he got his name."

Sure enough, Mr. Muggs walked over to Raymond's glass of

root beer, took a sniff, and eagerly took a few licks of the foam.

"Oh my God, that's so adorable. Now I get it, Mr. Muggs, from Mug root beer!" Jill laughed.

"Yup, it's Muggs with two Gs," Raymond said, "he's his own man, aren't you, my Mugginses?"

We all enjoyed our pizza, and after a couple of hours of talking, the girls decided to head home.

We reassured them once again they'd be all right, and that even though they might face a few challenges along the way, it was definitely worth it.

"Thanks again, guys, for tonight," Kimberly said. "You really helped make things more understandable going forward."

"Yes, thanks again," Jill said. "This was really fun. I hope we can do it again sometime soon."

"We'll plan on it," Raymond said.

We all gave each other a hug.

"You know where we are if you ever need to talk," I said. We all said good night, and the girls left for home.

"Well, that was interesting," Raymond said. "I know how they must feel, though. Remember when we thought like that, babe?"

"I sure do," I said. "Sometimes you start to question every-thing that's happening around you and wonder what the future holds. It can be intimidating."

"You sure can say that again." Eddie chuckled.

After working for another year, and graduating from college, the girls eventually got themselves an apartment of their own in another city that was still close by. We continued to keep in touch, and they became good friends with Raymond, Eddie, and me.

We affectionately nicknamed them "KimberJilly" when we would see them together.

"Wow, it's past eleven o'clock. Did you want to stay the night, Eddie? It's getting late. You're more than welcome to if you want," I asked.

"I think I will, if that's okay," Eddie said. "I always enjoy staying here with you guys. I told Bill I may stay over if it's getting too late, as it's almost an hour's drive, so he knows."

"I'm up early, but you and Raymond can sleep in," I answered.

"I'll get you a pillow and pillowcase, sheets, and a blanket," Raymond said and then returned with the bedding.

"I can do that," Eddie said. "I can make up the couch."

Raymond and I finally got into bed and turned out the light.

From the living room, we heard Eddie say, "Good night, Raymond. Good night, Dan."

Raymond responded, "Good night, Eddie. Good night, Dan."

"Who are we, the Waltons?" I said, loud enough for Eddie to hear. I finished with, "Good night, Eddie. Good night, Raymond. Good night, John Boy."

Eddie then quietly yelled from the living room, "Ha ha, very funny, don't quit your day job. Stick to training horse."

We all chuckled.

Just then, Mr. Muggs let out a very loud meow, and we all started to laugh. "And a good night to you too, Mr. Muggs."

CHAPTER 29
Early summer 1983.

After our gay-bashing chase encounter, we skipped going to the club for a while, waiting a month or so before we returned. This night we decided to wear our Blue Jays baseball jerseys again, just for the fun of it, as everyone there got a kick out of it.

We called Eddie and Bill, and they were willing to meet us there on the following Saturday night.

Once there, we had another fun night dancing and laughing with our friends. Since Raymond always drove, we limited our beers to only two each, due to the strict drinking and driving laws in our province. We decided to leave early, at around eleven p.m., and started heading to the door.

"Remember the last time we exited the club, babe?" Raymond somewhat joked.

"I don't even want to think of it," I said.

As we opened the door and started stepping into the street, another guy was walking in.

"Hey, aren't you the guys from the alleyway?" he asked.

Surprised, we looked and then realized it was one of the

guys who had helped us when I had tripped over the garbage cans after we were being chased.

"My neighbor Mark and I came to your rescue that night," he smiled.

"Thanks again for helping us," Raymond said, shaking his hand.

"I'm Frank, by the way," he said.

"I remember you now. It's nice to meet you again, Frank. I'm Raymond, and this is my boyfriend, Dan. Yes, thank you again, Frank. I'm not sure what would have happened if those guys had caught us," Raymond said. "You come here as well?"

"Sure do. I love coming here when I get the time off. I'm a firefighter, and my shifts often have me working on the weekends. This time, however, I got this weekend off," he said with a big smile. "Were you two leaving? Why don't you come back inside and let me buy you a beer?"

Raymond looked at me and we both smiled in agreement and went back inside with Frank.

Robert the doorman greeted us again, and we took off our coats and handed them back to the coat check.

"Frank!" Robert said, "What's going on, my friend?" They gave each other a big hug.

Robert then looked our way.

"Frank and I go a long way back," Robert said.

"This is Raymond, AKA the Pitcher, and Dan, AKA the Catcher," he mentioned to Frank.

Robert turned us around in our Jays outfits to show Frank.

"That's hilarious, guys. I love it, but we already know each other from a past experience, don't we?" Frank jokingly answered.

"Are you two Jays cutting in on my territory?" Robert joked as he took a step forward, allowing his six-foot-plus height to look down upon us.

He then put his big arms around us both and practically lifted us both off the ground. "Get back inside," he joked.

"I'll catch up in a minute or two," Frank answered, and continued talking with Robert.

"I think those two may have been a pair at one time by the way they're chatting," Raymond said.

"They certainly are in deep discussion," I jokingly replied.

After a couple minutes, Frank joined us at the bar. "What do you guys want?"

"We'll both have a Carlsberg," Raymond said.

Frank paid the bartender, and we sat down and began chatting.

"I was going to say that night when you fell in the alley, I knew you were coming from the club here, but the two of you looked so scared that I didn't want to cause you any more stress and thought it best just to leave it alone. Plus, I didn't really want my neighbor to know," Frank said. "I take it you made it safely home. Did you need stitches for that gash?"

"It was swollen for a couple of days, but I didn't need stitches," I said. "There's a nice older lady who lives across the hall in our apartment who used to be a nurse. She helped to clean it and bandaged it up."

"Who was chasing you that night, anyway?" Frank asked.

"We had come out of the club, and a couple of very large gay bashers started yelling at us from across the street," Raymond said. "So, we decided to come back inside. Robert suggested that we go out the back way. Once outside, we walked around and back to Sherbourne, hoping they had gone, but sure enough, we saw them across the street again. Once they noticed us, they started chasing us. We ran and somehow got lost and ended up in your back alleyway."

"Fucking bastards. I'm glad I came out when I heard you

knock over the garbage cans, Dan, after you fell. Some gay bashers are brutally mean. After I got back inside the house, I thought to myself that I should have walked with you back to your car for your own safety. I was hoping that you would make it home alright," Frank said.

"Yeah, it's a night I don't really want to remember, to be honest," I said.

Raymond knew how much it bothered me, reliving that evening, and eagerly changed the subject. "It sounds like you've known Robert for a while."

"Robert and I grew up in the same town and even went to the same high school together. Ten or so years ago, I was still living at home with my parents. I kept getting questioned by my father for never having a girlfriend. I was around your age, early twenties. I started feeling the stress of constantly having to hide my gay side, so I eventually started dating a girl."

As Frank spoke, we could tell how frustrating and unsettling it was for him to discuss his past.

"After a few months, we got engaged. I knew I had made a mistake, and that I wasn't being honest with myself, nor being fair to the girl. I knew it wouldn't work, so I broke off the engagement, came out, and basically broke ties with my family as a result. I had to get away from my hometown, so I moved here to Toronto. I haven't spoken to any of my family in over eight years," Frank sadly said.

"Robert and I happened to meet one day, and we, like you, started dating and had our romantic fun together, but it didn't work out. We're still great friends, though. I joined the Fire Department, bought a house, and I'm enjoying my life here in the city," Frank said.

"Your family life sounds very similar to ours, doesn't it, babe?" Raymond said.

"It sure does," I replied. "We're both in a similar situation with our families, like what you and Frank went through, especially Raymond, with his homophobic behemoth father."

"How long have you two been together?" Frank asked.

"Twenty-six months," I proudly exclaimed.

"That's great," he said. "Does your family know?"

"The only one in my family who knows is my sister, who's very supportive of us," Raymond mentioned. "No one knows about Dan in his family."

"You two are valiant for staying together for so long, considering how guarded it all is. The only advice I can offer is that no matter what, it's what you two want that's important. It may be a difficult struggle, and you may lose family and friends, but in the end, it's what makes you two happy that counts."

We finished our beer and then went and joined Eddie and Bill, who were nearer the dance floor.

We introduced Frank to Eddie and Bill as well.

After another couple of beers and a few more dances, we decided it was time for home. Raymond then went to get up from the table, tried taking a couple of steps, and uncontrollably flopped back down in his chair.

"Whoa, big guy," Frank said.

I started to chuckle at Raymond for being a bit drunk.

Raymond then began to laugh, looked at me, pointed his finger and politely told me, "Fuck off, babe." He continued to laugh and giggle uncontrollably.

"Are you alright to drive?" Frank asked Raymond. "The two of you are more than welcome to stay over at my place for the night," he said and jokingly added. "Do you remember how to get there?"

I was somewhat hesitant, but I knew we both had had too many beers since coming back into the club a second time. I didn't feel comfortable calling a taxi to a gay bar, plus the cost of driving the forty miles home in a cab would be expensive. "Raymond, do you want to stay at Frank's tonight, hun?" I asked.

Raymond leaned against me and said, "I can't drive, babe. I'm sorry."

"If it's alright, Frank, I think we'll take you up on your offer," I said.

Frank then helped me with Raymond as we put on our jackets, said goodbye to Eddie and Bill, and headed to the front door.

"Helping Raymond the Dance Man to the car, Frank?" Robert asked.

"I think it best for Raymond and Dan to stay at my place tonight. I don't want either of them attempting to drive while in this condition," Frank answered.

"Wise move, Frank. Take good care of my boys, and thanks," Robert said and held the door open while we walked outside.

The fresh air seemed to help Raymond wake up a bit, and he was at least able to walk in a straight line.

A few minutes later, we reached Frank's front door, where he welcomed us inside.

"It's a small place, but it does me fine. I'll get some blankets and a couple of pillows. I only have one single bed in the spare bedroom. Unless, of course, you want to..." Frank stopped his conversation, allowing us to continue to read into what he was referring. Raymond and I knew exactly what he meant, and we both looked at each other in wide-eyed curiosity.

"We don't want you to be uncomfortable," Raymond answered back.

"Nonsense, I'd feel more comfortable being with you two," Frank replied. "Besides, the bed in the spare room is so small. You need to be able to enjoy your stay."

He then put an arm around us both and walked us into his bedroom.

Frank got undressed and watched as we gazed at his big, naked, hairy frame, and big everything. Frank was big in one place, but not as big as Raymond was.

Raymond and I eagerly followed, and we all made our way to the bed.

"Wow, aren't you the lucky guy," Frank said, as he intently watched Raymond get undressed and drop his boxers. "Damn, son, I thought I was big down there, but you certainly have me beat! How big is that thing?" Frank asked.

"Big enough to explain why I always have a smile on my face," I joked.

For Frank's intimidating size, he was very submissive and enthusiastically asked Raymond and me to do whatever we wanted.

Frank then lay on the bed on his back while Raymond knelt between his legs. He lifted Frank's very hairy legs and placed them over his shoulders. Being the aggressive top he was, it wasn't long before Raymond was topping Frank and causing him to moan in delight with physical pleasure.

I was kneeling to one side of Frank's head, allowing him to both watch Raymond and enjoy me at the same time.

Now and then, I'd stand beside the bed, lean in, and passionately kiss Raymond, which seemed to turn Frank on that much more.

It was a night we wouldn't soon forget, and after what seemed like an all-night affair, we were soon satisfied and totally content.

"That was amazing," said Frank as he stretched out on the bed. "You certainly know how to use that thing!"

"Thanks," Raymond said. "I guess practice does make perfect, doesn't it, babe?"

"Most definitely," I joked. "We certainly have practiced a lot."

Frank then invited us to go shower, and although there wasn't much room, the three of us managed to get lathered up and cleaned off.

After drying each other off, Frank offered us a cold Coke, and we all sat around the kitchen table, talking about life.

We eventually went back to bed and soon fell asleep in a very friendly threesome.

The next morning, once we were all awake and dressed, Frank insisted that he wanted to take us out for breakfast.

We walked to his favorite diner, where we enjoyed a fun-filled breakfast.

"I had a great time last night at the club, and especially at home," said Frank. "I hope I didn't come across as being pushy or offensive in any way."

"Not at all," Raymond said. "We should be thanking you for your kindness and allowing us a place to sleep."

"Do you live around here?" asked Frank.

"We live in Milton, about forty-five minutes away," Raymond answered.

"We should be getting home, babe, as Mr. Muggs will be wondering where we got to," I said.

"Who's Mr. Muggs?" Frank asked.

"He's our cat. He has a liking for Mug root beer," Raymond jokingly replied.

"That's so strange." Frank laughed. "He actually drinks the stuff?"

"He likes the foamy part," I said, "and eagerly licks it up."

"Thanks again for a fun time, Frank," Raymond said. "Hope to see you at the club again soon."

"I'll be there when I can," Frank answered.

Before walking back to the car, we said our goodbyes, and shook his hand, which turned into a friendly hug.

Once inside the car, we immediately started talking about the previous night at Frank's.

"What did you think, babe?" asked Raymond. "I knew we had talked about having another one of those three-way escapades before, and the extra beers made me brave enough to go for it."

"I enjoyed it, but I'd never want to do it without you with me, hun," I said. "Actually, I'm glad you had those beers."

"I'm the same, babe. It was an adventure, but I know it's never going to happen without you being there, too," Raymond said. We both reached for each other's hand and continued our in-depth conversation about the event on our drive home. I mentioned to Raymond that when we were playing with Frank, I didn't seem to feel my jealously flare. Maybe it was because we were both helping to please both of us, and Frank didn't seem to favor one over the other.

CHAPTER 30

A few nights later, Raymond and I were sitting up in the grandstand in our usual spot, watching the races. He was on his break from the betting machines in the grandstand. I had no horses racing that night, so I was just watching the races.

I was looking at the racing program for the next day. I had a horse entered to race and had a good feeling that he'd do well. He was starting at 8-1in the pari-mutuel morning lineup, meaning for every dollar that you bet, you would get eight dollars back, plus your initial outlay. Based on the minimum of a two-dollar wager, you'd get eighteen dollars should he win. The odds, however, would fluctuate depending on how the public bet and who they thought had the best chance at winning.

"I think our horse has a good shot tomorrow, hun. I think I'm going to bet on him," I said to Raymond.

"Wow, in all the years we've been together, I don't recall you ever placing a bet," he said.

"Years ago, I met an old timer at the racetrack who had been a groom for most of his life. He liked the way I cared for my horses, and we became good friends. One day, he gave me some advice. He said if you want to be successful in the horse racing business, then you should stay away from habitual gambling, excessive alcohol, and fast women," I said, smiling.

"I know you don't drink excessively. I know you don't have a gambling habit, and I definitely know you don't chase fast women, not even slow ones. Damn, you're a good groom," Raymond answered, and we both continued laughing.

"I'll try to leave the women alone, but I still have a positive feeling about my horse. I'm going to bet a whopping forty dollars to win on him," I said.

Raymond leaned over and looked at the program, "I love the name of that horse," he mentioned and pointed to another horse in our race.

"He's a good horse, actually," I said. "Therefore, I'll bet a ten-dollar exactor of my horse to finish first, and yours to come in second, just for the fun of it. You do know that the definition of an exactor is when you pick the horses that will come first and second in correct order in the same race," I said to Raymond, trying to keep a serious face.

"I know what an exactor is," Raymond answered. "In case you haven't noticed, I work with the betting machines in the grandstand." He laughed back.

"I'm just teasing. Who knows, with any luck, maybe we can get that large color TV we saw in the window that one night," I joked. "Aren't you off tomorrow night, hun?"

"Yeah, I'm not working tomorrow. Why?" Raymond replied.

"Since you're not working, maybe you can place the wager tomorrow for us," I said.

"I guess I could do that," Raymond answered. "Even though I work right in the middle of everyone betting, I've never done it before."

"It's easy. Don't worry about it," I answered.

The next night, I gave Raymond the money, and he was going to place our bet.

"Now remember, forty dollars to win, and a ten-dollar exactor," I told him.

"Yes, yes, I'll remember," he replied. "You worry too much."

Later that evening, I walked my horse from the paddock onto the racetrack and wished the driver good luck.

As my horse was warming up and waiting for the starter to call them to begin the race, I kept my eye on the tote board, watching the odds.

My horse was going off at 6-1, meaning the public liked his chances also. I then looked at Raymond's horse that he had chosen, and he was around 15-1. *That would be a nice paying exactor, should it ever come in*, I thought.

Once the race started, my horse was in the perfect position the whole mile. Coming down the homestretch, my horse was neck and neck, and then finally pulled ahead and easily won. I was so excited about my horse winning, I failed to hear who was second.

I walked my horse up to the winner's circle to have our photograph taken for the win. It was then that I glanced over at the tote board that was in the infield by the finish line, which showed the odds and payouts. To my surprise, Raymond's pick had come in second.

I couldn't believe it. I stood there holding my horse by the bit in his mouth, trying to keep him still. I was also trying to calculate in my head how much we had won once they posted the results.

My horse paid $14.20 to win, and the exactor paid $93.60.

I did some rough calculations in my head and figured out that was about $600. I was ecstatic!

I happily took my horse back to the back stretch and to the urine barn. The urine barn was a small separate barn where the winner of every race had to go, along with another randomly selected horse, to have a urine sample taken and tested for drugs by the Ontario Racing Commission.

Many people are unaware, but when a racehorse is young and when you see him or her pee, you start to whistle. Over the course of time, the horse associates whistling with going pee. Once in the test barn, all you can hear are people whistling and waiting to get a urine sample. It may take several hours and lots of drinking water, trying to get your horse to pee. Urine is preferred, as the laboratory has a better chance of detecting forbidden substances.

If your horse fails to pee, then a blood sample is drawn by the racing commission's veterinarian to test for drugs.

Should a horse ever have a positive test for illegal drugs, he is disqualified and forfeits his purse winnings. It does not affect the pari-mutuel betting results, however.

After the race was over and my horse gave a urine sample, I took him back to my own barn to cool him down and put him away for the night.

The whole time I kept wondering how excited Raymond must be.

I bet he's at home with Mr. Muggs counting it out on the coffee table, I thought.

I eagerly finished by barn my work, and quickly drove the forty-five minutes back to the apartment, all excited to count our winnings.

Once back home, I raced upstairs and eagerly ran inside. "Hey, Mr. Rockefeller," I said. "Let's go celebrate with our winnings!"

Needless to say, Raymond was sitting there on the couch. He was slouched over with his elbows on his knees and his face in his hands. He looked up with an almost tearful look on his face.

"I fucked up, babe. Please don't be angry. I've never placed a bet in my life before, and I bet it wrong," Raymond said.

I wasn't sure what to say. "You bet it wrong? What went wrong?"

"I've never placed a bet in my life," Raymond said once again. "I got so confused and I messed the horses' numbers up all wrong and did it all backward. I'm sorry babe. I'll give you the fifty dollars back. Please don't be upset or angry with me. I'm sorry, I really am."

I must admit that I was disappointed, but at the same time, I also felt bad for the mistake he'd made, as he looked so disappointed. The look on Raymond's face broke my heart. He looked so sad, as if he'd failed us both. I desperately tried to make him feel better and forgot about the money aspect of it.

"Don't be silly, hun. Shit happens, don't worry about it. I'm not upset. Besides, what would we have done with the money anyway, other than probably put it toward rent?" I said.

"We'd celebrate, that's what we'd do, and then we'd go out and buy that big ass color TV!" Raymond yelled and jumped up off the couch.

He stuck his hand into his pocket, pulled out a huge, thick wad of rolled up bills, and threw them into the air. It started raining hundred-, fifty-, and twenty-dollar bills.

"What the fuck!" I yelled. "What happened, hun? What the fuck did you do?"

"Like I said, I totally fucked up. I was so nervous placing the bet that I got it all mixed up and reversed the bet. I bet ten dollars to win, and a forty-dollar exactor. I didn't realize what I had done till the race was over. That's nineteen hundred and forty-three fucking dollars, babe, and zero fucking cents!" Raymond yelled in laughter.

I could not believe what had happened.

We gathered up the money off the floor and sat there counting it out and putting it in piles of each denomination, doing it a couple of times just for the fun of it.

I think Mr. Muggs was enjoying it as well, as he kept touching the bills in the piles with his paw, causing them to fall to the floor again, where he would eagerly chase after them.

"Aw, Mr. Muggins likes the hundred-dollar ones!" Raymond joked.

I don't know how many times we counted it out.

"We can go buy that big color TV and still have lots extra," I said. "I'm glad you fucked up, hun."

"Don't mention it, babe. I'm always willing to fuck you . . . up," Raymond laughed. "Speaking of which . . ." He gave me that familiar, sly, come-over-here look.

We eagerly went to bed and talked about the TV and where it should go in the living room.

Eventually, we started to play, and then afterwards dozed off in each other's arms and had a wonderful night's sleep.

The following weekend, we went back to the electronics store in town.

"Can I help you boys?" asked the older salesclerk.

"We were interested in the large color television that's on display in the window," Raymond inquired. "How much is it?"

"That's a beautiful set," the guy said. "Somewhat expensive, however. It's $945, which includes tax, but it's the most technologically advanced set we have in the store. It even has stereo sound. Do you live close by?" he asked.

"Yes, in the one apartment complex here in Milton," Raymond responded.

"I'll make you a deal, purchase the TV, and I'll include

free delivery and set up. It's rather heavy and awkward to take upstairs due to its size," the sales associate offered.

"Deal," Raymond said and handed the guy the cash.

That afternoon, the electronics store delivered our new color TV, set it up, and adjusted all the channels.

Raymond was in his glory, watching the bright blues and reds of *Wonder Woman* in color.

CHAPTER 31

We sat there watching TV in color. "This is fucking awesome," Raymond kept repeating while I smiled and laughed.

"See, and it's all because you fucked up," I laughed.

We finished watching *Wonder Woman*, and Raymond relaxed while reading the latest edition of his *Billboard* music magazine. He loved all kinds of music and kept up to date on the Pop and Dance Club song charts, as well as any dance moves that he could think of.

"Hey, babe," and Raymond started to sing David Bowie's "Let's Dance." He stood and started his dance routine. "That's top of the charts at the dance clubs," he said.

"I've heard it at the club," I said. "I think we've danced to it before, but I still like Laura Branigan, and her song 'Gloria' best."

Raymond then went and got out our Laura Branigan album "Branigan," and put it on the LP player.

"Not too loud, hun. I don't want 'Mr. Old Fart' next door banging on the wall again."

We once had the LP stereo too loud, and our neighbor in the apartment next door started pounding on the wall.

Although we rarely saw him or even talked with him, I thought it only polite to go apologize.

The next day, I knocked on his door.

He opened the door and when he saw it was me, he instantly scowled.

"Hello, Mr. Jamieson. I apologize for playing our music so loudly last night. We'll try to—"

Before I could finish with my apology, he interrupted me and said, somewhat snarly, "Just keep it down." Then he immediately shut the door.

We never did find out why he was so unfriendly. He might have suspected we were gay, or maybe he just didn't like loud music, but for whatever reason, we tried to keep the stereo's volume at a respectful level just to appease him.

A few days later, we started listening to the stereo, always fearful of that dreaded wall-pounding we might hear, but luckily, it never happened.

This night we were listening to Laura Branigan, and I loved watching Raymond dance and his choreographed moves, especially to her song "Gloria." Once "Gloria" was finished, he put on Laura Branigan's "All Night with Me."

"I have to think of a dance move for this one," he said.

"I've never heard them play that song at the club. Besides, I don't really like that song's lyrics. She seems uncertain as to what her lover is thinking as they're lying together in bed," I said.

"And when we're lying in bed together, what do you think?" Raymond asked and smiled.

"That I'm the luckiest man in the world, of course. Remember what David up at the cottage referred me to? 'Lucky Dan, Lucky Dan,'" I said.

Raymond laughed. "I forgot about that." He raised his

arms high over his head and gave his torso a jiggle.

"I wonder how David is doing?" I said. "We should see if he'd want to come for a visit, maybe go to the club one Saturday night?"

"That's a great idea. I should give him a call," Raymond said. "I wonder if he ever moved to Kingston and moved in with Philip. Let me give him a call. It's only seven p.m. That's not too late, you think? Is it, babe?"

"I don't think so. Give him a call," I said.

Raymond looked his number up in our personal directory and called David's parents' place.

"Hello?" a voice answered.

"Is David there, please?" Raymond asked.

"Hold on a moment," the voice answered back.

Raymond gave a thumbs-up at me and put the phone answering machine on speaker.

"Hello?" David said.

"David? It's Raymond, Raymond Scott from up at the cottage," Raymond replied.

"Raymond! It's great to hear from you. I've been wondering how you and Dan are. How are the two of you doing?"

"We're doing great, thanks. How have you been? Have you moved to Kingston yet?" Raymond asked.

"Funny you should mention that, as Philip and I have been planning it. We think we found a place down there. It's a two-bedroom apartment, which suits us fine. Philip is here in the city for the week, and we're just getting things organized."

"That's great," Raymond said. "Dan and I were sitting here thinking about you and wondering if you and Philip had moved in together. We were also wondering if you two would like to go to the club with us this Saturday night for something to do—a fun night out."

"That would be awesome," David said. "Can you hold the

phone for a second? Let me ask Philip."

After a bit of a pause, David was back on the phone. "Hey, Raymond, Philip said he'd love to go and finally meet you and Dan. I've told him so much about you both, and how you two have managed to live together without too much of a hassle."

"Great, do you know where the club is in Toronto? Raymond asked.

"Yup, I know where it is. How if we meet out front there, say around seven p.m.?" David asked.

"That sounds great, David. Dan and I will be looking forward to seeing you and Philip there around seven this Saturday," Raymond answered.

"Thanks for calling, Raymond," David said. "Looking forward to it as well and say hi to Lucky Dan for me."

"I'll do that. See you Saturday," Raymond said and hung up the phone.

"I'm so glad David and Philip finally managed to get a place, hun," I said. "He's such a nice guy and deserves to be with his man."

That Saturday night, we drove into Toronto and to the club. As we walked up the sidewalk, we could see David and Philip waiting outside.

"Raymond, Dan, so good to see you again," David said, and he gave us both a big hug. "This is my boyfriend, Philip. Philip, this is Raymond and his boyfriend, Dan."

"Nice to meet you, Philip," Raymond said, and we all shook hands.

"David certainly went on about you while we were up at the cottage," I said to Philip.

"He spoke a lot about you two as well," Philip replied.

"Shall we go in?" David said, and we all went inside.

It was still early, and we were greeted by our doorman friend, Robert. "Hey, guys, good to see you again. You two doing okay?"

"Yup, all is good. Thanks, Robert. Let me introduce you to our friends David and Philip." They all shook hands.

"Pleased to meet you guys," Robert said. "It's still early, but there's lots of room at the bar if you want to go sit for a bit. I know Raymond's just itching to get onto the dance floor. Aren't you, twinkle toes?"

"I've been practicing a couple of new moves," Raymond jokingly said, and shuffled and danced his way toward the bar. We all followed. After we got our beers, we sat down at our favorite table and talked about work, family, and life in the gay world as we knew it.

As more guys entered the club, the livelier it became. Soon the DJ was playing his music, the room's bright lights began to dim, and the disco lights started.

The room began to fill with the familiar sound of very loud music, disco balls reflecting colored lights, and the overwhelming smell of shirtless men sweating and brushing up against each other while dancing.

Raymond, once again, danced the night away, while I tried to at least follow and keep up. David and Philip were amazed at Raymond's dance moves.

"You're an amazing dancer," Philip said. "Where did you learn to dance like that?"

"I think up the dance moves myself and will practice them at the apartment," Raymond said. "Dan's an honest critic and will tell me if something just doesn't fit with the lyrics or rhythm."

"Raymond's into music in a big way," I said. "He even gets *Billboard* magazine delivered to the apartment and has an amazing stereo system."

"That stereo is so old, babe. It really needs to be replaced," Raymond once again said. "It's so out of date."

Philip and Raymond started talking about the different stereos, equalizers, and speakers on the market, while David and I sat a little lost in their conversation.

"I enjoy music, but Raymond is way above me when it comes to the specific songs and the music stuff," I said.

"Don't worry, you're not alone, Dan," David answered. "Philip's into that stuff as well. Those two will be at it for a while yet," he said. "Let's go get a beer."

We both walked to the bar and got us and our guys another beer.

"This round is on me," David said.

"Thanks, David," I replied, and David gave me a smile.

We got our beers and walked back to the table. As expected, Raymond and Philip were still going at it.

"But the watts in that system aren't strong enough, in my opinion," Philip said. "I much prefer the Pioneer equalizer over the Aiwa."

"They have no idea that we're even here," I said. "They're off in their own little world of acoustics."

"I bet they don't even hear a word we say," David teased.

"Let's put it to the test," I jokingly said out loud,

"Oh, Raymond, hun, show everyone your huge horse dick." Raymond and Philip continued chatting, without batting an eye or missing a word, this time talking about subwoofers.

"See what I mean?" David replied, looking at me. "Oh, Lucky Dan, Lucky Dan." We both started to laugh again.

"What's so funny, babe?" Raymond asked as he looked over at us both.

"Here, hun. David got you another beer." I gave him his cold beer and a kiss on the cheek. "I just love ya."

"Thanks, babe, and thanks, David," Raymond answered,

and then leaned forward, pointed his thumb toward me, and surprisingly said to all of us, "and my huge horse dick loves this guy's sweet ass big time." He kissed me back.

"Oh my God! Lucky Dan, Lucky Dan!" David said, and we all started roaring with laughter.

"I'm having such a fun time, guys. Thanks again for inviting us along," Philip said.

At around two a.m., and after a couple more rounds and some more dancing, we all decided to call it a night and head for home.

"Please keep in touch, guys," David said. "Philip and I had an amazing evening. Once we are settled in our apartment in Kingston, I hope you two can come down for a weekend visit."

"We'd love that, wouldn't we, babe?" Raymond answered. "We'll definitely keep in touch. Call us anytime."

We all gave each other a hug, then went outside into the hot, muggy night, and headed for home.

CHAPTER 32

On our way home, we started talking about Raymond's sister, Rozz. In our eyes, she was a complete sweetheart in every sense of the word.

With money left over from our big win, even after our new color television purchase, we decided to do something special for her, as she was always there for us.

"Let's take your sister Rozz out for dinner, hun, while we still have some extra money," I said. "She's always there for us both."

"That's a great idea, babe. She'd love that! Her thirtieth birthday is coming up, and I know she likes to go to that one Italian restaurant near her place," Raymond said. "I'll give her a call in the morning."

"How much of our winnings do we still have left over?" Raymond asked.

"Well over $800, and I know what you're going to ask." I looked at him and smiled. "How much is it?"

"Oh, babe, it's on sale at the one stereo store in Toronto. I saw it in their flyer. I can keep my LP player, but I'd really love to get the receiver and equalizer. It was around $300,"

Raymond said, with the most adorable look on his face.

"How can I say no to that face?" I answered.

It made me happy seeing Raymond happy, and although the big color TV was for the both of us to enjoy, I knew that a new stereo system would make him feel totally ecstatic.

We had a small, locked metal case that we kept spending money in, which was well hidden in the bedroom closet. After our big win, it was like our secret treasure chest full of fun money. It came in handy whenever some unexpected cash was needed. Other than that, we would always use the money that we'd deposit into Raymond's bank account to pay the rent and bills.

"We can drive into Toronto next weekend and get it if you want, hun," I said. "What kind is it?"

"It's an Aiwa," he said, "a great brand."

"I've never heard of that name before, but I'm sure you know what you're talking about. I remember you and Philip talking about that stuff at the club that one night."

The next day, Raymond got on the phone and called his sister. "Dan and I want to take you out to dinner for your birthday." Then, after a slight pause, he said, "Bring him along also. Okay, sounds good. See you on Saturday night. Love you, Rozz. Bye." And Raymond hung up the phone.

"Apparently, Rozz has a boyfriend named Peter, who asked her out on her birthday already, so I asked her if he would like to come along," Raymond said. "He was there with her and said he'd love to join us."

"Do you think he'll be alright with our living arrangement?" I said.

"If Rozz is there, then we're safe," Raymond answered. "She won't allow any negativity toward us."

Raymond and I would occasionally go out for dinner

with another gay couple that we knew, but we never went on a double date with a straight couple for the simple reason of not knowing what their reaction would be to seeing two guys together.

But Raymond was right. We knew everything would be fine if Rozz was there, as she would never allow, nor tolerate, any gay-bashing or slander toward us.

Luckily, Raymond and I did not have to work that Saturday evening, and we eagerly looked forward to going out on the town. Once Saturday night arrived, we sat relaxing on the couch while we waited to get ready to go meet Rozz and Peter.

"We should go shower and get ready, hun. We don't want to be late," I said.

"Wait, I have something for you, babe." Raymond went into the bedroom and came back with a flat box wrapped up in bright paper.

"What's this for?" I curiously asked.

"Do you need a reason to give the person you love a gift?" Raymond replied. "I've been keeping it for a special occasion. Go ahead and open it, babe."

Once again, I slowly lifted the tape and carefully unfolded the wrapping paper.

"Oh my God!" Raymond laughed.

I then opened the box. "My tie! My pink tie! Babe, where did you get this from?" I was so happy and excited. I remember sitting on the couch, bouncing up and down. I was so thrilled. Raymond started to laugh and sat down beside me.

"After our big win that night, I quickly drove back to the same store where I had bought the first one and got it. Apparently, they still don't sell many pink ties." Raymond chuckled. "They only had the one in stock, and that was the one on display again."

I was so happy, and gave him the longest hug, never wanting to ever let him go. The tie was the most beautiful shade of shiny pink with tiny, raised dots.

"Oh, hun, you have no idea what this means to me," I said. "I love this tie. I really, really do!"

To me, my pink tie represented and expressed how much love and care we had for each other.

First, by Raymond secretly going to back to buy it for me when we went Christmas shopping that one day, when he saw how much I loved and wanted it.

Then, with him helping me when I fell and hurt myself, the result of the gay bashers chasing us after seeing me wearing my pink tie, and once again now, when Raymond took the time to go back and buy yet another one.

He did all this out of the true love he had for me, a simple act of love, caring, and wanting to make me happy. A love that came from deep inside his beautiful heart.

"Time to shower, babe!" Raymond said, and he eagerly undressed in front of me. With his excited "big" bounce, I eagerly followed him into the bathroom.

We were both feeling so excited and happy that our usual shower time together turned into a much extended, and a very pleasurable and very satisfying one.

Afterwards, we got all dressed up and drove into Toronto. I was wearing my white shirt and proudly showing off my new, bright, shiny, bubblegum pink tie. Maybe it was somewhat bold to wear a pink tie in public, but I considered it sharp and fashionable, and I eagerly wore it.

Raymond had made reservations for seven p.m., and we arrived on time. We sat down and ordered a beer while we waited for Rozz and Peter.

After a few minutes, Rozz and Peter arrived. "Dan and Raymond," Rozz said, "this is my boyfriend, Peter. Peter, this is my younger brother, Raymond, and his partner, Dan."

I was unsure how that statement would go over with Peter, but at the same time, I felt my chest swell with pride upon hearing her say "partner."

Peter extended his hand, and we all shook hands. Peter was a few years older than Rozz, around thirty-five to forty.

"I'm so glad to meet you two," Peter said. "Rozz has told me so many good things about you both, and I'm pleased to see that you two are a couple." Peter then glanced over at Raymond. "My views are the same as your sister's, Raymond. I'm totally supportive of you guys. So please relax and feel at ease around me."

"I greatly appreciate that, Peter, and I speak on behalf of Dan as well. We're always very leery of going out on a double date, for fear of reprisal from anyone who doesn't accept our lifestyle," Raymond answered.

"The world is full of phonies, hypocrites, and bigots," Peter said, "and don't even ask my opinion of the Catholic Church regarding same-sex relationships."

Raymond, Rozz, and I almost burst into laughter.

"What's the joke?" Peter asked.

"You and the boys are going to get along just fine," Rozz said to Peter.

She then went on to explain to Peter about Raymond's, and my own experiences while growing up in a Catholic household, as well as their father's terrible stance on homo-sexuality and his displeasure with all gay people.

"That's terrible," Peter said. "Remember to let me voice my opinion to your father when I finally meet him."

"God, NO!" we all basically cried out and began to laugh. Rozz then described her father in more detail to Peter.

"He's not worth wasting your breath on that discussion, Peter," Raymond said.

Just then, the server came over to take our orders.

"Order what you want, guys. It's Dan's and my treat," Raymond said.

"What?" Rozz surprisingly asked. "It's very expensive here, Raymond. You two can't afford this place on your own. We'll pay our share."

"Nope," Raymond said, and gleefully started to tell them about his gambling story.

"First off, we never bet on the horses, but Dan liked his chances, so Dan and I bet on one of his horses, and being the professional gambler that I am, I made a mistake in the way I placed the bet. Dan told me he wanted to bet forty dollars to win on his horse, plus a ten-dollar exactor of his horse first, and my horse I chose, simply because I liked its name for, second. I incorrectly bet ten dollars to win and a forty-dollar exactor. The horses finished first and second, one, two, and we got back over $1,900!" Raymond excitedly explained, "so, dinner is on us."

We all started laughing and continued having a good time.

"I feel like I want to contribute somehow," Peter said. "Let me at least pay for the bar tab. I'd feel better."

Over the course of the evening, we discovered how they met at the bank, while Peter asked how we met.

Raymond then gave Rozz a birthday present and a card. The card was signed, "With Love from Raymond, Dan, and Mr. Muggs."

It was a family picture of Raymond and me, along with Mr. Muggs. The two of us were sitting on the couch in the apartment and sitting perfectly between us on the back of the couch was Mr. Muggs. We were all smiling at the camera.

Raymond had taken it with one of his timed cameras on the tripod, had it enlarged, and then had it framed.

"I love this," Rozz said. "It means so much to me, my three

boys together. I'm going to put this on my night table beside my bed and slip it in the drawer in case Mom or Dad ever come over."

"Wise move, Sis. I never thought about that." Raymond said, somewhat concerned, and he raised his beer in acknowledgment.

"I remember it took quite a few shots as Mr. Muggs kept trying to lick Raymond's ear," I laughingly said, as I nonchalantly put one hand under the table and patted Raymond's thigh, agreeing with his comment to Rozz about hiding the picture.

Rozz then showed the picture to Peter and explained to him how we got Mr. Muggs, and how Raymond named him.

"That's so cute," Peter said.

The server brought us our food and another round of drinks. We had a great night talking about the many fun stories Raymond and I had, as well as stories of Rozz and Peter.

After a couple of hours, we ended our evening together, and upon leaving, Rozz gave us each a hug. Raymond extended his hand to Peter, who in turn reached for his hand and pulled him in close and gave him a hug as well. He then gave me a hug.

"I told you, I'm not afraid to show my feelings and thoughts about you two. I'm proud of you both," Peter said.

We said goodnight to Rozz and Peter and drove back to the apartment.

Once home, Mr. Muggs scolded us for being so late by meowing and not pausing until he was completely satisfied with his lecture, and he finally stopped. Raymond and I got undressed, washed, and settled into bed. Mr. Muggs eagerly joined us, and we all had a peaceful night's sleep.

CHAPTER 33
August 1983.

Shortly after Rozz's birthday, it was my own birthday. Raymond knew that I wasn't into the birthday party thing, and he always was willing to allow me the peacefulness of just him and me going out to our favorite pub to celebrate.

The odd time I would have my birthday at my parents' place, but mostly it was Raymond and me going out for dinner somewhere.

What I liked about my birthdays back then was that my birthday had been a couple of weeks before I had met Raymond, and I was more interested in celebrating the day Raymond and I had met, than I was in celebrating my own birthday.

I'm not sure why, but I've always been that way toward my birthday. Maybe it's because, as a kid, I don't ever recall having a birthday party, or anything, but even to this day, I'm not overly excited about all the celebrating.

There was a book shop in the grandstand at the racetrack that sold different books about horses, drivers, and the horse racing industry, and for my birthday that year Raymond had gotten me a couple books about famous standard-bred racehorses.

We also went to our favorite pub, and naturally, Kimberly came over and greeted us.

"Hey, guys. How's your day going? Want the usual?" she asked.

"Yes, please," Raymond said. "It's Dan's birthday, so we're here to celebrate!"

Kimberly came over and gave me a hug, "Happy birthday, Danny!" she said.

Raymond of course laughed and smiled as he always did whenever he heard her call me by that name. We enjoyed our meal and afterwards Kimberly brought us over two large pieces of chocolate cake, one with a lit candle on it.

"These are on the house, guys," she said, and she placed them on the table in front of us.

"Happy birthday," she said again, and gave me another hug.

We sat there enjoying our cake when I suddenly remembered something. "We never went into Toronto to get your stereo receiver thingy," I said.

"I was going to say something, but it slipped my mind as well," Raymond answered.

"Is it still on sale, hun?" I asked

"Yeah, the sale runs for another week," he said.

"Why don't we drive into Toronto next Sunday for something to do and check it out it?" I said. "There's no racing, plus, I'll be finished extra early because it's Sunday. Maybe we can even visit Rozz at the same time."

"Really, babe? You won't believe the difference in the sound quality once I get it all hooked up. I could kiss you right here and now," he said. "Plus, I always like seeing Rozz."

"Sure, why not?" I said. "I always love your kisses."

I could see the joy radiating off Raymond's face at the thought of upgrading his stereo system.

"Thanks, babe," he said.

We paid our bill to Kimberly, gave her another hug, and left for home.

Once home, Raymond found the flyer with his Aiwa equalizer in it.

"Plus, I need a couple of these special cables to hook it all together," he said.

"What if we took $400 out of our treasure chest? Would that cover it, hun?" I asked.

"That should be more than enough, babe," Raymond said.

The next Sunday morning, we drove into Toronto and to the electronics store.

As we looked around, a nice guy came over to help us. "Can I assist you with anything, guys?"

Raymond brought out his flyer and mentioned he's interested in his Aiwa receiver and equalizer thingy.

"Great choice. They're over here." The clerk took us over to the Aiwa section.

"Here it is." He showed us the one on display.

Raymond and the salesman got into the mumbo jumbo jargon of receivers, equalizers, and speakers, all a foreign language to me.

After locating the right wires and cables, we headed up to pay. While at the cashier, the salesman once again came over to us. "Hey guys, I forgot to tell you, we're also having a promotion that if you spend over three hundred dollars, you get a twenty-dollar discount off the purchase of any LPs," he said.

"Awesome," Raymond said. "Can I go have a look at your albums then?"

"Sure," and the salesman showed us their LP section.

After looking over the entire selection, Raymond decided on Pink Floyd's album, "The Wall," and a Duran Duran LP. "I've always wanted these, and I'm surprised I never got them already."

We took it back to the cashier, and Raymond paid for our purchase.

"Thanks, guys," the cashier said, and we carried Raymond's equalizer to the car.

"That wasn't as much as I anticipated. We still have about eighty dollars left. Did you want to visit Rozz, hun?" I asked.

"Sure, we could stop by and say hello. Maybe I should call first just to make sure it's ok," Raymond answered.

We put the albums, receiver, and equalizer into the trunk of his Monza, and searched for a payphone so Raymond could call Rozz.

Raymond searched his pockets for looking for some loose change and came up empty.

"Do you have a quarter, babe?" I dug into my pocket and pulled out some loose change. Luckily, I had a couple of quarters.

"Hey, Rozz, it's Raymond. Is it okay if Dan and I drop by for a quick visit?" I heard Raymond ask.

"Oh, okay, we don't want to interfere," he said. "Are you sure it's alright?

"Great, we'll see you in a few minutes." Raymond hung up the phone.

"What was that about?" I asked.

"Peter stayed the night and he's still there." Raymond chuckled. "But Rozz said it's alright and to come on over anyways."

"Let's find a bake shop and get some bagels or something," I said.

"Good idea, babe."

We managed to find a coffee shop that had some freshly baked bagels and purchased a dozen to take to Rozz's place.

Raymond and I got to Rozz's apartment, buzzed at the lobby, and went upstairs.

We were greeted by Rozz and a shirtless Peter.

"Peter, go get a shirt on, for heaven's sakes," Rozz said.

"I'm sure the boys have seen more than one shirtless man before," he joked.

"It's all good, Rozz," I said. "It's a guy thing. In fact, at our place you're lucky to find Raymond wearing anything at all when we're home alone."

"That's not true!" Raymond said, somewhat embarrassed, and I looked over and raised my eyebrows at him.

"Okay, well, at least not when company is over," he jokingly replied.

"That's reassuring," said Rozz. "Remind me always to buzz from the lobby first." We all had a fun laugh.

Rozz then made some coffee and tea, and we enjoyed the freshly baked bagels.

"Is everything going okay with you guys?" Rozz asked.

"Yup, all is great," said Raymond. "There is one thing I've been wanting to ask you."

He then went on to explain about that day when he and their mom were cleaning out the garden, and her asking how I was.

"Do you think she knows about us?" Raymond asked.

"Yes, Raymond, Mom knows about you and Dan," she said. "She asked me if you two were a couple a long time ago. I didn't want to tell you as I was worried that you might be more scared than ever, wondering if Dad knew or would find out. Maybe, I should have told you, but I know Mom was always worried about Dad finding out."

You could tell Rozz was deeply concerned about how

worried their mom was regarding their dad.

"Mom said her biggest pleasure was seeing how happy you two are when you are together. She mentioned she could see the joy and bond you have when you are with each other. I personally know she'd never tell Dad, simply because it would cause you, and her, too much heartache and grief if he was to find out."

Rozz continued, saying, "She's put up with a lot of crap from Dad over the years, and I know she would never tell him. Mom would never give him the satisfaction of being so cruel by letting him know, as she knows Dad would unleash his evil, homophobic hate."

Raymond and I looked at one another in bewilderment.

"Don't worry," Rozz said. "That was well over two years ago that she asked about you two. She isn't going to say anything now. Besides, I hate to say it, but I know that she is physically afraid of Dad as well, so her secret is best kept silent."

We finished our visit, and we all gave each other a hug goodbye.

While driving home, Raymond was quiet.

"Are you alright, hun?" I asked.

"I'm okay, babe, but for some reason, I really have a dislike for my father right now. I don't like how he's kept a stranglehold on my mom, on me, and even now on you. I feel like telling him about us, and that I'm as gay, as gay can be," Raymond said. "I know he'd never be happy for us, but I'd love for him to find out that he in fact fathered a gay man."

"Don't, hun. Don't do that," I answered. "It would only cause grief for your mom, as she is the one who has to live with him. Your mom would probably go to your defense if your dad found out and think of how he would react to her then. No, I think it's best we keep it quiet, like Rozz says."

"You're probably right, babe," he answered. "I just hate the thought of him in control."

I reached out my hand and held onto his. He smiled back, and I knew he felt better after thinking it through.

"Let's go listen to how 'Gloria' sounds now," I said, "or even the Righteous Brothers."

"Damn, that's the album I should have gotten. I only have 'Unchained Melody' on cassette. Sounds totally crap," Raymond said.

After we got home, Raymond set up his new stereo and connected all the necessary cords, wires, and cables. "Now that's a beautiful sound," he said, as Laura Branigan filled the apartment with sounds of her singing "Gloria."

I had to admit to Raymond that he was right. The sound was phenomenal compared to before.

CHAPTER 34
Late spring 1984.

Over the next few months, it seemed as if the pressure was mounting about allegations from work and our families regarding Raymond and myself being together so much.

Persons at our work and family members kept asking why we never dated women.

A close relative of mine came right out and asked, "I've never seen you with a girl. You're not a fucking faggot, are you?"

I always answered the same. "I'm concentrating on the horses. I don't have time for a girlfriend," which kept them satisfied for the time being

Raymond was also getting some heat at work. There was a chance for a promotion within his company, but his one manager, who was a complete homophobe, always treated Raymond poorly, criticizing the gay community whenever Raymond was present, almost taunting him to admit it.

"Hey, Ray, I see in the paper where another queer got beaten up last night. They're only good for that, you know. I have absolutely no sympathy for them. It's a waste having them around. Believe me, if I knew there were any queers working here, I'd fire them on the spot."

This was basically what his manager told Raymond one day in his office. Back then, there were very few laws protecting people from sexual discrimination or sexual discrimination in the workforce. Even when these new laws were in place, it wasn't easy to come out as gay in the workplace and face your coworkers. Many gay people felt safer and more comfortable simply not coming out at all and remained silent.

Although it was no longer illegal to be gay, there were still many negative stereotypes and prejudices around it. Raymond desperately wanted to get ahead within the company, as the computer industry was rapidly evolving, and he was deeply knowledgeable in the field. While in the apartment one evening, Raymond started talking about work. We were lounging on the sofa, relaxing after dinner, when he mentioned how frustrating his boss could be.

"I wish my manager wasn't so homophobic," he said. "I swear he thinks I'm gay and deliberately tries to taunt me over it. There are a couple of positions for advancement in the company, but I would need his approval and recommendation to apply. I'm certainly not ashamed of being gay, but why do some people make you have to hide it just to get their acceptance?"

"I know, hun. It's much like David, from up at the cottage, was talking about. Hopefully, one day it will change. But for now, what if you play his game? What if you asked a girl out on a date and then told him about it the next day?" I asked. "Do you think that would make a difference?"

"I think it would be more believable if I was able to show him that I was with a woman," he said.

"I'm also feeling uncomfortable when I'm at my parent's place. Maybe we both need to ask a girl out," I answered.

We decided then and there that if we both dated a woman, it might relieve some of the negativity that seemed to be hanging around us, and ease anyone's thoughts that we were together, or gay.

I can still remember my personal feelings about looking for a woman to ask out, only to appease a certain few. I felt as if I was not only being untruthful to my born lifestyle, but also being cruel to whom I was looking to date.

Raymond thought of a woman at work, and I also thought of someone in the backstretch at the track. The thought of either of us dating a woman was somewhat horrendous, to be perfectly honest, but we could not change the world, so we thought we should try to blend in with the status quo. We could remain single, but we knew by being single, we would continue to get the same reaction from home and friends. Why aren't you dating? Are you going to remain a bachelor your entire life? Let me hook you up with someone.

I recall asking a girl out on a date. I certainly was not attracted to her, but I knew I had to try, or at least make a visible effort toward the opposite sex to satisfy, or reconfirm to some, that I was straight.

She worked for a trainer as a groom in the same barn as me, and we would often buy the other a coffee if we were going down to the cafeteria.

Being my gay, naive self, I never considered her friendliness or very flirtatious nature, anything more than two people just being friends.

She lived in the girl's dormitory at the racetrack, and I later learned, not that it bothered me any, that she enjoyed her many man friends.

One day, not aware that her previous flirting was a sign that she was already interested in me, I asked if she would be interested in going out for dinner.

She agreed, and a couple of nights later, we went for dinner and a movie. I had never felt so awkward at being in my wrong element in all my life. All I kept thinking about was Raymond at home.

While in the movie theater, she kept trying to get closer and would touch my hand or thigh, making me extremely uncomfortable and nervous. We finished with the movie and headed back to the racetrack. She said there was something she wanted to show me in her dorm room, and again, being the naive gay guy that I was, and unaware of a female's intention, the first thing I thought of was it must be something horse related.

We entered her room, and she immediately started kissing and groping me. *What the fuck is this?* I thought.

She pulled off her sweater and undid her bra. Her boobs were staring me in the face.

Terror started racing through my mind, and I felt like yelling, "Raymond, help me! I'm trapped!"

She started undoing my pants and taking off my shirt. "Fuck, you're hairy!" she said. "I love that."

I didn't know what to do. I wasn't turned on sexually at all. She took my manhood into her mouth, trying to wake him up. Eventually, after thinking of every gay fantasy that I'd ever wanted to try, and with my eyes shut, I was aroused.

We got onto the bed, and she pulled me on top of her. "Do me, Dan. Do me!" she kept repeating.

I recall seeing some straight porn once, so I thought I should kiss her boobs. After concentrating on them, she started pushing my head toward her down below.

"Go down on me," she begged.

Oh My God. No! I thought. *I've never even seen one of those before in person.*

I went back to her boobs. where she said, "You're a boob man."

I'm a boob man? At first, I thought she was somewhat joking about my lack of experience and referring to me as a boob. *Get me out of here,* I thought.

She then persistently pushed me back down and pulled her waist up. There it was; something I dreaded doing. Just the thought of having to continue was making me soft. I couldn't do it. I just couldn't. *Raymond!*

Before I lost total arousal, I climbed on top and tried putting him inside her. I closed my eyes and went back to my gay fantasy world. She finally got him inside, and we started.

What am I doing? I kept repeating to myself in my mind.

We just kept going at it and at it. I knew I would never reach the finish, as I wasn't interested in, nor did I want to climax.

After about half an hour, she said, "Stop, it's starting to hurt."

I am unsure what her reaction was, but I recall I never kissed her good night, and quickly got dressed and ran back to the car. All I wanted to do was to go back to the apartment and be with my Raymond. I raced home, ran upstairs, and went inside. Raymond was already in bed and awake, waiting for me.

"How was it, babe?" Raymond asked.

"Let me go have a quick shower first," I answered.

I went and showered, and soaped, and soaped, and soaped, all over, toweled dry, then joined Raymond in bed.

"So, how was it, stud?" Raymond teased.

"Have you ever seen a woman's pussy in real life?" I asked. "They look complicated as to what is actually going on inside of it," I said.

Raymond started to laugh and said, "You had sex on your first date? What a stud!"

I lay beside my Raymond and held his hand.

"She kept pushing my head down toward her woohoo, and I'd keep trying to move it away," I told him. "It was awful, even with just one look. I thought I was going to toss my dinner."

By now, we were both howling in laughter.

"Did you stick the beast in?" Raymond said, laughing so hard I thought he was crying.

"I put him inside her and just kept going till she begged me to stop," I said, all the while trying not to laugh so hard that I couldn't at least speak. "No matter how hard I tried, I couldn't blow. I just shut my eyes and went for the ride. What do guys see in those things? Yuck," I said.

"Did she orgasm?" Raymond asked.

"Fucked if I know. That never entered my mind to ask her. She never said anything if she did," I replied. "I think she was mad at me."

By now, Raymond and I couldn't stop laughing.

"You, totally gay, but trying to be straight, adorable newbie," Raymond said, holding back the tears of laughter. "You don't ask her if she had an orgasm. She'd moan and groan while having it."

"In that case, she definitely did not orgasm." I laughed. "She sounded like a bit of a tramp, to be honest, as she kept saying, "Fuck me, fuck me.""

We both lay back down on the bed together, laughing and giggling, and holding onto each other.

In a world full of straight people expecting you to be equally as straight as they are, my first thought was, *Holy crap, this is going to be difficult and frustrating. I'm not sure if I can convince anyone that I'm straight.*

I then started to question myself. *How difficult would it be to come out and tell everyone that I'm gay? How much criticism, rejection, bullying and possible physical abuse could there be to tell the world the truth?*

I was glad to be back in the apartment—back to what I deemed "my home, my normal, my life," and, more importantly, with "my Raymond."

CHAPTER 35
Late fall 1984.

A few weeks after my first female encounter, I was having a rough day at the track, and all I could think about was going home to the peace and comfort of the apartment, and to Raymond.

It was a cold, rainy morning with thunderstorms, and everything was muddy and soaking wet, including me. I had finished my daily chores and eagerly wanted to get home and out of those cold, wet clothes. It was just one of those days when nothing seemed to go right. My one horse was coming up lame with a new injury, and I had a wicked headache due to the pouring rain.

I just wanted some quiet time at home, snuggling up with my guy and forgetting about the world. It was Saturday, and neither of us had to work that night or on Sunday.

All I thought about was curling up on the couch and watching a movie with my hun.

I decided to stop and get Raymond and myself a cheese pizza for lunch. I then drove to the apartment and parked my car while the rain continued to pour down among the lightning and thunder. The rain was coming down even harder than before. I waited a couple of minutes for it to ease off, but it kept coming down in a torrential downpour.

After a gigantic boom of thunder, I decided to make a run for it. I raced the hundred feet or so to the front doors, holding the pizza upright, trying to avoid the rain.

Once in the lobby, my cardboard pizza box was completely drenched, and was already starting to get soggy and bend. The water was dripping down off me and making a puddle by the elevators. The elevator doors opened, and I went upstairs, looking forward to nothing more than the comfort and peace of being home.

I got off the elevator to the loud sounds of the Ramones singing, "I Wanna Be Sedated," echoing down the hall.

Once inside the apartment, I saw Raymond doing his best Johnny Ramone air guitar impersonation while singing out the repeated lyrics of "I Wanna Be Sedated" and putting on a rather impressive, energetic show.

I quickly lowered the volume, trying to ease the pounding in my head that it was causing.

"What? What's the matter, babe? Too loud?" he asked.

"Just a bit. I could hear it getting off the elevator," I said.

"No fucking way? Really? Crap, I didn't realize I had it that loud. I hope the old fart next door doesn't complain," Raymond said and turned it completely off.

"I don't think he's home, hun," I answered. "His parking spot is next to mine, and his car hasn't been there for a couple of days now. I hope he's alright."

"We'll ask Mrs. H. She keeps track of everyone on this floor. She'll know," said Raymond.

Just then, a huge rumble of thunder shook the apartment.

"Hopefully, with all this loud thunder, our neighbors didn't notice the live concert going on in here," I joked.

"Are you okay, babe? You look like a wet lost puppy," Raymond asked.

"I have a terrible headache, I'm drenched to the bone, and I'm totally exhausted," I said. "I had a rough day at the track, hun. I just want to be home, put the day behind me, and be with you."

I put the soggy pizza on the kitchen counter and turned to look for Raymond. He took me by the hand, and we went into the bedroom. He got me out of my wet clothes, toweled me dry, and then helped me slip into my comfy gray fleece sweatpants. I then just wrapped my arms around him. "Thanks, hun. I just want to be with you," I said, and we went and sat on the couch under our favorite blanket.

"What went wrong today, babe? Just a bad day?" he asked.

I snuggled up close against Raymond's shoulder.

"The one horse we have stumbled coming off the trailer, and afterwards, he was walking with a noticeable limp. I had the vet look at him, and he thought it wasn't anything too serious, but he may have to be scratched from racing on Monday. We'll see how it goes, but I think it's best to rest him, rather than take a chance on further injury by racing," I said. "What did you do today, hun?"

"After you left at six this morning, I sleepily went back to bed, then afterwards did the dishes, and around ten a.m. I called Rozz to say hi," Raymond said.

"How is Rozz doing?" I asked.

"Great. She asked if we wanted to join her and Peter for dinner on Wednesday at her place. Do you feel like going, babe?" Raymond asked.

"Sure, we can go," I replied. "We haven't seen them in a while. I'll get some flowers to take."

"Let me get the pizza," Raymond said and went into the kitchen. "It's cold, babe."

"I'm not really that hungry now, hun. Can you bring me a Tylenol and a Coke?" I asked.

Raymond brought me my Coke and Tylenol, and a root beer for himself. We settled into watching TV, with a very content, and very loudly purring, Mr. Muggs sitting on the back of the couch. A short time later, I fell asleep on Raymond's shoulder. He gently laid my head down on a pillow on his lap and covered me up with the blanket, while he continued to watch TV.

I must have slept for a couple of hours as when I woke up, Raymond was at the door talking with Mrs. H. I heard Raymond thank her and then he came back into the living room.

"What did Mrs. H want, hun?" I asked.

"She brought us over your favorite casserole for dinner. You know, the one with the ground beef, and mac and cheese all mixed up together, plus a chocolate cake. She thought you could do with some comfort food, having to work outside in such rotten weather," Raymond said. "We can have the pizza for breakfast."

"She is such a sweetheart," I said. "She's always thinking of us. Remind me to get some flowers for her as well."

"Feeling better now, babe?" Raymond asked.

"Yeah, thanks for letting me sleep," I answered. "I think I was just overtired from all the late nights of racing this week. I'm hungry. Shall we eat?"

Raymond got some plates and put it all on the small kitchen table we had, but naturally we ended up taking it to the couch and the coffee table.

"I don't know what this is called, but Mrs. H sure does make a delicious mac and cheese and beef casserole," I said.

Mr. Muggs had his usual sniff and a couple of sips of Raymond's Mug root beer, and the three of us all settled in for an enjoyable, relaxing night of watching TV together.

CHAPTER 36
Spring 1985.

The next few months rolled by, and although Raymond dated a couple of women, he never had sex with them. He even took one girl home to meet his parents. They were very pleased to finally see him with a girl, and they certainly approved of her.

Yet, whenever I was around, his father never seemed to let up questioning Raymond about me, and why I was constantly around.

One day, Raymond was all excited about a job posting he had heard about through his work. By this time, he was more deeply involved with the computers at work and was becoming very computer savvy.

"It's a posting out west, babe, in Vancouver. The pay is phenomenal, there's a chance for a promotion, and we can get away from my overbearing father," Raymond said. "I even made it a point to show up with that one girl at my manager's office, to calm his homophobic ideas. He's suggesting I apply."

My heart sank. I was dreading hearing this. Just the thought of us not being together upset me.

I wanted Raymond to get ahead and to especially get away

from his father. Even though I was deeply committed to the horses at this point, I somehow wanted out of the horse racing business altogether in order to be with Raymond.

Raymond and I talked about what we could do. I thought about going back to school and taking computer repair, at least have a trade if I were to go with Raymond out west.

I didn't want to go out there and train horses again. I was tired of the work hours and commitments needed in the horse-racing industry. It was a never-ending job of long days, having to tend to the horses 24/7, and in all types of weather. I often wished I had chosen a different profession, stayed in school, and gotten a better education.

I talked to my father about leaving the horse industry and going back to school and learning computer repair. I even applied for funding at one of the computer colleges in the city. He wanted me to stay with the horses and couldn't understand my sudden interest in the computer field.

I was the trainer of our horses now, and deeply involved with them financially. My father and I had an interest in about eight horses of various worth, including one who was one of the best racehorses on the grounds, and worth close to six figures.

It was a confusing time for me. I wanted to leave the horses and go with Raymond, should he get that position, but I was uncertain about what I'd do once I got out there. I put it out of my mind and waited to hear what Raymond was going to do and see what would happen.

Raymond applied for the position in Vancouver and surprisingly got a rave recommendation from his current, homophobic manager. The next few weeks were one of uncertainty. It was like living on pins and needles, waiting for any correspondence from out west.

In order to carry on the illusion, Raymond and I both continued to date women just to satisfy family and coworkers.

One day, I entered the cafeteria at the racetrack and saw a very pretty blonde-haired girl sitting with the family of the groom who worked for me.

She instantly attracted my attention. She was incredibly attractive, with fluffy, curly blonde hair and an amazing smile. I immediately thought, *Those women were only attracted to jocks and sports-affiliated guys. I'm neither, nor do I have a hope in hell of her ever pursuing me.*

Later I asked Paul, the guy who worked for me, who the attractive blonde girl was.

"That's my cousin, Susan," he said. "She's interested in horses, so I told her to come to the track one day."

"Maybe you could introduce her to me the next time she's here," I said. "She could always come see our horses if she wants to."

I was getting more confused by the day. Why was I suddenly attracted to a young lady now, especially at a time when I feared I could lose my partner and the love of my life?

"She's coming with my father to see Bob's horses," he said.

Bob was a good friend of mine and an experienced trainer. We had been stabled beside each other a couple of times in the past. Bob co-owned a horse with Paul's father, who was Susan's uncle, hence the connection.

I remember asking Susan out on a date on two occasions, and each time she said that she was busy. This only confirmed my suspicions of not being jock enough for her. I once again asked her out, and for the third time, and not surprisingly, she was busy once more, but she did say that she was free on her birthday.

I was feeling so lost. I still couldn't understand my attraction to her but thought fate must know why. After three attempts at asking her out, I finally gave up. I convinced myself that she only dated jocks, which I knew I wasn't.

I sat in my car and thought about how my life was in shambles. At that precise moment, I wanted to yell, "What the hell is wrong with me? How can life be so difficult?"

For some strange reason, I suddenly got very mad at my own family. I got angry at not being able to tell them what my "real life" story was about, about my love for Raymond, and about me being gay all these years.

I was so confused and unsure of what I should do, and what my future held. I knew deep down that I probably would never be able to tell them, which made me that much more frustrated and angry.

After calming down a bit, I began thinking about Raymond. If Raymond were ever to get that job in Vancouver, and if I were to go to live with him, what would his father say? He'd know that we were together. What would the financial consequences be for Raymond? What would Raymond's new employer say if they ever found out we were gay lovers?

I then thought about Susan. Maybe she truly was busy, as she previously told me. At least she had given me the option of taking her out on her birthday.

I thought the best thing for Raymond and myself, would be to allow Raymond to go out west. I just didn't want to think about it anymore, as it totally depressed me and brought me to tears.

I felt like driving home and telling my parents, "Mom, Dad, I'm getting out of the horses and going to sell all my interest in them, sell my truck and trailer, everything. I'm then going to be moving out to Vancouver with my boyfriend, Raymond. Yes, my boyfriend, meaning that I'm gay. So, deal with it!"

The thought of me ever doing that made me feel happier and at peace. Then why couldn't I do it? I started having a conversation with myself. *Because you're a coward. That's why.*

At that moment, I desperately wanted to be with Raymond.

CHAPTER 37
Early summer 1985.

A few weeks later, we got the news.

I got back to the apartment, and Raymond was sitting on the couch with a letter in his hand. The look on his face explained it all. I felt myself go white and cold.

"I got the job, babe," he said. "They won't be needing me for quite a few months, probably not till early next year. They've asked that I take some extra computer courses, which they're willing to pay for."

"Oh, hun, I'm so proud of you. I really, really am." I went over and sat beside him. We both knew what this meant. We hugged each other and sat there quietly. I tried to hold back the tears. Although we knew we would eventually be separated, at least we still had some time together.

Eventually, Raymond started taking computer courses at one of the computer technical institutes regarding programming and a certain software course. He no longer pursued his interest in dating any women.

I eventually asked Susan out on her birthday. Why she ever agreed was a mystery to me, as I was no jock. We went to dinner and, surprisingly, I had a nice evening, even if the server accidentally dropped our entire meal on the floor beside us.

We had what seemed to be a fun night out together, and I thought about seeing her again. I drove her home, and I somehow felt a bit more comfortable, as she was such a nice, honest, and fun person to be around.

I walked her to her front door, and, out of total nervousness, I believe I gave her the fastest kiss humanly possible. Little did I know at the time that this beautiful young lady would forever change my life going forward and I'm forever in her debt. She saved my life from a ruin that I was sure to follow if we hadn't met.

I now know for certain that without Susan in my life, I would have ended it all, as the closeted gay lifestyle, combined with the never-ending thought of not being with my Raymond, would have been too depressing for me to deal with, and I easily would have taken my own life out of regret.

Raymond and I continued with our daily routine, with me in the barns, Raymond in the grandstand, and our life in the apartment as we always had.

Raymond had told his parents about the job offer, and they were pleased for him.

I continued to see Susan over the next few months. Even though my connection to Raymond was still very strong and solid, I found I was getting accustomed to being around Susan and looked forward to seeing her. I didn't tell her about my connection with Raymond.

One night, Susan was at the track, and Raymond dropped by as well. Raymond stayed at the opposite end of the barn. I walked over to him when I noticed him standing there.

"Hey, babe, I just wanted to see what Susan looks like," he said. "She's very pretty."

"Let me introduce you to her," I said.

"I don't think that's a good idea. She'll ask who I am, and then we'd have to make up something."

I felt sad, as I knew what Raymond and I were both thinking. It was the beginning of one relationship and the closing of another.

I nonchalantly pushed Raymond out of view and kissed him. "You'll always be my Raymond, hun."

"Will you be at the apartment tonight?" he asked.

"Yes, hun, I'll be home," I answered.

Raymond smiled, grabbed my hand, and left.

I went back to Susan and eventually drove her back home to Toronto, then immediately drove all the way back out to the apartment in Milton.

I so much wanted time with Raymond alone.

CHAPTER 38
Late summer 1985.

Once back home in the apartment, Raymond and I curled up on the couch and started watching TV.

"How are things with you and Susan working out?" Raymond asked.

"So far, it's been fun. We seem to enjoy each other's company," I said.

It was awkward for me to talk to Raymond about it, for I felt as if I was betraying him by also seeing Susan. I knew it was difficult for him as well, as we both felt as if we were holding on to each other for dear life, knowing one day we'd have to let go.

"Could we talk about something else, hun?" I asked.

"Sorry, babe. Forgive me. I know what you mean, and I won't bring it up again," Raymond answered back.

"Thanks, hun," I replied. "I wish we could get away somewhere, you and me together for some alone time. Like up at the cottage, or maybe even go camping somewhere. We need a break from this constant overthinking about the future."

"That's a good idea, babe. My folks are constantly up at the cottage lately. Camping does sound fun, though," Raymond answered.

We both agreed that we needed some relaxing fun time with just the two of us, without anyone around. Both of us had been camping a few times before, but we were no outdoorsmen.

"I'll stop at the information center on the highway on my way home from the track. I'm sure they must have some info on the different provincial parks around," I said.

We eventually went to bed and spent the night talking and cuddling each other. Whenever Raymond and I cuddled up close, it always felt as if an emotional wall of security encompassed us both, and it blocked out all of life's troubles and hurt.

The next day, I stopped at the tourist kiosk, gathered up some information pamphlets that were available, and took them home. That night, while we watched TV, Raymond and I looked through the information at the different provincial parks.

"What about Algonquin Provincial Park?" I asked.

"That's a long way away, plus it's so big. I'd be afraid of getting lost or getting eaten by a real bear," answered Raymond. "What about something closer, and not so intimidating? I always thought of Algonquin as so remote with no others around."

"True," I said and continued looking.

We finally decided to go to Halfway Lake Provincial Park, about four and a half hours away.

I arranged to have someone look after the horses, and Raymond booked the weekend off so we could get away.

I brought a heavy old canvas tent from home, sleeping bags, blankets, and a Coleman stove and lantern. We also took our small hibachi barbeque, which we used on the balcony.

I had gone grocery shopping and got the basics of bread, pop, bacon, eggs, potatoes, hamburgers, and a couple of steaks. I put it all in a couple of coolers topped with blocks of ice and wrapped in our blankets for extra insulation.

Once again, our beloved Mr. Muggs was cared for by his Auntie Rozz. She came over and stayed at the apartment while we went away for the weekend. We packed up the car and headed out on our wilderness adventure one Friday morning.

"Have fun, guys," Rozz said as she waved us off.

"Thanks, Rozz. Love you," hollered Raymond from the car.

"This is going to be fun," he said, as he settled in the driver's seat with me in the passenger seat.

After a couple of hours, we both needed a break.

"I'm getting hungry, babe. What about you?" Raymond asked.

"Yeah, I'm hungry as well, plus I have to pee," I answered back.

It was early afternoon, and we decided to stop for something to eat after reaching the next town, which seemed as if it was in the middle of nowhere. We went inside the small diner, sat down at a table, and reviewed their menus, which were in a small picture frame on the table. It wasn't too busy, with only about a dozen other patrons enjoying a meal.

A young girl came over. "Hi guys, can I take your order?" she asked with a very friendly smile.

"We'll have two cheeseburgers with fries, a Coke, and I'll have a root beer, please," Raymond answered.

She took our order and handed it to the guy through the kitchen window.

"She certainly had her eye on you," Raymond said quietly and teasingly gave me a wink.

"What do you mean, on me?" I replied. "If anyone should attract the stares, it's you."

"All I know is she kept looking at you and smiling," Raymond said with a grin.

The young server came back with a cold bottle of Coke and a root beer with two glasses.

"Enjoy, guys. Your burgers are almost ready," she said.

I looked up at her, and sure enough, she was smiling and staring back at me. "Thanks," I said.

"Always a pleasure," she replied.

Raymond sat there with a big goofy grin on his face. "Told ya." He chuckled. Then he leaned forward and whispered, "Don't worry, babe. I'll tell her you're gay when she comes back."

I shook my head and smiled while Raymond tried to contain his laughter.

We ate our burgers and asked for our bill. The young girl placed the bill by Raymond.

"She didn't charge us for your Coke. Not fair!" Raymond quietly protested in fun. We left a five-dollar bill for the meal and another dollar bill toward the Coke and tip.

I looked over at the young server, and I gave a wave. While walking out, I whispered to Raymond, "I swear she won't stop looking at me."

We got back in the car and started back driving.

"You don't give yourself credit, babe. You turn guys' heads," Raymond said.

"Yeah, right, but she wasn't a guy, was she? Great, I'm attracting women now. How depressing," I jokingly answered.

"Works for me," Raymond replied, "plus I don't want guys eyeing you up anyway."

We both laughed and continued driving.

Soon, we reached the park and drove up to the gate. The park ranger came out and took our license plate number, names, and our deposit.

"It's pretty quiet here this weekend, guys. You can have site E4. It's a nice site, up high and dry. Just follow the road to the end, turn left, and it's the site on the bend overlooking the river. You better hurry, as it looks like it's going to start raining soon," he said.

"Thanks a lot," Raymond replied, and we drove into the park.

"He was right about no one being here," I said. "It's somewhat creepy."

"I agree," Raymond answered. "The forest zombies probably came out in the middle of the night and snatched everyone while they were sleeping in their sleeping bags. Human sausage rolls."

"Would you stop that!" I said. "I hate the thought of those things. Besides, if anyone is going to get your sausage, it'll be me!"

We both laughed as we slowly drove through the campground until we got to site E4 and started to unpack the car. We could hear thunderclaps off in the distance.

"Crap, we'd better hurry, babe. That sounds like it's getting really close," Raymond said.

We quickly set up the tent and securely tied the tarps to the ground and surrounding trees just as the wind picked up. Once inside, we blew up the air mattress, opened the sleeping bag, and placed some blankets and pillows on top. We brought in the coolers and lantern just in time for the rain to start.

"We made it just in time, babe," Raymond said as it started to downpour.

The two of us watched out the front mesh window opening. The front door tarp was propped up on poles, protecting us from the storm as the rain poured down.

We were thankful for this site as it was on a hump, and the rain simply rolled away from the tent and down toward the river behind us. By now, it was early evening with hardly any daylight left. It was starting to get dark.

"So much for a fun camping trip," Raymond said as he took off his t-shirt, showing off his hairy self while continuing to look outside.

"I love the rain, hun," I said, now lying on the air mattress. "You and me inside, warm and dry, while we listen to the rain outside. Sounds very romantic to me." I reached over and tickled his side.

Suddenly, Raymond jumped and cried, "Oh my God, babe. Look, look over there. There's a bear!"

I quickly jumped up and again looked out the mesh window. "Where? Where is it, Raymond? I don't see it," I said, frightened out of my wits as one of the signs on the way into the park said, "Please, do not feed the bears. Clean up all garbage."

"I don't see any bear!" I continued looking out the window, searching through the rainstorm, trying to get a glimpse of it. "Raymond, are you shitting me?"

"It's over here." Raymond laughed. "A 'bare' me!"

I looked around, and there he was, now in his glorious nakedness, lying on the blankets.

His beautiful hairy physique was at full attention, with the toes of his size-twelve feet wiggling in anticipation.

I crawled over and lay on top of him.

"Are you going to eat me, Mr. Bear?" I asked.

"Damn right I am. As soon as I get you naked!"

We quickly stripped off my clothes, and once again, I lay on top of my hairy man bear. Whether it was the fresh air of the wilderness, or whatever, we both were very eager to satisfy each other.

I lowered myself onto his chest as we kissed and kissed. I felt Raymond's hands all over my behind.

Now and then, he'd give me a quick slap on my rear end, which always heightened the experience.

I then settled into my favorite position. I felt him underneath me as I lowered myself down. It didn't take us long to get into an exhilarating rhythm.

We continued making love as the rain poured down and the thunder roared. It was beautiful, plus we could make all the noise of "encouragement" we wanted, without having to worry about anyone hearing us, which heightened the experience.

After we finished, it was still raining. We lay under the covers listening to the thunder and watching the flashes of lightning. I clung close to Raymond, with every lightning flash, anticipating another round of thunder.

It continued to rain as the late afternoon turned into evening and started getting dark outside.

"I better light the lantern, hun." I pumped up the Coleman lantern and gave the flint starter a few quick turns to ignite the gas.

Although we were stuck in the tent due to the storm, at least we felt content having the soft glow of the lantern and the cooler filled with food. I managed to make us some cheese and bologna sandwiches, along with a Coke and root beer.

It was quite cuddly and relaxing being together, secure and dry with the rain coming down. I had packed a deck of cards and our Scrabble board to pass the time away.

We decided to play "dirty" Scrabble till we got tired. We would often play dirty Scrabble in the apartment, where any word you'd ever heard could be used. It always made us laugh, especially intersecting dirty sexual words.

Suddenly there was a huge clap of thunder, and we both jumped, which spilled the Scrabble board, sending all the pieces flying.

"Fuck!" Raymond said.

"Well, if you insist," I replied, and we both giggled.

I turned the lantern down low, so there was at least some light, just enough to create a mild glow against the pitch black of the outside darkness. We both felt safe, secure, and content as we listened to the steady pelting of the rain on the tent's roof, with the sound of thunder and the sudden flashes of lightning.

We soon fell asleep curled up together in each other's embrace.

CHAPTER 39

The next morning, we woke up to a clear sky and no rain. It was a bit muddy, but was drying up quickly in the bright sunshine.

We set up a tarp over top of the picnic table, got out the Coleman stove, and I started making breakfast. On one burner, I had the frying pan with bacon and eggs, while on the other, the kettle was boiling water for tea. Once tea was made, I toasted some bread. Soon, we were enjoying our breakfast in the warmth of the sun.

"This is almost as comfortable as the apartment," I said jokingly.

"I love it out here, babe," Raymond answered back.

"I have to admit I was a bit afraid last night as it was so dark, and that thunder was so intense," I said.

"I'm glad I had you beside me, that's for sure. What shall we do today, babe?" Raymond asked.

"Once I clean up here, let's walk up to the park's general store. It's here on the map the park ranger gave us," I said.

I cleaned up from breakfast, and then we walked along the road to the store. The sun was hot, and after the previous day's rain, it was very humid, creating that wonderful wet smell that only comes from being in a forest.

We passed by a couple of other campers who waved and said, "Good morning!"

We never realized it, but now and then, we unconsciously held hands while walking. I don't think anyone saw us, and if they did, at least they were kind enough not to say anything. It felt so good to be holding each other's hand. I later thought about how something as simple as holding hands with the one you love could look so awkward to so many others. Two men holding hands just wasn't done back then.

At the general store, we looked around before deciding on our purchases: a small container of milk, a bag of ice, barbeque charcoal, and some dry firewood for a campfire later. We walked back to our campsite and put the firewood and charcoal by the picnic table, and then went inside the tent. I put the ice and milk in the cooler while Raymond flopped down on the air mattress. He decided to read his *Billboard* magazine while I took out my journal and wrote down some words about our day.

I look down and our hands are clasped as one,
A symbol of love and security that can't be undone.
As we walk, I can easily see
Why so many guys would be jealous of me.
What they'd give to be by your side,
Filling themselves with honor and pride.
But it's your inner beauty and looks that outshine
   them all,
Being beside such a handsome man makes one
   stand tall.
But I'm the luckiest man among any crowd,

*As I'm your forever-loving man and I'm
forever proud.*

Raymond, I love you.

That afternoon we basically just relaxed and laid around. We eventually walked down to the river and waded knee deep in the water until I saw a couple of leeches trying to swim toward me, and we hurriedly got out.

"I hate those blood-sucking things," I said as I shook all over. "They're disgusting!"

Raymond laughed, and we quickly looked over each of us to make sure none were attached.

I purposely pulled open the front of Raymond's bathing suit and looked inside. "Just checking for those nasty critters," I said. "A family of them could dine on him."

We laughed, walked back to our tent, and sat at the picnic table in the full heat of the sun. We decided to start getting dinner ready as it was getting late in the afternoon, so I lit some charcoal in our trusty hibachi.

I cut up some potatoes, mixed in some onions, green peppers, and butter, and wrapped it all up in some aluminum foil, and placed them on the hot coals to bake. After a while, I placed the two T-bone steaks on the hot grill.

Once everything was ready, we sat down at the picnic table to a great steak dinner and roasted vegetables.

"Remember that night we went for a steak dinner, babe, across the street from the track, and later on, you took me back to look at the horses?" Raymond said. "And then later, when we went to the tack room and you seduced me?"

"I seduced you?" I jokingly asked. "From what I recall, I think we basically ravished each other." We both nodded and laughed.

"Babe, can I ask you something?" Raymond said, staring at me.

"Of course, hun. Ask away," I replied.

"If we could, in this fucked up world of ours . . . if I asked you to marry me, would you?"

I stared at Raymond, knowing it was only a matter of time before the tears started rolling down my cheeks. "Oh, hun, I would marry you right here and now if I could. You know that I would," I answered.

Raymond then took hold of my hand and said the following words:

"I, Raymond Anthony Scott, take thee, Daniel Joseph Reynolds, to be my wedded husband, to have and to hold from this day forward, for better, for worse, for richer, for poorer, in sickness and in health, to love and to cherish, till death do us part, according to God's holy ordinance, and thereto I pledge thee my faith and pledge myself to you."

By now, tears were rolling down my face as I sat there holding Raymond's hand while staring into his beautiful eyes and listening to his every word.

"I guess being constantly told to pay attention all those years as a kid in church made me remember a few things," Raymond said.

We stared at each other, and not knowing what else to say, I said, "I do."

Raymond smiled, and rarely did he get too emotional, but I could see the tears starting to build up in his eyes as well. I leaned in close and rested my head on his shoulder.

Raymond had rolled up some small pieces of gold aluminum foil, from the baked potato, into two rings and slid one on each of our ring fingers. We hugged and sat side by side, finishing our wedding dinner, with a squirrel as our best man, and a couple of chipmunks chirping as witnesses congratulating us from in the trees above.

I then went back to my latest poem and changed its ending from "man" to "husband."

> *I look down and our hands are clasped as one,*
> *A symbol of love and security that can't be undone.*
> *As we walk, I can easily see*
> *Why so many guys would be jealous of me.*
> *What they'd give to be by your side,*
> *Filling themselves with honor and pride.*
> *But it's your inner beauty and looks that outshine*
> *them all,*
> *Being beside such a handsome man makes one*
> *stand tall.*
> *But I'm the luckiest man among any crowd,*
> *As I'm your forever-loving husband and I'm*
> *forever proud.*

> *Raymond, I love you.*

We finished dinner, cleaned up, and decided to go for a walk. We started walking along the road, and knowing we were alone, I purposely held Raymond's hand tightly in mine.

We passed by the campsite of two young women, lying side by side, each on their own outdoor chaise lounge.

Raymond and I both waved while still holding hands and gave a friendly, "Hi, girls!"

They then held hands, waved back, and with friendly smiles, said, "Hi, guys, have a nice evening!"

As we walked away, we mentioned how we could relate to the girls and probably vice versa.

Back at our campsite, we started a fire and sat around it. Off in the distance, we could hear the howl of either coyotes or wolves, which made me want to be held tight by Raymond.

I lit the lantern and stove, made some tea, and we sat down as a happily married couple, on our make-believe wedding night, watching the fire.

After a while, we decided to go to bed. Raymond jokingly lifted me up off my feet and carried me over to the tent.

"You're such a romantic, hun," I told him.

"And I'm lucky you don't weigh a lot." Raymond laughed.

We kissed each other as he put me down and went into our bridal or groom's tent.

That night, we made love once again for the longest time. It's difficult to explain how much joy and pleasure you can feel when the both of you are in love to the depths that we were.

The next morning it was starting to cloud over, and we decided to pack up early, while everything was still dry, and avoid any rain. We dismantled the tent and packed everything back into the car just in time before the rain started coming down once again.

We drove back the same way we had come and stopped at the same restaurant for something to eat. The same server came over to take our order and smiled.

"Hey, guys, you're back," she said.

Raymond mentioned we were camping for the weekend, but it looked like rain, so we decided to get back home.

"I love camping," she said. "What can I get you?"

Since it was still early, around ten a.m., we both decided on some eggs, bacon, toast, and tea.

Once we were finished with our breakfast, we paid our bill, left a tip, and waved to our server.

We drove the few hours home and were feeling somewhat better about life and ourselves.

CHAPTER 40

At home, we were greeted by Rozz and the never-ending meowing of Mr. Muggs.

"Does he always sleep with you two?" Rozz asked. "He never left my side. Not once did he sleep in his cat bed but curled up with me all night. I think he really missed you guys and was lonely."

Raymond picked up Mr. Muggs and held him to his chest. "How's my Mr. Mugginses?" He gave Mr. Muggs some well-deserved kisses. "I missed you sooo much."

I swear Mr. Muggs almost smiled as he started to purr very loudly.

"Why don't you stay for dinner, Rozz? We can order pizza," I said.

"Sure, don't mind if I do. I have tomorrow off, so I can stay for a while," Rozz said. "So, how was the camping trip?"

"We had a great time," Raymond said. "We even managed to get married, didn't we, babe?"

"What are you talking about?" Rozz asked, surprised and totally confused. Her expression was priceless, as if she had missed the memo that gay marriage was now legal.

"Yup, Raymond and I are officially married," I excitedly said. "A squirrel was our best man, and a couple of chipmunks were witnesses. Raymond performed the ceremony at the picnic table while we got dinner ready, and we both said, 'I do!'"

Raymond and I were so excited, telling it to Rozz as if it was a real wedding and wanting to tell her all the details.

We then explained the ceremony, and Rozz mentioned how we were both so cute it was almost sickening, but she loved us all the same.

Later, I began thinking about what it would be like to be a married couple. The freedom that a straight married couple had and took for granted, not having to worry about any prejudice or negative thoughts against them. However, it was a totally different story if you were a gay couple.

I'd be happy just to be accepted for being gay, let alone being part of a married couple.

I so much wanted to come out of the damn closet but felt suffocated in my attempt to tell others, especially my family, about Raymond and myself. I was still uncertain as to what I should do.

I still felt deep down inside that if I ever did tell my parents or family, I'd regret it, as they would forever condemn it and never recognize nor accept Raymond as my loving partner.

When will society open its eyes and hearts and allow the love between two men to be acceptable? I constantly thought.

I often wondered, *What would society think of as more acceptable: would society be willing to accept two men who loved and cared for each other, who wouldn't harm anyone, or would it be more willing to accept a husband and wife relationship, even if they knew the husband habitually beat his wife?*

It was a question that I would often ponder, as I knew

what most people would choose, and with their decision in mind, I felt bad for the wife. To this day, many people have an unchanging mindset, and they find it easier to condemn someone forever than to accept them.

Love is love, and it should never be pushed aside nor ignored simply because of someone's "expectations."

CHAPTER 41
Early 1986.

Another autumn and then Christmas had come. Like previous Christmases, we spent our time together on Christmas Eve exchanging presents and visiting Mrs. H. She knew about Raymond's leaving and was glad for him, but sad for us both.

One day, she asked me, "Dan, how much do you love Raymond?"

"More than anything I know of Mrs. H. I only wish I could go with him," I replied.

"That's why I'm asking," she said. "Make your life complete and go. Forget about what anyone else thinks."

If it was only that easy, I thought. I gave Mrs. Hutchinson a big hug and thanked her. Her thoughts would often come back to me over the years. "Make your life complete and go. Forget about what anyone else thinks."

To this day, those words will often echo in my mind, not only regarding Raymond and what might have been, but with many other aspects of life. It's for this reason that I often tell people—especially young people—if you are passionate about something, then go for it or at least give it a try.

Knowing this New Year's was our last together, I managed to be with Raymond and came up with an excuse to give to Susan. A few weeks into the New Year, Raymond got a letter from Vancouver again. He was advised that his job would start on May 1.

The company had recruits to assist in finding a place for him to live once he arrived.

We sat down and tried to get our lives together.

Raymond decided to drive out to Vancouver as he needed a car once he got out there anyway.

We had given our notice to the landlord that we would be moving out, and he was very sad to know we were leaving. I believe he knew we were a gay couple and always showed us kindness.

Some of the furniture in the apartment was stored at Raymond's parents' house, and some would be used up at their cottage. The new TV we gave as a gift to Mrs. H, which she was delighted to receive.

Our queen-size bed we gave to Eddie and Bill, and we knew it would be put to the test, like it was meant to be with us.

Rozz, the amazing sweetheart she was, was going to take our beloved Mr. Muggs.

As much as I wanted to take Mr. Muggs to my parents' place, we already had a cat. Plus, I thought it would be too stressful emotionally for me, as every time I'd see Mr. Muggs, I'd think of Raymond.

It was planned that Raymond would leave for Vancouver on Saturday, April 5, 1986. Time enough to drive out there and a couple of weeks to find a place. He was staying at a hotel once there, paid for by his new employer.

I dreaded the next few weeks. My mind couldn't concentrate on anything other than my Raymond. A couple of times, I missed the entry deadline for entering my horses in races, much to the displeasure of their owners.

Finally, the Friday that I feared the most came: the day before he was to leave. That night we just lay in bed talking. We weren't in the mood for lovemaking, but instead remembered the times we shared together. The apartment was almost empty except for the bed, which Eddie and Bill were picking up that same Saturday.

The next morning, Rozz met us downstairs. Raymond's car was packed full. This was the moment I had feared for the last few months. I never envisioned it happening, or us parting. All those years we had together as a hidden couple, so much in love that nothing could separate us. Now I felt that I had let both of us down—too much of a coward to go with him.

I wrapped my arms around Raymond, and we both started crying. "I'm sorry, hun. I should be going with you," I said.

Raymond held me tighter. "Fate brought us together, and this is what it had in store for us both, babe. I know you want to come, and I wish you could, but I understand how difficult it would be to tell your family and to leave the horses. I'll never forget you for as long as I live."

"I'll think of you every day. Hopefully, one day in the future, we will meet again," I tearfully replied.

"I love you, Dan."

"I love you, Raymond."

Raymond then hugged his sister Rozz and jumped into his car. With a quick wave and a slight honk, he was gone.

Rozz and I stood near the curb on the roundabout in front of the apartment's front entrance.

I started sobbing uncontrollably.

Rozz held me close.

"What am I going to do without him, Rozz? We were together for over five, almost six years." I cried.

Rozz stepped back, and with arms outreached, held me by my shoulders and looked at me.

"Look at me, Dan," Rozz said. "Life will continue. Raymond will forever be part of your life, as you will forever be with him in here." She placed her hand on my heart. "But don't forget to live. Don't pine away, but live life, along with your memories of the both of you."

She then gave me a big hug, and I continued to sob on her shoulder for a while.

"You have my number and know where I live should you ever need me," she lovingly said.

The next few days were a living hell for me.

I tried to stop thinking about Raymond, but the thought of never seeing him again kept me in an almost depressive state of mind. It was as if a big empty void was inside me, like part of me was gone. I also worried about Raymond traveling across the country on his own and wondered if he'd be lonely.

What did the future have in store for us both? I don't want another man if I can't have Raymond. He was my first love, and I wondered if it was possible for me to love again after loving him so intensely and deeply.

Even as I write this, it's difficult for me to remember those times without getting emotional.

CHAPTER 42
Late winter 2001.

I had put Raymond on such a high pedestal that, after he left, no other man was his equal. I still looked and thought about men but had no desire to date or become emotionally attached to another man.

Susan and I continued to date, and after a couple of years, I asked her to marry me. We have been fortunate to have a great marriage. Over the years, we worked hard, bought a nice home in the suburbs, and raised two wonderful daughters.

After getting married, and with the birth of my first daughter, I decided to leave the horse-racing industry. It had become a sport of winning at all costs, without any regard for the health of the animals. I sold all my interest in the horses, my truck and trailer, and left. I have no regrets about doing so.

During those years, and without my wife knowing, I had secret affairs with men. It's something I'm not immensely proud to admit, but nonetheless, it happened. They superficially satisfied my desires, but in no way did I become romantically involved with anyone, nor did I want to.

Through everything, I never forgot about Raymond, and often wondered how he was doing. Whenever I was having a bad day or was frustrated with my inner turmoil about being gay, I'd always think back to those days when we were together. How we met, the adventures we had, our life in the apartment together—these memories always made me smile.

Later, I got a job reading hydroelectric meters in the City of Toronto. It was a very steady job with a good income. Whenever I read the hydro meters on Church Street in the Gay Village, I always felt "at home and in my element."

It's a feeling that happens even today. When my man friend and I visit one of the gay bars in Toronto, my mind will race back to being with Raymond and the freedom one feels by being with one's fellow gay brothers.

Recently, while we were at the club one night, they started playing the song "Gloria." It instantly took me back to that night on the dance floor with Raymond and Eddie. I started looking to see if Raymond was on the dance floor. I knew he wouldn't be there, but it satisfied my curiosity. What if he was?

I then looked around to see if anyone was dancing to Raymond's dance moves for the song. This put a smile on my face, made me laugh, and got me dancing.

I recall reading the electric meter at a gay bar one afternoon. Back then, meter readers had to wear a uniform of a blue shirt and pants. As I was leaving, the bartender jokingly mentioned, "I love a man in uniform."

I replied, with a smile, "See, that's where you and I are different. I much prefer a man completely out of uniform." I gave him a thumbs-up while the patrons there at the bar laughed.

On another occasion one summer, I was reading meters and knocked on the door of the house to gain access to their meter in the basement. At the time, many meters were installed inside the home. A big, burly, shirtless bear came to the door. After catching my breath and staring at the furry chest in front of me, I finally blurted out, "Good morning, here to read your electric meter."

"Sure thing, no problem. Come on in, it's downstairs," the beautiful bear replied, and he led me to the basement. He opened the meter cabinet on the wall and stepped back.

I stepped forward and started reading his meter. I immediately felt the bristles of that beautiful hairy chest lean against the shirt on my back. I'm sure he felt me tense and quiver as he asked, "Did I use a lot of electricity this month?"

"It's coming in as a normal reading. All is good," I stammered and tried to make my way out. The big bear of a man then raised his arms and put them over my shoulders to shut the meter cabinet door. For a moment, I could smell his musk and paused.

He gently pushed his crotch against my backside, and I could tell he was aroused.

I then got extremely nervous about what was happening, and I quickly ducked under his arms, nervously thanked him for his help and started to leave.

"Hope to see you next time," he said. "Have yourself a good day."

I was so afraid of situations like this simply because I didn't want to put my job in jeopardy. Plus, I was always scared of being in a stranger's home, not knowing who or what their intentions were.

I quickly went up the stairs and went back outside.

CHAPTER 43
Late winter 2001.

One day, while in Toronto reading meters, I recall having a very hectic and frustrating day, as all the people calling back were unavailable to meet me that day. I can't remember the exact date, but I recall there was still some snow on the ground.

I would often leave my cell phone number at different places of business or with superintendents of apartment buildings, requesting they call me so I could return to read their electric meters. This would result in a more accurate bill instead of an "estimate."

I had gone to numerous buildings that day and was unable to gain access. Once again, my cell phone rang.

"Hello?" I asked.

"Is this Dan? Dan Reynolds?" the male caller asked.

"Yes, this is Dan. How may I help you?" I replied.

"It's Raymond. Raymond Scott," the caller answered.

A strange feeling overwhelmed me. I was instantly taken back to the apartment, and the two of us still together.

I felt short of breath as my heart started to race. "Raymond?" I practically shouted over the phone. "Is this really you? My Raymond? My hun? Where are you?"

"I'm in Toronto for business and was hoping to see you. Where are you?" Raymond eagerly replied.

"I'm in Toronto as well," I stammered. "I'm just finishing up work at Toronto Hydro on Carlton Street. Where in Toronto are you, Raymond? How have you been?"

My heart was racing with joy and confusion.

"I'm good, thanks. I'm staying at the Days Inn, on Charles Street. Do you know where that is, Dan?"

"Yes, that's just a few blocks north of where I am. I can be there in about ten to fifteen minutes."

"Great, I'm so looking forward to seeing you. I'll meet you in the lobby."

"I'm on my way," I answered and eagerly headed to my car.

I couldn't believe what was unfolding. My first reaction was wondering if fate was trying to bring us together again. I jumped in my car and drove the few blocks to his hotel. I parked the car on Charles Street and started speed walking to the hotel. With every step closer, I got more nervous and excited. I wondered if I would recognize him and how much we had both probably changed. I entered the lobby, and there, once again, sat my beautiful Raymond.

I instantly recognized his beautiful smile and wavy hair.

He jumped up and quickly started walking toward me. Our eye contact was like that first day we'd met as his sparkling blue eyes met mine.

We embraced and held each other close.

"You look the same as the day you left," I said as we broke our hug and looked at each other at arm's length.

"Plus, ten pounds extra, and you look the same as well. How long has it been?" Raymond asked.

"Fifteen years," I said, "and hardly a day goes by without me thinking about you."

"Let's talk more in my room," he answered, and we went upstairs to his room. He threw his arms around me again and stared into my face.

"I've missed you beyond belief," he said. "Tell me what has happened in your life up till now, as I have something I want to ask you."

I looked at Raymond and felt my heart warm. Once again, I was trying desperately not to cry.

"I married Susan. Remember the blonde girl I'd started dating? I got out of the horses and got a job reading electric meters here in Toronto. We moved to the suburbs, have two daughters, aged seven and four, plus a dog named Spencer," I said.

We lay down on the bed facing each other, just like the old times, Raymond on my right and me on his left.

"How did you find me?" I asked.

"I called the racetrack, and the one guy in the race office remembered us being friends and found your cell number," Raymond said.

"Are you still living in Vancouver?" I asked.

"Yes," Raymond said, "I'm still in Vancouver, have an apartment now. I dated a few guys, but it just didn't work. There was no click with any of them. I married a girl about ten years ago out of pressure, but we divorced a couple of years ago. Luckily, we had no children."

"Sorry to hear that." I then made the mistake of asking him the reason for his divorce.

"She and I were always having issues. We'd often quarrel sometimes, then one day a few summers ago, I came home, and she was sitting on the floor with a stack of torn-up photographs beside her. She was throwing them into the lit fireplace.

"I asked her, 'What the hell are you doing?'

"She replied, 'Who the fuck is this?' and she showed me a picture of you and me at the club on Valentine's Day, kissing. She grabbed it out of my hand and threw it into the fire. Another picture was of us in bed at the apartment together, taken with my Polaroid camera.

"I was enraged at her throwing away those photos of us and our past. I went to take a swing at her, but luckily, I stopped. We had a heated argument, and I gladly told her everything about us and how long we were a loving couple," Raymond said.

"She was another homophobe," Raymond continued, "and I should have known better than to marry her, but I thought my gay desires after marriage would stop. Needless to say, they never went away. That day, she called both a lawyer and my father. We divorced shortly after. It caused quite a problem in my family, as she was more than happy to tell my dad all about us.

"I eventually came out to my father, and surprisingly, he said he suspected that you and I were a couple for all those years. He and I rarely speak now, but my mother said he is willing to 'try to understand.' At this point, I don't really care anymore what he may think of me. He burned his bridge with me a long time ago. Mom said it was Rozz who sat him down and told him about us."

"I'm so sorry you went through that, Raymond," I said. "That must have been terrible to go through. Are you currently seeing someone?"

"No, I'm not seeing anyone," Raymond quietly answered.

I could hear and sense the loneliness in his voice. He was lying right beside me, yet he sounded so far away and distant. He then rolled onto his side, so we were face to face. "That's one of the reasons I contacted you. I desperately wanted to see you again, but also, I'd like to know if you want to get back together. My life seems alone and empty. I understand if you can't. I didn't realize you had a family now. I'm happy for you, I really am, but I had to ask you."

My heart sank, and everything inside me felt like it bottomed out. Here I was, happily married, and yet even during my marriage, I often thought about Raymond and wondered how he was doing. In those times of wondering, I would think what life would have been like if we were born in a different generation, a generation where being gay was more acceptable and tolerated. I too often thought of getting back together as well.

I then began thinking of my two little girls. *What would their lives be like if I were to leave? What would happen to my wife when she had to tell our family and friends that I left her for a man?* Once again, I questioned if fate was challenging me.

I placed my hand on Raymond, and my mind went back to the older days.

"I can't, hun. It kills me to say this, but I can't." I tried to hold back the tears, but I was thinking not only about Raymond but also about my wife and girls.

"I can't leave my family, hun." I started feeling the tears roll down my face.

"I understand, Dan. I totally do. We had an amazing time together, and we will forever remember those times."

Raymond and I continued to stare at each other as we lay on the bed. It was as if he was defeated and had just lost his last friend but tried to conceal his feelings.

"You and your tears. You haven't changed," and he smiled and wiped his finger down each cheek, wiping them away.

We started reminiscing about the many fun things we had done and began to chuckle and smile, which helped break the drama of the moment.

"How's Rozz?" I asked.

"She moved out west to Vancouver as well," Raymond mentioned. "She's still with the bank, and we still see each other quite regularly."

"Please tell her that I said hello," I asked.

"She'll be so glad to hear that you're doing well," Raymond said, "and I'll certainly tell her."

We got up off the bed.

Raymond reached into his suitcase and said, "I have something of yours that I want to return." He then pulled out a pink tie. "This is yours, babe. I knew you were looking for it back when we were moving out of the apartment, but I kept it. I desperately wanted something of yours for myself to hold on to. I'm sorry. Here, take it."

"You mean that's my actual necktie, hun? The same necktie you bought me all those years ago, and you've kept it all this time?" I said and stood there in amazement. It was an odd feeling, one of being happy to see it, but one of sadness in knowing its memories were only that, memories of times gone.

"I couldn't part with it, babe, but I know how much it means to you. Here, please take it." He slowly stretched out his hand as if giving something up that he treasured. "Please, please take it," he said

Again, the tears started streaming down my face. I took hold of the beautiful pink necktie and held it to my face and shut my eyes. I instantly remembered its smell and texture, and suddenly all the hidden stories it held flashed before my eyes. The nights of dancing, going out to dinner, the love and fun it was witness to, even the late-night chases that were all the memories associated with my pink tie.

I could see the tears building up in Raymond's eyes. I took the tie and wiped the tears that started rolling down his face.

"Hun, this means the world to me, but I want you to keep

it," I said. "It should be with you,"

Raymond smiled, gladly took it back, and tucked it into his suitcase. "Thanks, then do me this favor, babe? I somehow always want to be with you. Take this."

He then took the silver ring off his finger and gave it to me.

I put in on my right hand, and it was a perfect fit. "I'll never take it off, hun, never."

We stood there looking at each other, both of us with tears in our eyes. I didn't want to leave, but somehow knew that it was time to part. The emotional hurt we were feeling was getting too unbearable to control. I felt as if I was going to collapse if I soon didn't leave.

We then hugged each other one last time.

I gave him a kiss, let go of his hands, and started to leave. I opened the hotel room door, looked one last time back at my Raymond, and pulled the door shut behind me with a heavy thud.

Once out in the hotel hall, I tried to compose myself and stop crying. I leaned my back against the wall before going to the lobby. I decided to take the stairs. As I walked down the stairwell, I started thinking back to those days of running down the stairs in the apartment, rushing to the basement to hide from his father.

I stopped at almost every floor, still trying to compose myself. I didn't want anyone to wonder what was wrong once I got back into the lobby. My old stereotypical ideas came back. Men shouldn't cry in public. If someone saw me crying, they would presume I was a total wuss or worse.

I finally managed to stop the tears and get to the ground floor. I straightened my hair and walked through the lobby without looking at anyone and aimed directly for the front door. I remember walking outside into the cold air, which somewhat woke me up from my stupor. I sat in my car for the longest time, trying to comprehend what had just happened.

How could fate be so wonderful as to bring Raymond and I together, and then be so insensitive and cruel in tearing us apart?

I kept thinking about my little girls at home and my wife, which reassured me that I had done the right thing. I also kept thinking about Raymond and what it must be like to be all alone, like he'd told me.

I had to restrain myself from not returning upstairs and going back to him. God knows I wanted to, but my wife and girls, wife and girls, I kept repeating to myself.

I can still distinctly remember that long drive home from work that day. My mind was adrift in an emotional undertow. My thoughts would go from sorrow for leaving Raymond, then guilt for thinking about him and my gay past while being both married and a father, to the love that we both had eagerly shared with one another.

I then got angry at my own family, and toward society in general, for not being gay-friendly and tolerant all those many years ago. Yet through it all, it was the love of my wife and two daughters that gave me the strength to release the past and continue to move forward in life.

I remember I even gave some credit to our loving dog, Spencer, for his love and support, which made me sit there and chuckle and helped break the serious mood I was in.

I somehow managed to get my act together and made my way home. Once there, I immediately went upstairs, changed out of my work clothes, washed my face, and went back downstairs to my family as if nothing had happened.

In all my years together with my wife, I had never mentioned anything to her about my gay past, nor told her anything about Raymond.

Upon wearing Raymond's ring, I told her that I'd found it one day in the snow while at work and liked it, so I kept it on.

CHAPTER 44
Spring 2017

Over the years, my desire for men has never left.

With the advent of gay hookup websites and gay hookup apps, I secretly met up with men while constantly living in fear of my wife ever finding out.

With every hookup, I would acknowledge, within my own mind, an apology to my wife and girls for what I was doing. Somehow, it helped me to ease the inner weight of guilt.

One night, in the spring of 2017, for reasons unknown to me, fate turned my thoughts once again toward Raymond.

In my sleep, I dreamed I was staring out our bedroom window at home and looking into the backyard. I had been having dreams about my gay past and had contemplated ending this turmoil inside me once and for all. I'd also thought about it a couple of times while awake. The constant struggle of hiding my gay side, the never-ending urge for men, and the heavy guilt that would follow every sexual encounter, was just getting to be too much of a burden for me to deal with.

I wanted it to end, but how could I end my life and do it in the quickest way possible? The easiest way, I thought, would be to quickly tie a necktie around my neck, so tightly that I couldn't undo it even if I changed my mind in the process.

I stood there in a daze, staring out the window, thinking of what I should do, when suddenly, I was startled to see Raymond standing beside me, holding my pink necktie.

"I'm not going to let you do this, babe. Don't do it. Please, don't do it."

I couldn't understand what was happening. Raymond was standing there as true as life beside me. Was I dreaming, or was I awake?

I swear I could have reached out and touched him.

I must have fallen back asleep, but when I woke up and got out of bed, I was shocked to see a pile of my neckties on the bedroom floor. Somehow, I must have taken them out of the walk-in closet while I was dreaming. In my daze of waking up, I questioned if it had been someone else.

I soon came to my senses and realized it was me.

Wondering why they were there, I soon started recalling my dream. I don't remember ever getting up out of bed that night, and slowly my dream started to come back to me. It was then that I remembered seeing Raymond standing beside me, and what I had intended to do with the neckties.

My wife got out of bed and said, "What are these doing here?"

I was terrified of what had just unfolded and started to shake.

"What's the matter?" she asked.

I then had to tell her about my dream, and about Raymond. As shocked as she was about my gay side, and about my living with Raymond, she said, "Let's go to the ER at the hospital and talk to a psychiatrist. This scares me with the neckties."

We went to our ER and sat waiting for a psychiatrist. I

recall the psychiatrist being a very understanding lady, who basically said that my mind wants peace and for my inner turmoil to stop and that my "true gay self" needs to come forward for that to happen. She mentioned that I had some deep psychological issues that I wanted to reveal.

There was no denying that I was a gay man, and that I could no longer continue to hide those feelings from those around me.

"This is your true identity, Dan," she said. "You've been hiding this for your entire life, and it's about time you showed everyone who you really are. Be proud of yourself, and be proud of your time with Raymond, but most importantly, be truthful and come out."

I honestly believe that Raymond's mind and my mind, somehow subconsciously came together that night. It was as if he knew what I wanted to do, and he was there, like before, to be my knight in shining armor and to come to my rescue once again. Knowing Raymond as I did, it was his way of at least getting me through the night in order to get the help I needed.

Seeing him holding my pink necktie confirmed to me that he knew what I had planned.

The psychiatrist gave me the contact information for a therapist my wife and I could talk to.

I had a few sessions alone with my therapist and discussed my past with him: me growing up gay and hiding it, and my terrible jealous streak, which I discovered was the result of extremely low self-esteem.

He said that over the years, and probably since I was very young, I had come to believe that I was insignificant to others and that I thought others saw me as nothing more than someone who could be picked on or abused.

Back then, it was drilled into me that all gay men were

abnormal, and no one would love them anyway. It wasn't until I met Raymond, who showed me the love and respect for which I was so desperately looking, that I got any feeling of self-worth. Hence the reason for me putting him on such a high pedestal and comparing him to every man I would eventually cross paths with.

My therapist also helped my wife and I get over what most people viewed as a "conventional marriage," and gave us some scenarios of what we could do.

We could divorce, and go our separate ways, where I would pursue my desire to be with a man. We could separate, in our attempt to deal with me being gay, while I enjoyed my gay lifestyle. Or, we could stay together, with the understanding that I had certain needs that only another man could fulfill, and that I could enjoy my gay side with my wife's approval.

My wife and I have a hot tub in our backyard, which we soon called our "Hot Tub Confessional."

We would sit in the hot tub and discuss all aspects of our marriage, of Raymond, and of my past.

I knew all along that I could never leave my wife, as it would be too difficult emotionally.

I recall asking if she were ever interested in wanting to be with another man, to which she said no. I would often say if she were to have an affair with another man, then I would leave. My jealousy would not allow me to be able to deal with it. What could another man give her that I couldn't?

I mentioned if it were to ever happen, then I would want to move far away, so I wouldn't know or see. However, if she were to have an affair with another woman, then it wouldn't bother me at all, for the simple reason being that I couldn't give her what she desired.

As strange as this line of thinking was, my wife understood and agreed with me.

Over the next few months, I eventually told my daughters about Raymond as well. Being brought up in a younger, and more understanding generation regarding LGBTQ, they were completely understanding and hugged me to show their support.

After telling my wife and daughters, I felt as if an anchor had been cut loose from me, and I finally felt free. I love my wife and daughters more than anything and I'm happy knowing that I can keep my memories of Raymond without any feelings of negativity from them.

Over time, my wife and I have discussed all aspects of my gay side. I confessed to my extra-marital affairs with other gay men and admitted my continued desire to be with a man.

I could never leave my wife, as she is the single reason I am still here. I know the inner gay turmoil in me, just like that of so many other married men, would have led me to destruction at my own hand, but she gave me a reason for living.

I often wondered about Raymond, where he was, what he was doing, and if he had ever met another man.

My wife once asked me, "What would you do if Raymond ever showed up at our front door?"

That is a question I find very troubling to answer, for it goes through me like a double-edged sword.

If he were with someone, I'd be happy for him, yet at the same time, I'd always be questioning myself, saying that the guy he was with should be me. If he were single, I'm unsure what I would do.

Again, I know I could never leave my wife, but I often think of what "could have been," and it makes me question myself and the decisions that I made those many years ago.

For that reason, I am content to remember my memories. I still recall what Rozz advised me on that heart-breaking day when Raymond and I said goodbye to each other.

"Life will continue. Raymond will forever be part of your life as you will forever be with him. But don't forget to live. Don't pine away, but live life along with your memories."

Over time, I have met and become friends with some of the nicest gay men I could ever imagine. Some who have bravely escaped persecution from their home countries and built a new life of freedom and pride here in Canada.

Some who have escaped persecution from their own family, and some who are still hiding in the closet, contemplating about coming out, while others who are totally out and as proud as can be.

I also enjoy going to my favorite gay club in the city for a fun night out, which my wife knows about and is totally supportive of.

In the gay culture, I'm often referred to as a Daddy Bear. I have a sentimental spot in my heart and care a great deal for the younger generation of gay men.

From my "Handsome Cub," to my "Squeeze Squeeze," and my handsome "Baby Bear," I greatly respect and love them all, as I was once in their shoes

I'll see young gay men dancing together, and it warms my heart, and I'm so pleased and proud for them.

It often reminds me of my time dancing with Raymond, and I thoroughly enjoy going.

I even proudly attended our Pride Parade here in Toronto and had an incredibly fulfilling day with one of my gay man friends.

EPILOGUE

Upon looking back over my life, I realize how wonderful and beautiful it has been and still is.

I truly have been blessed: first by finding my loving Raymond, and then meeting my incredible wife Susan, and being the proud father of two beautiful daughters.

Even though it came with many challenges, and many tears, my ability to love and be loved by those very special individuals in my life makes me forever grateful to them all. Fate was truly on my side.

Many times, when a married man comes out of the closet later in life, he is often praised and congratulated for his braveness in doing so. A great number of people sympathize with him regarding his lifelong internal struggle and greet him with open arms of support and acceptance, which is totally understandable.

But when handing out praise and support, one must also remember his wife, who he married in faith those many years ago. Often, she is forgotten and is now left to deal with her own internal struggle of wondering what has happened.

Was her marriage really a marriage of love, or simply one of convenience to hide her husband's gay side?

Many women stay with their husbands, like mine has, in hopes of keeping their marriage together. Others, however, angrily separate or divorce for reasons of their own, like Raymond's did.

Should the wife stay with him in support, or leave in frustration or anger, either way, they too need someone's open arms to be encouraging and comforting.

Personally, my wife has told me that if she had known about Raymond being my partner while we were dating, she would never have married me.

Whether you are a gay man or woman, young or old, married or single, confused or frustrated by living a closeted lifestyle, only you can decide to make that change and come out. But if it is possible, don't live your life only to satisfy the expectations of others.

It's a cold and lonely lifestyle, forever living in the closet and having to hide from your true inner self. Allow yourself the opportunity to come out and feel the inner freedom of who you truly are. Come into the sunshine and the warmth of our beautiful rainbow that encompasses us all.

I'm proud to let anyone know that I am a gay man and that I always have been. I was born gay, grew up gay, and I am immensely proud of that quality.

I lovingly and very proudly wear two wedding bands. On the ring finger of my left hand, I wear my wife's golden band, while on the ring finger of my right hand, I wear Raymond's silver band. Beside Raymond's ring, and on my middle finger, I also proudly wear my multicolor rainbow ring for all to see. It's my way of always reminding me of the struggles, the love, and the togetherness Raymond and I had as a proud gay couple. I've never taken my golden band off, nor have I ever taken Raymond's off, since that day he gave it to me, those many years ago.

I finish my story with one more piece of writing about Raymond and our time together.

*Growing up gay in the seventies and eighties was a
    challenge, at best,*
*With so much prejudice and hate you kept hidden
    from the rest.*
Then, when I least expected it, he came into my life.
Our love and our loyalty helped keep away the strife.
*Over the years, we loved, laughed, and some-
    times cried,*
Even wanted to marry, but that was denied.
Then that dreadful day came when we had to part.
*It was pressure from family and society that broke
    our hearts.*
*When you find your true love, keep him close, and
    keep him near,*
Be gay proud of yourself, and don't live in fear.
*For it's the love from each of us that helps keep
    us strong,*
I'm proud to be a gay man because now I belong.

Raymond, I love you.

If there were ever two men more loving, and sentimentally silly than Raymond and me, then bless them both, for they will truly understand how the act of love, caring, unselfishness, humor, and sheer goofiness can combine to create a never doubting and committed relationship.

I have altered some names in my story to protect anyone who may think it is about them.

Many of the venues, cities, and street locations in the story are also different for privacy and protection.

Raymond, I love you.

CPSIA information can be obtained
at www.ICGtesting.com
Printed in the USA
LVHW100039280323
742726LV00005B/137

9 781039 155800